Praise for *Wine Wit*

Filled with grit and vulnerability, MacLean examines the hardest parts of being a woman in a man's world with honesty and poise.

— VICTORIA JAMES, bestselling author of *Wine Girl*

Zesty, vibrant, meditative, edgy, structured, intense — these words Natalie MacLean might use to describe wines all apply to her *Wine Witch on Fire*. With clear-eyed honesty and needle-sharp probing, her memoir covers a time of personal and of professional crisis, much of which rose from the astonishing sexism of other wine writers. Dire, yes, but the book is funny and a page turner.... Anyone at a crux will be buoyed by this writer's grit and grace.

— FRANCES MAYES, *New York Times* bestselling author of *Under the Tuscan Sun*

Rousing, funny, and insider-y, Natalie MacLean's soul-baring memoir paints an evocative and compelling picture of what it's like to be a woman in wine.

— NELL MCSHANE WULFHART, bestselling author of *Off Menu* and *New York Times* columnist

Courageous — that's the first word that comes to mind while reading Natalie MacLean's new memoir. MacLean is an accomplished wine writer, but this deeply personal book takes us behind the scenes, revealing one woman's journey and extraordinary determination to become herself.

— KAREN MACNEIL, bestselling author of *The Wine Bible*

Natalie MacLean has been through hell and back — misogyny, sexism, social media trolling — but her words are heartfelt and her journey inspiring.

— BARBARA FAIRCHILD, former editor-in-chief of *Bon Appétit*

With a voice full of humour and keen honesty, wine writer Natalie Maclean pairs the personal with the political in *Wine Witch on Fire*. In the process, she exposes the sexism of an industry while coming to understand her own hard-won strengths. A delightful read with or without a glass of wine.

— SUZANNE EVANS, author of *The Taste of Longing*

In *Wine Witch on Fire*, Natalie MacLean opens her heart with authenticity to the pain of love lost, the joy of discovering new love, and the endless questions of balancing parenting with being a working professional. Her love of language is a joyous counterpart to her love of viticulture. I learned so much from this fine memoir and I have a strong sense its appeal to the artist in all of us is limitless.

— KEN GOLDSTEIN, bestselling author of *Endless Encores* and *From Nothing*

Natalie MacLean is living a life that is the definition of resilience. In her empowering new memoir she takes us on her incredible journey filled with love, anguish, and fearless determination. Natalie's story is an inspiration and guide to living well and fearlessly. A fabulous read!

— TRACI MELCHOR, judge, *Canada's Drag Race*, and senior correspondent, *Etalk*

Natalie Maclean has written a harrowing, heartfelt, and often hilarious account of the backlash she endured breaching the largely male-dominated world of wine writing. This highly personal odyssey is an eyes-wide-open take on betrayal, the insidious lure of addiction, and the sheer mettle required to rise above those seeking to cast a poisonous spell.

— ROSA HARRIS, bestselling author of *Boomerville*

Natalie MacLean offers readers a look into the magical world of wine, addressing head-on its problematic treatment of women throughout the industry. I came away from this book feeling less alone, as if I'd shared a great bottle with a friend and talked through the life problems we all experience at some point.

— RACHEL SIGNER, bestselling author of *You Had Me at Pét-Nat*

Wine wizard wordsmith, enchanting interviewer, battle-tested survivor, fierce mother, witty, wise — Natalie MacLean is the whole package. Sip a great wine while you savor her memoir.

— GUS CLEMENS, wine columnist, *USA Today*

MacLean is well known for her vast wine knowledge and for sharing that knowledge but with this work she shares a plethora of personal life crises with humour and compassion teaching that anyone who experiences similar troubles and mid-life crisis can also transform their lives. Middle-aged men can learn a lot about how to support their female partner by encouraging her self-worth. It's a must read for everyone over thirty years old.

— JOHN J. MAHONEY, PH.D., C.W.E., author of
Every Bottle Has a Story, *Wine for Intellectuals*,
and *Wine: The Source of Civilization*

Vulnerable, honest, personal … with a touch of humor (and best paired with your favourite glass of wine). Natalie's beautifully written memoir shares an empowering story of her journey that reminds us just how powerful we are as women, and how we can always dig deep to find a little determination and faith, even when those things seem nowhere to be found.

— AMY PORTERFIELD, podcast host,
Online Marketing Made Easy

Natalie MacLean had it all — an accomplished husband, a high-profile wine writing career, and an email signature of "Chief of Wine Happiness." But her life fell apart when her husband departed, she started to drink too much, and a social media mob came after her. *Wine Witch on Fire* is the triumphant story of how MacLean pushed back against sexism in the wine industry, found love, and drew on her female "witching" powers to turn obstacles into opportunities.

— FRANCES DINKELSPIEL, bestselling author of *Tangled Vines*

Natalie has crafted her experience into what could pass for an unputdownable thriller. It's all the more jarring because it's based on fact. I loved the tension and fast-paced writing. Any man who has a daughter, sister, or mother should read this book. Women with a little witch and fire within them will enjoy it too.

— STEVEN LAINE, bestselling author of *Dragonvine*

There's a lot of underbelly in this memoir. Someone will inevitably say it's about score-settling, but that's less an opinion than a gaslighting. Natalie bent over backwards to be fair. This book is a significant gesture to push the wine industry toward greater inclusion of people who've been marginalized. While this memoir will be torn and shredded by many persons of ill will and with minds less acute than hers, I hope she stays resolute. I wish her strength and contentment. Natalie, you done good.

— TERRY THEISE, bestselling author of *Reading Between the Wines* and *What Makes a Wine Worth Drinking*

WINE WITCH
on FIRE

NATALIE MACLEAN

WINE WITCH on *Fire*

Rising from the Ashes of Divorce, Defamation, and Drinking Too Much

a memoir

DUNDURN
PRESS

Publisher: Kwame Scott Fraser | Acquiring editor: Russell Smith
Cover and interior designer: Karen Alexiou
Cover image: wine glass: nito/shutterstock.com; fire: Valeev/shutterstock.com; ash: xpixel/shutterstock.com
Interior image: Celtic tree: artdock/shutterstock.com; wine glass: rawpixel/freepik.com

Library and Archives Canada Cataloguing in Publication

Title: Wine witch on fire : rising from the ashes of divorce, defamation, and drinking too much : a memoir / Natalie MacLean.
Names: MacLean, Natalie, author.
Identifiers: Canadiana (print) 20220494959 | Canadiana (ebook) 20220495114 | ISBN 9781459751194 (softcover) | ISBN 9781459751200 (PDF) | ISBN 9781459751217 (EPUB)
Subjects: LCSH: MacLean, Natalie. | LCSH: Wine writers—Canada—Biography. | LCSH: Sommeliers—Canada—Biography. | LCSH: Women in the wine industry—Canada. | LCGFT: Autobiographies.
Classification: LCC TP547.M33 A3 2023 | DDC 641.2/2092—dc23

We acknowledge the support of the Canada Council for the Arts and the Ontario Arts Council for our publishing program. We also acknowledge the financial support of the Government of Ontario, through the Ontario Book Publishing Tax Credit and Ontario Creates, and the Government of Canada.

Dundurn Press
1382 Queen Street East
Toronto, Ontario, Canada M4L 1C9
dundurn.com, @dundurnpress 𝕏 f ⊚

*For my mother, Ann, who taught me how big
my brave is, and to let my words out.*

❧

Author's Note

I wrote this book with positive intent for everyone in it, even those involved in traumatic moments. They've all made me who I am today, as flawed as that remains. Some people's names, physical characteristics, and company affiliations have been changed for privacy. Otherwise, this memoir is a true narrative. The events and dialogue are based on my memories, conversations, journal entries, emails, texts, online posts, screenshots, and recordings. I asked family, friends, colleagues, and several lawyers to review the manuscript. The opinions in this memoir are mine alone and are intended only to share my experience. I don't represent any brand, company, or organization mentioned. My story isn't unusual, but I hope that my journey helps others who travel this way to feel less alone. I raise my glass to you.

DOMAINE MACLEAN

UNRESERVED OLD VINES

PINOT NOIR
(THE HEARTBREAK GRAPE)

2012
(A TERRIBLE VINTAGE)

After writing about wine for more than twenty years, I can't resist suggesting several bottles that'll pair well with this book. I don't sell wine, and those in this memoir have been selected independently. I'm also not recommending wine to deal with whatever life throws at you.

For me, that was divorce, motherhood, later-in-life dating, and boozy girlfriend get-togethers blended with anxiety, depression, hope, joy, and wiser love.

Pour these wines at your book club, wine group, or coven moon circle. You'll find tips for informal wine tastings in a free discussion guide at nataliemaclean.com/witchwines or scan this QR code:

It pays to read a bottle's back label for more clues about what's inside. In the wine world, we talk about *terroir*, a French word referring to the magical combination of soil, geography, climate, weather, and winemaking decisions to create a wine. Terroir is like a writer's voice. It embodies word choice, point of view, humour, dialogue, and digging in your own dirt to create a memoir.

This book is different from my first two. It's more personal and, in parts, more serious. We'll travel through the terroir of my industry, contoured by sexism, to look for a kinder landscape on the horizon.

Why the witch theme? Witches resonate with me because their strength comes from within, not from external validation. They also embody the unity of women, the power of the feminine, and the healing connection to nature.

Did I end up embracing the positive powers of my inner witch? It wasn't that straightforward, and labels can be misleading. I was forced to battle my darker impulses. That's the real magic I want to share with you.

Pour yourself a glass and let's dive in.

Natalie

WILD YEAST FERMENT
UNFINED AND UNFILTERED

CONTENTS

Begin at the Season's End

Boil and Bubble

I wake to the smell of burning. Heat runs up and down my body. My tongue feels like sandpaper. Why are my eyes glued shut?

Ahhh. Last night.

It started with two glasses of champagne to kick off dinner, then three (four?) glasses of pinot noir. The real culprit must have been that glass (okay, two) of port.

My family passed the decanter around the table clockwise to symbolize the passing of time with the ones you love. A beautiful ritual binding us together. Now all that booze is splitting my head in two. The little drummer boy starts pounding on my cerebral cortex.

Wait.

That's not burning, it's smoked bacon.

My eyelids creak as I pry them open.

Notes of Andy Williams singing "It's the Most Wonderful Time of the Year" drift up the stairs to my bedroom. I tune in to the sounds and aromas of morning happiness.

It's ten days to Christmas 2012, and somehow I've made it to the end of the year from hell, not just intact but … *could it be?* … yes, happy. The thought makes me spring out of bed, which I now regret, and sit back down.

Why doesn't Andy just shut up about jingle belling? He's clanging against the other soundtrack in my head: I'm queasy, queasy like Sunday morning.

Damn. Why did I drink so much?

Hey, it's December 15, and everyone celebrates a little more than usual during the festive season. Why shouldn't I?

I ease off the bed, wash my face, and brush my tangled seaweed hair before inching downstairs.

"Good morning, princess," my boyfriend, Daniel, says as I enter the kitchen.

I wince, but not at his pet name for me, as it comes from a good place. This hangover doesn't.

He smiles and flips the bacon. Daniel is Prince Charming in my fairy tale, with curly brown hair and a football-quarterback build. He loves to cook and he even cleans up afterward. I affectionately call him my Cinderfella.

Mom sits at the kitchen island with my fourteen-year-old son, Cameron, playing crazy eights. She's come up from Nova Scotia to stay with us for the holidays.

"Oh, you rascal, you," she says, as Cameron makes her pick up six cards. She looks at me from behind her steel-rimmed glasses and nods. My family's warmth eases the pain in my head. All the heartbreak, depression, and anxiety at the beginning of this year seem to fade with the closing credits of 2012. I've survived the separation, found love, and I'm still writing. My life has somehow magically come back together.

```
There are just fifteen hours left
   until my world implodes.
```

"I'm making rosemary chicken with roasted artichoke for dinner," Daniel says. "Got a wine for that?"

"Not yet, but I will." Sure, I have a cellar, but I love seeing what's new on store shelves. Also, did I mention that I'm a professional? I can shop for wine while nursing a hangover.

I'm not worried about the chicken, which plays nicely with wine, but artichoke is one of the problem children of the pairing world. It contains an organic acid that fools us into thinking everything we eat or drink afterward is sweeter than it is, including wine. This kind of mission impossible is something I do frequently for my family.

"Cameron, come with me after breakfast … we still have a few gifts to get."

His crystal blue eyes are hopeful. "Like a PlayStation?"

Damn. I've been trying to keep him away from video games for as long as possible. But it feels mean, with my separation from his father at the beginning of the year, and now the holidays are approaching. He has weathered our split well.

"Perhaps you should ask Santa for it." I wink.

"Good idea. Do you think the elves can throw in a console stand?" He grins.

Back in my office, snow swirls outside the window. I email another writer to confirm that I'm updating the way I post wine reviews on my website so he'll stop pestering me. This is part of a long stream of nasty comments I've received over the years.

```
There are only twelve hours and forty-three minutes
   before my Nightmare Before Christmas begins.
```

My books, *Red, White, and Drunk All Over* and *Unquenchable*, celebrate the pleasure of wine. Many readers embrace my loopy tales. Some older male wine writers loathe them. Silly chick lit — their equivalent of "women's wines": chardonnay, pinot grigio, prosecco, rosé. Bitch pours. The opposite of their sophisticated sommelier selections.

To hell with them.

I am woman. Watch me pour.

That's why I've long been fascinated with literary witches who didn't care what labels society put on them, from the three sisters in Shakespeare's *Macbeth* to the women in *The Witches of Eastwick*. They were persecuted for their "powers" — or, more likely, their misunderstood (and feared) skills.

Even Maleficent, in the 2014 Disney film, was originally a good fairy with powers over plants and herbs, until the man she loved most betrayed her. Same old playbook. There's a happy ending, though. She regains her strength through the phoenix, the mythological bird that rises from the ashes of its predecessor. Maleficent's kiss, not one from a prince, wakes up Sleeping Beauty.

I write for people like me who relate to an occasional tipsy evening — and dealing with the aftermath. Like right now. Ow.

It wasn't the buzz so much as the upwelling joy that pulled me to wine. I remember the September evening years ago when I visited Merry Edwards Winery and Vineyards, in Sonoma. The sweet smell of grapes and alcohol hung heavy in the air of the barrel room. As I walked into the vineyard, the slanting amber rays slid over my shoulders. Wine drew me outside again, connecting me with the earth. It got me out of my head and away from the computer I was chained to in my previous tech job. Some employees there slept under their desks to work longer. We were "mole people," I used to joke. We shrank from sunlight.

When I returned to the tasting room, I drank the wine to make the sun and soil part of me. Then I wrote about it to metabolize my feelings and digest its sensuality.

~∾~

After Cameron and I pick up the gifts, we walk into the liquor store. I remember when he was just four. He had looked up at me and asked loudly, "Why do we always go to the *boos* store, Mommy?"

"Because Mommy writes about wine. It's her career," I told him in an equally loud voice, avoiding eye contact with other customers. Then I looked up at the lady with an over-oaked merlot. "That's why no one needs to call Child Services."

Cameron and I stroll down an aisle of sauvignon blanc. Bone-dry, with racy acidity and herbal aromas, it'll be a lovely counterpoint to the artichoke, while cutting through the tender roast chicken.

With other dishes, I use the lemon or butter rule. If I squeeze some lemon juice on the food, for example, seared halibut, then I drink a wine with edgy acidity like sauvignon blanc or grüner veltliner. However, if I slather melting butter on my entrée, say a big juicy steak, then I pair it with a rich, full-bodied cabernet, or even a barrel-aged chardonnay. Yes, white wine with red meat. How rogue. The buttery, toasty notes of the chardonnay will complement the caramelized flavours of the meat.

As I stop to pick a bottle, a young couple a few feet away debates whether a sauvignon blanc or chardonnay would go better with pasta in a cream sauce. I really shouldn't interfere, but my instinct as a wine superhero kicks in. Just as a doctor would clear a crowd to use a defibrillator on someone who has collapsed from a heart attack, I want to say, "Please stand back, everyone, I can help these people. I'm a trained sommelier."

I wait for a pause in their conversation to jump in. "If you like contrasting flavours, I suggest you go with the sauvignon blanc. It'll slice like a knife through the cream. But if you want to layer richness on richness, a toasty chardonnay is your ticket."

"Oh that's great, thank you," the woman says. She takes a sauvignon blanc from the shelf.

"Yeah, thanks. We were really stumped," her partner adds.

Their happy, shining faces make me want to soar up into the clouds and use my infrared vision to scan other liquor stores and save more indecisive drinkers. Alas, I must return to my family who need me more than the throngs of wine enthusiasts. My life's work to relieve their first-world problems will have to wait another day.

~∞~

Back home, I try on one dress after another, throwing the rejects on the bed before choosing a fiery red number with sparkles. While I'm usually in yoga pants, I want to wear what I feel tonight: glittery and happy. Glappy.

Four hours and six minutes.

The savoury, golden aromas of Daniel's rosemary chicken and artichoke fill the kitchen. Although it's only mid-December, we toast to the end of 2012 (good riddance) with the crisp sauvignon blanc. Watching the movie *Elf* after dinner, we laugh at the oversized adult Will Ferrell sitting on his father's lap.

Eleven minutes.

Calling it a night, Mom and Cameron get all nestled and snug in their beds. Daniel sleeps in the guest room rather than drive home after another very merry dinner. We've been dating for only two months, so we're not ready to share the intimate nature of our relationship with Mom or Cameron. Besides, when sugarplums start dancing in their heads, Daniel's just down the hall.

It's getting close to midnight, and I'm still feeling festive. In my small dark office, the multicoloured lights twinkle through the window. The buttery notes of Ella Fitzgerald's "Have Yourself a Merry Little Christmas" melt into the background.

The perfect end to a perfect day. But this day isn't over — and it's going to be anything but perfect.

`Time's up.`

I'm checking my email one last time before heading upstairs to bed when a Google alert pops up with the headline:

Google Alerts

"Natalie MacLean"
As-it-happens update December 15, 2012, 11:42 PM

NEWS

Natalie MacLean: World's Best Wine Writer or Content Thief?

Toil and Trouble

---

*C*ontent thief?

The text quivers as I try to register what I'm reading. *What is this? Where did it come from?*

My heart pounds.

I click through to Palate Press, a large American wine and spirits website. There's a long rant about me with phrases that burn into my retinas. "Copyright infringement" ... "Intellectual theft" ... *What the hell?*

Their words merge and blur: "those so offended is a 'Who's Who' of the world of wine journalism ... brings discredit upon any of us ... scourge on journalism ... cannot be tolerated."

This isn't simply a nasty comment. I'm being accused of the one thing a writer dreads most — stealing someone else's work. Doctors lose their licences for malpractice; lawyers are disbarred for misrepresentation; writers get their careers cancelled for copyright infringement.

I now earn my living online since the income from my books has long since dried up. Those of us who work online can't simply "turn it off" any more than a brain surgeon can operate outside a hospital. The difference is that online there are no separate workplaces. There isn't even separation between work and home — everybody eventually knows everything about everyone.

11:44 p.m.

I'm on my second read through the article. I realize that everything I've written over the past thirteen years — all those words — are now fiery cinders flying up around me as my professional reputation burns.

My feet feel cemented to the middle of a long ribbon of highway, the oncoming eighteen-wheeler hurtles toward me.

The authors of the article have asked other writers to weigh in on me. No one has commented yet. Maybe I can still defend myself, stop this disaster before it becomes worse.

Hands shaking, I start writing a comment below their post. Then I stop. Panic ricochets inside my skull. *What can I even say?*

I can't see through my tears, anyway. Closing my eyes, I wrap my arms around where I've been gut-punched, rocking silently.

Oh my God.

I stumble to the kitchen to get water, spilling half of it onto my chest as I gulp. The glass slips and smashes on the floor. Shards scatter in all directions. I hold my breath but don't hear anyone upstairs move. Throwing the pieces in the garbage, I notice the blood. I wash my hands quickly, ignoring the fragment in my palm.

Back in the office, the lights outside merge into a sickly swamp. Something dark is seeping in through my side vision. Can you suffocate in ink?

As I stare at the screen, my mind races back over the past year, starting with the implosion of my marriage, finances, health, and sanity. Was all that just a warm-up for what was to come? As I feel an unnamed dread close in on me, I clasp my hands around the back of my neck.

Out of nowhere, I see him: Motorcycle Guy. I'm nine years old. Mom's driving me back from a Highland dancing competition in Nova Scotia. He crosses the highway median in front of us and careens into a truck, flying up into the air. He comes straight back down on the asphalt. No helmet. No movement. Legs and arms where they shouldn't be. Eyes open, not blinking.

Mom pulls over to the shoulder and slams on the brakes.

Don't look.

I look.

Now I can't look away.

11:52 p.m.

I take a deep breath and continue writing a response. I'm not a thief or a cheat. This sure as hell isn't plagiarism. *My God.* I'll be rational. I'll calmly address the accusations and this will all go away. Right? The blood from my palm drips onto the keyboard.

12:06 a.m.

Done. Sent.

12:29 a.m.

When I get up from my desk, my knees buckle. I run for the bathroom. After throwing up twice, I find myself standing in front of Daniel's bedroom. I must have walked upstairs, but I can't remember doing that.

12:39 a.m.

I put my hand on his door handle, then stop. Our relationship is unfolding perfectly, but it's still so new. I don't want to destroy this honeymoon with Prince Charming. Telling him about the online mess wouldn't just be showing him my warts; it would be admitting to him that the world thinks his princess is really a witch — a wine witch.

When Adam, my husband of twenty years, left me suddenly at the beginning of the year, I resolved not to trust any man romantically.

I was too heartbroken to be angry. There are, and have been, many good men in my life, from my son to my grandfather and more in between. I just didn't want to go back to months of sobbing silently so Cameron wouldn't hear me. Questioning my sanity, drinking to cope.

Daniel doesn't need to know about this, especially since he doesn't go online much. I can control the narrative. But what if someone else tells him? How much time do I have?

Maybe I can still have a happy ending, even if I have to eat this poisoned apple alone. Somewhere deep down, that old, terrible thought shudders up through me …

Love leaves when it sees all of me.

12:46 a.m.

I stagger back to my room. The dresses thrown on the chair are like past lives lived, personalities tried on, then discarded. None of them will fit me now.

I fall into bed in a hollowed-out heap but lie awake for hours. The barbed words from the article march from one side of my mind to the other.

How has this entire year become so mucked-up?

3:24 a.m.

I stare blearily at the clock until, finally, the weight of exhaustion drags me down into sleep. I dream of men without faces standing in a circle around me.

～❦～

It takes several moments before I surface from the murkiness of my dreams to realize last night — my Nightmare Before Christmas — was real. I want to go back to the computer but first I run to the bathroom again.

The television interview is in just a few hours. It was scheduled weeks ago and will be broadcast on a live news show with more than a million viewers. What if the anchor asks me about the online meltdown instead? I can't cancel. That would make me look guilty. Plus, the anchor would never forgive me for creating a last-minute hole in the program. I have to go. What can I say?

Dragging myself back to my office, I see the scalding article and the comment I wrote. Rather than defuse the situation, it has inflamed it.

I scroll through the comments, which pile on more accusations, but I can't dwell on them because I hear Cameron coming downstairs. Daniel glances at me as I enter the kitchen. He doesn't recognize the horror hiding behind my forced smile. He can't hear me howling inside my head, *Ask me, ask me about last night, make me tell you!*

He knows I'm often preoccupied with my own thoughts — or the aftermath of another "sociable" evening.

"You must love that dress, princess," he says. "It looks great on you!"

I look down and realize I'm still wearing the sparkly number.

"Oops, guess it was just so comfy."

Mom smiles as she looks up from the *Ottawa Citizen* newspaper on her tablet.

I expect to see the headline "Local Writer Exposed as a Fraud." I pace around the kitchen island. Can't eat, can't sit down.

"Everything okay, Mom?" Cameron's eyes search mine.

"I'm fine, hon. Think I might have a cold." I push my smile a little wider. How can I tell him the truth? *The world thinks your mother is a cheat and a fraud!*

I don't know if I can clear my name. Even if I could, what would it matter? After years of working online, I know that nothing on the internet dies — except reputations — and my reputation as a writer is all I have.

After Cameron goes back upstairs, I say nothing about the online attack. I don't want to stress Mom and aggravate her heart condition. And what am I supposed to say to Daniel: *Welcome to my realm of online hate?* I talk mechanically about the news and weather.

While Mom and Daniel linger over coffee, I slip back to my office to watch my career execution. There are a few more comments, mostly from other wine writers, cheering each other on. The anonymous comments have also started. I look for anything positive — anyone coming to my defence — but nothing.

Much as I want to stay and stare at the pile-on, I must be at the TV station at 12:30 p.m. We're supposed to discuss holiday wines and spirits, but I feel about as festive as the Ghost of Christmas Past.

In the shower, I turn the nozzle to full blast, a cold rinse in fear. Stepping out onto the mat, I'm still shivering. After dressing, my hand trembles as I put on lipstick. Who is that pale, terrified woman in the mirror?

In a flash, I realize that the last twenty-four hours have irrevocably changed my life. I awoke yesterday a princess in my fairy tale, albeit one with a hangover. I never was traditional. Now I'm the witch, and the villagers are coming for me, pitchforks and all.

∽⊚⌀

In the TV parking lot, I sit in my car, staring up at the giant lightbox sign:

Your 24-Hour News Station That Digs Deeper

A mist of tears covers my face. I scream to stop them. Can't go on air with black streaks of mascara running down my cheeks. Finally, I drag the bottles — and my body — into the building.

"Welcome, please take a seat beside me," Monique, the host of the show, says.

"Thanks, this is going to be so much fun!"

She gives me a sugary smile, giving no signs of having seen the article. But has she? She doesn't seem that friendly, either. Is she going to ask me about the accusations on-air? Should I bring it up and get ahead of the story? Would that give it an unnecessary spotlight? I feel a fiery ball of panic rising in my throat.

Decades of training as a Highland dancer kick in. No matter what was going on around the stage or in my life — rain bucketing down, sheep wandering between the judges and me, or my neighbour kicking her swords into mine — keep smiling, keep performing.

The bright overhead lights flash on as several large cameras roll toward us. The producer gives us the countdown: "In three, two, one ...

"You're live!"

But for how long?

Back to the Season's Roots

Tasting Sham-Pain

A s I stare at a bottle of pinot noir on the table between Monique and me, my mind flies back to the last time I tasted it, at the beginning of 2012. This year had started like the previous twenty that my husband, Adam, and I had been together. We went to a local restaurant for dinner every Sunday. Our son, Cameron, joined us. Dining out was our family sport. We'd chat about business, books, Adam's work in high tech, my writing, and Cameron's school projects.

"Will you be having your favourite pinot tonight?" our server, Sheila, asked, staring intently at me. She was trying to avoid eye contact with my husband. A few snowflakes fluttered outside the restaurant on this January evening.

"That would be great, Sheila." I handed the wine list back to her. Adam and I had both chosen the duck à l'orange with wild mushroom risotto. The gamey flavours of the dish would pair beautifully with the earthy notes in the wine.

As she left the table, Adam's stormy blue eyes followed her all the way to the kitchen. When he turned back to me and saw that I had watched him watching her, he shrugged. "You can't fight a billion years of evolution."

I laughed it off as *men will be men*. Isn't that what you do when you've been married so long?

But it stung. I wasn't enough to hold my man's attention. I hate the word *sexy* and how it objectifies women. In that moment, though, I wanted to be sexy.

"What's a billion years of evolution?" Cameron asked.

"It's about dinosaurs." I stared at Adam. He smirked.

I used to be the one who caught his eye. We met in London, Ontario, at Western University's Master of Business Administration program. He was tall and pale, with dark spiky hair, arousing both sexual and maternal feelings in me. I wanted to get him a glass of milk. Instead, I asked him about our programming assignment since we were in the school's computer lab.

He gazed at me for a few moments. "I'll show you." He bent over and typed on my keyboard.

I smiled at his just-do-it attitude and thanked him.

"No problem."

After a few chance encounters at a local coffee shop, he asked me out on a dinner date. I dropped out of the law portion of the combined degree at Western so I could graduate with Adam. I didn't want to be a lawyer, so I figured I wouldn't need legal skills. How wrong I was.

We moved to Toronto, where we blew through my law school savings on travel, dining out, and rent. I paid for a separate apartment for the first four months, loath to tell my mother I was "living in sin" with a man. That apartment was the most expensive answering machine I ever had. While we had both lined up great jobs, he at Citibank and I at Procter & Gamble, there was a gap between graduation and our first paycheques. I was proud to be the one supporting us financially for those months.

Five years later, Adam encouraged me to apply for a job in the Canadian office of a California-based supercomputer company. It specialized in powerful computers used to model scientific, aerospace, and other applications.

"I don't know anything about computers."

"You're smart, you'll figure it out. Besides, you won't be programming. It's marketing."

I loved that he believed in me more than I did. I assumed he'd always be at my side, cheering me on.

The computer company staff was mostly post-doctoral engineers and computer scientists. Young men in sales, paid on commission, were fast-talking, hard-hitting, coin-operated. Their favourite quote from Scott McNealy, co-founder of Sun Microsystems, was "Eat lunch or be lunch."

Almost a year after joining the company, I attended a sales conference in California that featured nights of hard drinking and virtual reality games. The corporate buildings, painted in red, blue, yellow, and green, spread across sprawling lawns where young men in T-shirts played Frisbee. They called it the campus. It had a frat-boy culture.

On the first night of the conference, about sixty of us gathered in a packed room where the air conditioning was no match for the sweltering July heat. The music boomed.

In the centre of the room was a long table for computers, now cleared and filled with bottles of beer and spirits. Jack, one of the most successful sales reps, yelled something and put a lemon wedge in his mouth. He grabbed the arm of Denise, our administrative assistant, who had been with the company for years. The men started chanting.

Denise danced her way to the table with Jack, jumped up on the edge, then shimmied her way backward to lie down on the table full-length. He got up on the table as the chanting intensified. The men clapped and whistled. Jack leaned over Denise, both hands now on the table. Using his lips and tongue, he transferred the lemon from his mouth to hers. They stood up and cheered. The crowd went crazy.

I knew Jack was married. Were he and Denise "together" on business trips? What did I know? This was my first conference.

The men started chanting again. Jack put another lemon wedge in his mouth and was, to my horror, heading for me. I stood in a corner talking to my boss, George.

"What's he doing?" I whispered.

George shrugged and smiled.

"Do I have to do this?"

George just shrugged again.

I froze.

The chants rang in my ears.

As one of the few women in the company, I wanted so badly to fit into this fail-forward-fast culture. The ethos urged developing new products at warp speed, whatever the damage.

Jack grabbed my forearm and pulled me through the crowd of men. The chanting swelled. Everything was a blur. He spun me around so that my back was against the table. I leaned away from him as far as I could, arching backward as he kept leaning toward me, until I, too, was on the table.

He jumped up on a chair and fell toward me, catching himself with both hands on the table in a push-up a few inches over me. His sweaty weight slowly pressed into my body. He exhaled hot, beery breath. His salty lips curved around mine as his tongue pushed into my mouth with the lemon. I felt his tongue move around inside my mouth. I couldn't move. I couldn't think. I waited for it to be over.

Jack jumped up on the chair, shaking both fists overhead. The crowd went wild.

I stood up, took the lemon out of my mouth, and walked slowly to the back of the room. Jack was going after his final conquest. No one saw me leave.

I was still trembling when I got to my hotel room and filled the tub with the hottest water I could stand. I sank slowly under the surface and finally let the tears fall.

In retrospect, I recognize this for what it was: the sexualized subjugation of the few women in the company. Perhaps Denise felt the same way despite acting like a "good-time gal." We didn't talk about things like that back in the late nineties. What was the point?

This was years before movie producer Harvey Weinstein, and others, were convicted of sexual assault, and many men reconsidered this behaviour. It was also before Facebook chief operating officer Sheryl Sandberg would advise women to lean in and take a seat at the table. I didn't lean into the table. I was on top of it, garnished with lemon for the men surrounding me. I was lunch.

~◎~

While working in tech, I'd spent several years taking the Sommelier Certificate program courses at Algonquin College during the evenings so I could graduate before Cameron was born, near the end of 1998. Now I was curious about how to get started in the wine writing profession.

While on maternity leave, I called a Canadian author of many wine books. Tech had taught me to be bold and call high, so why not ask advice from the most famous wine writer I could think of?

"Just don't expect to earn a living from it," he told me, after we'd spoken for a few minutes. "Treat it like a weekend hobby, sweetheart."

Sweetheart.

My face burned furnace-hot. Cameron was sleeping in his bassinet beside me in the living room.

There was a long pause on the phone.

"Thanks for your advice."

I screamed silently into Cameron's teddy bear.

I knew that creating a business out of a passion for wine wouldn't be easy, but that conversation fuelled the fire inside this little "sweetheart." The next day, I pitched an article about finding wine and food pairings on the web to a local magazine. The editor asked if I had published previously. I said yes, thinking of my high school newspaper. Thank goodness she didn't ask me to send samples.

The day the magazine came out, I ran to the store and flipped the pages furiously to find my column. There it was — and my name — in print! I was a *real* writer now. I bought all twelve copies of the magazine on the rack and mailed one to Mom. Someone had actually paid me to write!

That assignment led to a regular column and to my cold-calling other editors. It worked, though I got twenty noes for every yes. At the end of my maternity leave, I didn't return to the supercomputer company. I loved writing and being home with my son. For this introvert, leaving that high-octane office was like bathing a mosquito-bitten body in calamine cream.

I also found more meaning in writing about wine than in my work on the cooking oil brand at Procter & Gamble. Homogeneity is the benchmark in producing most packaged food, but good wine is about wild diversity in taste that changes every year depending on the weather. That's why we put wine, not cooking oil, on the dinner table in its original packaging. It matters who made the wine, where it was made, and what happened that year.

The assignments trickled in slowly at first. Over the years, they developed into regular columns for various newspapers and magazines. I hadn't gone to journalism school and had no contacts in either the wine industry or the media. Even Adam, with his tech network, couldn't help me. In the wine world, I was a nobody from nowhere who created a career out of nothing. Despite this, I built a brand and identity that were my own.

I loved my life or, at least, my work life. It was entirely online and headquartered in my tiny home office. No commute, no inane water-cooler chatter, no overstimulation. My conversation with the veteran wine writer should have alerted me that my new industry had its own issues with sexism. I was too battle-worn from tech to see it.

Several years in, another wine writer posted a link on my Facebook page to a website that had photoshopped my head on a bikini body, along with other women wine writers in skimpy attire. Facebook automatically added the photo from the website to his post. He wrote, "So sexy Natalie!" and tagged me.

"What's that on Facebook about you?" Mom emailed me.

Ugh.

"It's fake, ignore it."

My aunt, my high school volleyball coach, and several girl-friends also saw it, direct messaging me. "WTF? Have you seen this?!"

"Yes, apparently, everyone has." I drew in a sharp breath. "Please ignore."

Part of my fear and frustration with the bikini pic was that I'd thought I'd escaped the blatant misogyny of the tech world. If a colleague taped that photo to the cafeteria wall of my workplace, I could have taken it down before most people saw it. I wouldn't have worried that my son would eventually see it. I could have asked my boss and human resources for help. I would have talked with supportive colleagues rather than face it alone. I could have driven home at the end of the day and not seen it again.

False news on social media spreads six times faster than the truth, according to a 2018 Massachusetts Institute of Technology study by professors Deb Roy, Soroush Vosoughi, and Sinan Aral. You slowly become the search algorithm's amalgam of fact and fiction. That doctored bikini photo became part of my online identity even after I deleted the post from my timeline and blocked the writer. More friends and family members emailed me about it.

What could I do? Even in my own home, I couldn't avoid the male gaze online, where I worked, any more than the server, Sheila, could avoid my husband's wandering eye. Now, sitting at the restaurant table across from my husband, I thought about the night of the lemon and the day of the bikini, but with less sting. I could shake off my husband ogling a waitress and the occasional online sexist comment. Couldn't I? I thought I had girded myself for any assault but didn't realize how easily armour is pierced with a slender sword between the plates.

～☙～

The next morning after our dinner I was up at 5:00 a.m. My favourite time to write. It was still dark. The desk lamp cast a golden spotlight on my steaming green tea.

Although Ottawa is Canada's capital, it still felt like a small town far from the big media cities of Toronto, New York, and London. I loved that. It helped me avoid the constant stream of wine tastings.

I had never met most other wine writers. I treated writing like one long, gloriously extended English class. Kept my head down, worked hard, got good grades — alone. I also didn't go on many media trips to wine regions, which added to my isolation and happiness. Wineries usually paid for these. Often the stop at each winery was just long enough for the winemaker to deliver the standard slideshow, starting with the family timeline in 1848 and ending with how the new generation was revolutionizing viticulture, yet also bringing it back to the fundamentals of great-great-great-granddad. Same old press release.

Besides, travelling on a bus for a week with fifteen people, writers or not, was my definition of hell on wheels. Some writers interpreted my absence as a personal insult.

"Natalie's too good to be on the same bus with us," one writer posted on Twitter a few years back.

How could I avoid groupthink with everyone clustered around the winemaker hearing each other's questions and scribbling down the same answers? It was the difference between looking at a rhinoceros in the zoo versus tracking it yourself on the Serengeti. Most winemakers were cagier with their comments when in public-relations captivity versus roaming down a vineyard row with just one other person.

I believed, and still do, that conversational intimacy develops one-on-one. This allows for unguarded comments. After a long day together, the winemaker finally forgets that you're a writer and talks freely.

I travelled to wine regions only a few times a year on my own. Even these solo trips were packed, from early morning tastings to late-night drinks after dinner. They felt like a sensory assault. There was no time for wellness, not even a walk. But isn't wine about enjoying a happy, relaxed life with friends and family?

Sometimes I felt guilty I didn't become a nurse or a doctor. I was caring for the helpless rich who wanted to know which vintage to buy. Of course, there were many more wine lovers who were looking for good value. They worked hard, didn't have gobs of cash to throw down for a cult wine, but still wanted pleasure from what they drank.

Over time, I also discovered the vital place wine has in the economy. It's now a $500-billion industry worldwide. In the U.S., the wine sector contributes $276 billion to the country's economy and employs 1.8 million people. The Canadian industry is small, with only seven hundred wineries producing less than one percent of wine globally, according to a 2022 report by the industry association, Wine Growers Canada. However, it contributes $11.6 billion to our country's economy every year, also supporting industries such as restaurants, hotels, theatre, tourism, transportation, manufacturing, and retail. It employs forty-five thousand people, many in rural areas where more people can afford to live, supporting mostly family-owned farms from coast to coast. Every bottle of wine made from 100 percent Canadian grapes contributes about eighty dollars to the economy versus eighteen dollars for an import.

It's a high-stakes business, requiring expensive farming equipment, grape presses, fermentation tanks, and oak barrels. Unlike a chef who can quickly remake a dish that doesn't work, winemakers have just one chance each year to get it right. Every harvest, they face make-or-break decisions.

As I continued to connect with drinkers through my writing and online food and wine pairing courses, I realized that appreciating wine was not only part of enjoying it, but also of moderating it. My father was indiscriminate in his alcoholism and family relationships. I believe that what you know, love, and truly understand, you're less likely to abuse.

I understood myself better through writing. Even now, when I write, I make sense of the world on the page. This flow-state sparks creative connections, the opposite of my shrivelled primal brain worrying about being perfect and needing a drink to calm down.

I've always loved the challenge of long-form narrative, especially when I immerse myself in the subject. New Journalism writers, such as Truman Capote, Norman Mailer, and Joan Didion didn't believe in objectivity. They inserted themselves into the narrative. I'm not in their league, but I love their approach. This was unorthodox for wine writing and another reason some writers dismissed me.

In my first two books, I took that day-in-the-life approach by becoming a sommelier, working in several wine stores, and helping with the harvest. I tried to do what those who worked in these positions did, to feel what they felt. Readers can't identify with experts who remove themselves entirely from their writing. They touch your mind with their analysis like a cold point of steel, but they don't open your heart with empathy.

My earliest inspiration was the romantic poet John Keats. His belief in "negative capability" — when a person can stay in uncertainty and mystery — was the topic of my final paper at Oxford University. He tried to become one with what he observed to capture pure experience in words. I also wanted to capture the *feeling* of wine in words, not reduce it down to a fruit salad with a number.

On a walking tour of Rome's lesser-known food haunts several years ago, I discovered Keats's burial place. Leafy trees canopied the crumbling grey stones of those who wanted to be buried in Rome but who weren't citizens back in the eighteenth century. Call me morbid but walking through the graveyard on my way to a cheese shop made perfect sense: blending life and death; eating and satiation. I've kept up this practice of visiting cemeteries while on wine trips — my version of the circle of life. Later, I found out it's called graving and is practised by taphophiles, from the Greek *taphos*, meaning burial or funeral.

The heartbreaker is that Keats didn't want his name on his tombstone. Instead, he was simply identified as a young English poet. Keats felt he had contributed nothing to the world before he died at just twenty-five, from tuberculosis. He came into literary glory decades after his death.

Also on his tombstone: *Here lies One Whose Name was writ in Water* — a melancholy musing that everyone would forget him. Perhaps mine could be "Here lies one in time whose name shall be consumed with wine."

Keats's good friend Joseph Severn arranged for his own grave to be next to the writer's so he could indicate that the nameless stone beside his was that of his "death-bed companion, John Keats, whom he lived to see numbered among the Immortal Poets of England." I wondered if anyone would remember me when what I wrote about was so fleeting? Perhaps the most I could hope for was that they thought of me when they tasted a wine I'd recommended. In one article, I joked I had enough Air Miles to fly to Hawaii based on wine purchases alone. My tombstone would read:

Here lies Natalie MacLean
37,879,981 Air Miles
Too bad she expired before they did.

A Pox on Your Prose

Adam left the house at seven most mornings in early 2012. He rarely said goodbye. We were both focused on our work. Cameron was a night owl like his father. Rousing him required a SWAT (special warmth and tactics) approach. Bedroom lights on, curtains open. A groan from under the blanket.

"Good morning, hon!"

After Cameron was out the door, I got back to writing. Bottles sat on my desk to the left and right of my computer and filled the gaps in my bookshelves. In the back of the kitchen was a hallway I called Tasting Alley. Hundreds of bottles stood on the counters, in the cupboards, and inside a full-sized wine fridge. Three thousand more were under my feet in the basement. Cases of wine arrived daily from wineries and wine agencies. Several unopened boxes were always stacked in the front entrance.

Surrounded by wine, I lived in what an oenophile would consider paradise. That's why I've never made wine off limits to Cameron. I didn't want him thinking it was taboo.

"What's that?" Cameron pointed to my cabernet sauvignon at dinner one night when he was just three.

"It's wine, hon. Would you like to taste it?"

He nodded, putting his tiny hands on mine, holding the glass as he took a small sip.

"Yuck!" His small tongue tried to spit out the bitter liquid from his mouth.

Confession: Had I been drinking a sweet wine, I wouldn't have offered him a taste. I didn't want him thinking it was liquid candy. The tannins in the cabernet gave it a bitter, furry mouth taste and feel, like eating walnuts.

I think I overdid it though, as two decades later, Cameron still doesn't drink any alcohol. When I asked him if it was because of my drinking habits or career, he said no. He just wasn't interested. I wasn't either at his age.

Wine was never my first love; writing was. Wine gave me the confidence — liquid courage — to write. Now, I had an expertise that would interest publishers. The flip side of loving long-form narrative was loathing short-form wine reviews, most of which I found were fifty shades of dull.

When I left tech, my income dropped from a salary that had been a strong contributor to our household to almost nothing. While Adam supported my decision to be home with Cameron, I still felt the need to pull my weight financially. I pitched publications obsessively, trying to get back to my previous income. I contributed to the *Sydney Morning Herald* in Australia, *Canadian House & Home*, and the *Chicago Tribune*. It still didn't make much difference monetarily. It would have been faster opening a lemonade stand.

In 2004, I signed book deals with Random House in Canada and Bloomsbury in the U.S., the latter having published a little book series called *Harry Potter*. I wanted that magic dust. When we met the editor in New York City, he asked me how long it had taken me to write my book.

"All my life."

He laughed but realized that all of me was in it.

As we wrapped up the meeting, Anthony Bourdain, author of the bestselling memoir *Kitchen Confidential*, stood in the doorway of the editor's office. At six foot three, towered over me. I was tongue-tied, but he was disarmingly down-to-earth when we spoke briefly.

Entering this rarified world of New York publishing, with its giants both real (Bourdain) and fictional (Potter), I felt like I'd wandered into a fairy tale. *Jack and the Vine Stock*? *The Princess and the Pinot Noir*? Who needs a prince when you've got a book deal? In 2006, *Red, White, and Drunk All Over* made it to number four on the national bestseller list, though the income was still less than half of my tech salary.

❧

At 5:00 p.m. I headed down to Tasting Alley, where I sampled about thirty wines a day. A never-ending backlog of two hundred bottles waited on the counters. I realized then, and now, that there aren't any tiny violins playing for my "workload."

Lining up twenty-seven red blends from British Columbia enabled me to make better comparisons than mixing different regions. My wall-mounted corkscrew minimized the effort to open them. Otherwise, I'd have the wine writer's equivalent of tennis elbow.

My other tool of the trade: a big-ass glass, one with a large bowl rather than those pathetic golf ball–sized ones. Why do I still have one of these stamped with *Lucky Lotto 88* in my glass menagerie of shame?

The extra space allows me to swirl the wine without sloshing it on myself before I smell its aromas. We can detect millions of aromas via smell but only five tastes in our mouths (sweet, salty, bitter, sour, umami — a savoury character). Smell is the only sense that connects directly to the parts of the limbic system responsible for memory and emotion: amygdala and hippocampus. Our other senses don't have this direct connection. That's why smell can take you back to a memory more powerfully than can sight, sound, touch, or taste. I smell some wines and immediately I'm back where I first drank it, who I was with, what we were eating and discussing. It's the key to my memory palace, unlocking rooms I've forgotten for years.

Tasting wine means concentrating on individual components: aromas, flavours, acidity, tannin, structure, texture, weight, and finish. As I tell my online course students, the difference between tasting and drinking is *thinking*. Much like the movie critic who analyzes plot, dialogue, and character development for a review, the wine critic's approach to a glass differs from someone who's simply enjoying it. I can do both, though I find it hard to turn off the critical brain and sometimes find myself unconsciously swirling orange juice.

I took my time with each wine, entering notes on my laptop. I found this as tedious as paperwork. Spitting every sample kept my thinking from getting fuzzy. I got excited only when I loved the wine, and said so with non-technical notes like "Love, love, love this pinot noir — so luscious and smooth. To die for with roast chicken!" Fun and friendly didn't mean dumb and tasteless. I still added details about the wine's core aspects.

I also wrote about the people behind the wine. In my lineup was a bottle from Nk'Mip Cellars (*in-ka-meep*), in the Okanagan Valley, the first Indigenous-owned winery in North America. Winemaker and band member Justin Hall later told me that the name refers to the southern tip of the Osoyoos Indian Reserve where the vineyards are planted. It's one of the warmer areas in the region and where his ancestors spent their winters. Snow-capped mountains encircle a stunning desert landscape.

Nk'Mip Cellars Winemaker's Series Talon is a sumptuous, full-bodied blend of syrah, malbec, cabernet sauvignon, merlot, and pinot noir. Talon is named for the eagles that nest in the area. They call to mind the Thunderbird, a supernatural creature that's part of North American Indigenous Traditional Stories. The creature was so large and strong it could pick up a whale with its talons and had the power to protect people from evil spirits. The Thunderbird reminds me of the phoenix.

When I started writing, the farm-to-table movement connecting food producers with consumers was gaining momentum. More and more restaurant menus noted where their ingredients were sourced. That's what makes wine magical, too, moving it away from money and scores to people and places.

Wine was my calling card to talk to fascinating people around the planet. It gave me permission to ask incredibly nosy questions. It made me feel things I'd never felt.

This was the opposite approach from some older critics who believed you shouldn't have feelings about wine; you should be objective. I don't believe this is possible, as wine is such a subjective, sensory experience. Objectivity can also be a shield against vulnerability and connection.

Why shouldn't I get emotionally wrapped up in my work? Do you have to be serious to be professional? Must levity be the opposite of gravitas when the two make a more complex blend? Science has shown that the moment after we laugh, our attention to a message is highest. Entertain before you educate.

For me, wine starts with the person. How does this wine make you feel? Writing about wine consumes my whole body, like dance once did. When the dance finishes, the wine consumed, all that's left is memory. Wine involves all of me in a way that food cannot. It touches all the senses, like food, but wine is also a drug that creates new mind states. The full-body buzz of wine sends lightning out under my skin.

Talking about the effect of alcohol in wine was another way I broke the rules, as well as admitting to my likes and dislikes, memories and misunderstandings, blind spots and biases.

My problem? I was thinking like consumers, wondering how to get a good wine that didn't cost a fortune or embarrass me if I took it to a friend's house. Sure, most critics will tell you they're consumer advocates. But some aren't talking to consumers with empathy for their anxiety, confusion, or disappointment with wine. Instead, they talk to a wine lover like a displeased parent.

That's why I never aspired to be a critic like Robert Parker, who popularized scoring wine in the U.S. in the 1970s. Most reviewers now use the 100-point scale. For the first three years I wrote about wine, I refused to do so. How can you trap a subjective experience in a number? But after numerous requests from my readers for this shorthand that they could easily understand to buy wine, I started using them.

The financial crisis of 2008 gutted traditional wine criticism. Many newspapers and magazines cut their wine columns and other lifestyle content. Others just went out of business. These days, I can think of only three U.S. newspapers employing a full-time wine critic: the *New York Times*, the *Wall Street Journal*, and *San Francisco Chronicle*. The last one I know of in Canada was Beppi Crosariol, who left the *Globe and Mail* in 2017 and was replaced by a freelancer. The few writers who have a wine column get paid an average of a couple hundred dollars per column, hardly a living. Most just post their reviews on their own website and on social media, where everyone expects them to be free.

At the same time, my site was growing quickly. Every day, I'd run downstairs like it was Christmas morning to check how many people had signed up for my free newsletter — five hundred, five thousand, fifty thousand. I couldn't keep up with my inbox, which was flooded with more than a hundred emails a day. I hired a virtual assistant, then another one, and then contracted a web developer.

New wine sites popped up to fill the vacuum left by the demise of traditional print columns. In 2009, the financial investor behind a website I'll call Wine Corp emailed me multiple times before I finally agreed to talk to him by phone. After making his fortune in tech, he had set his sights on reinventing the wine world.

"How come I never heard of you before I got into this business?"

"I don't know." I blushed at his question.

"Well, I found out I have ninety-two thousand reasons to talk to you." He was referring to the number of people who received my free newsletter. He then explained how big his site would become and why I should be part of his online posse of mostly male critics, several of whom had lost their print columns.

"Why would my readers continue to subscribe to my reviews if they can get them on your site?"

Silence.

"Well, you can be part of this or not, but it's gonna happen."

After our chat, he sent me detailed launch plans unsolicited, confident that I'd become part of his endeavour, even though I'd spent a decade building my own site and community.

I declined. I figured that was that. We'd all move on.

In 2010, I shared on Twitter that I had been to a tasting of eighty wines, recalling being overwhelmed at my first tasting years ago of just twelve wines. With time, you develop the stamina to taste more wines, just as you improve at almost anything with practice.

Wine Corp's investor tweeted back that I must have a "supernatural" tasting ability. It clearly wasn't a compliment and something I never claimed. Of course, a witch would have special powers, so why not accuse her of being unnatural?

I am, however, technically a "supertaster." Dr. Linda Bartoshuk, at Yale University School of Medicine, discovered the supertaster phenomenon in 1999. Women are more than twice as likely as men to be supertasters. Women have more fungiform papillae, the tiny structures on the tongue that hold taste buds. This doesn't mean that we're *better* tasters — that comes with practice — but it does mean that we're more sensitive tasters.

Dr. Bartoshuk dipped a thyroid medication on study partici-pants' tongues to test their sensitivity to bitterness. She divided the population into three groups: non-tasters with limited palates (25 percent), tasters with average palates (50 percent), and supertasters with very sensitive palates (25 percent). Supertasters possess more than a hundred times more taste buds per square inch than do regular tasters. She compares this to having five hundred fingers rather than just ten, noting that supertasters live in a "neon world of taste."

Tim Hanni, a sensory taste specialist and Master of Wine in California, measured the density and number of my taste buds for an article I was writing. Being a supertaster also means being extra-sensitive to your entire environment. Hanni knew without my telling him that I cut the tags out of my clothing, prefer tea over coffee, and have thermostat wars with family members. It's also why I probably didn't start drinking alcohol until I discovered wine in my late twenties. Beer and whisky were both too bitter.

The combination of being an isolated woman with what others perceived as suspect skills reminded me of *The Scarlet Letter*. Nathaniel Hawthorne's classic novel is set in seventeenth-century Salem, Massachusetts. Hester Prynne, accused of adultery, is shamed on the public square scaffolding with the letter *A* embroid-ered on her dress. She's as much an outcast as Ann Hibbins, who encourages her to practise "witchcraft" — learning about healing herbs. Hibbins is later executed.

That was fiction. In reality, my Generation X friends and I assumed our mothers had won the battle for women's rights in the 1970s. As we got into our careers, we discovered the laws may have changed, but the mindsets hadn't. When we made it to middle management or took up too much space in the media landscape, we weren't nice girls anymore. I asked a sommelier friend what I'd done to make them hate me so much.

"Nothing. They want your piece of pie since they can't be bothered to bake their own."

~☙~

When I noticed some critics on Wine Corp giving wines negative reviews, I was relieved I hadn't joined. I was fine with low scores if they were deserved, but not with what appeared to be nasty comments about the winery. To me, the site's approach didn't come off as radically honest, but as festering brutally bad karma. Wine and food are part of hospitality; they're about welcoming people to your table and forgetting your cares for a while.

That's why when I came across a wine that I believed was poorly made, I didn't review it. Some people thought I should, to warn consumers from buying it. Call it Whine of the Week. But my readers had enough challenge remembering the thousands of great wines I recommended. They didn't need a long list of bad ones. I wanted to attract good energy by celebrating the pleasures of life.

I did, however, review expensive wines even when I believed the quality didn't match the price. Then collectors could judge for themselves if they wanted to buy that vintage. I'd signal this low quality/price ratio with a warranted low score. For example, a one-hundred-dollar bottle got a score of 87 points out of 100. I believe that given its price, it should have a score in the 90s because of its higher investment in production, from the quality of the vineyards to the oak barrels.

I wasn't a wine snob; I was a writing snob. I got sniffy at anyone who misplaced a semicolon. What a *grammateur*. Wine reviews were the classified ads of the wine world: mundane facts strung together with commas. You might start a career writing these, like reporting on house fires for a newspaper. If you had any potential, you didn't stay on that beat. Opinion columns were where the real talent bylined.

When I started writing a column for *Ottawa Magazine*, I convinced the editor to let me write narrative-driven columns without wine reviews. The magazine's sister publication, *Toronto Life*, took the opposite approach, focusing almost exclusively on reviews. Yet another gulf separating me from the Toronto crowd and their approach to the craft.

In 2011, a different email alert popped up in my inbox. It was for one of my own reviews, but the link took me to Wine Corp. I found a dozen of my reviews going back several years.

As I continued to click around the site, I noticed they were not only copying my reviews, but also those from many other writers, including Jancis Robinson, Ian D'Agata, and Robert Parker. Had they secured permission from them? I doubted it.

Wait a minute, I thought. I've read some of these reviews before, somewhere ... Ah, the LCBO site! The Liquor Control Board of Ontario (LCBO) is the government-owned corporation that sells wine in the province. It's the second-largest buyer of alcohol in the world after Costco, with retail sales of over six billion dollars a year.

Wine Corp was copying the reviews from the LCBO. Were other writers doing this as well? Yes. At the top of the Google search results was another site doing the same thing and posting my reviews. I assumed the reviews must be in the public domain as they were posted on a government site. The LCBO had never asked me for permission to post my reviews. No one had ever complained. Nothing about it on social media. It must be okay, I thought.

That assumption was my first mistake.

I didn't even consider that Wine Corp might be violating my copyright by publishing my reviews. I was a glass-half-full kind of gal, so I started posting the latest LCBO reviews on my site rather than asking the other two sites to remove mine. I believed that if I quoted multiple reviews, like Rotten Tomatoes did for movies, I'd be providing my readers with more context for each wine beyond my review.

That was my second mistake.

I began with newly released wines and didn't go back in time to publish the thousands of reviews the Wine Corp and the other site had already posted. I didn't subscribe to other writers' sites to access all their reviews behind their paywalls. The reviews I posted were only from the liquor store site and they were not behind my paywall.

While the LCBO's Vintages catalogue spelled out the writers' names and publications, their other print and online publications used their initials beside reviews with a separate directory to spell them out. For instance, Robert Parker was RP, Wine Spectator was WS, and so on. I followed that format and included the full names in a directory on my site. My readers, already familiar with this directory, could reference it for the full names.

That was my third mistake, though not my biggest.

∽◎◇

Near the end of 2011, I couldn't believe I was sitting at the same table as Lettie Teague, the executive wine editor of *Food & Wine* magazine. Susan Kostrzewa (*Wine Enthusiast*), Bruce Schoenfeld (*Travel + Leisure*), and Richard Bradley (*Worth*), among other top-notch editors, were also at the Napa Valley Wine Writers' Symposium. Although my hermit self recoiled from most gatherings, I couldn't resist the heady excitement of talking to these thought leaders in the industry.

This private event was hosted at the Meadowood Napa Valley resort, which backed onto a mountain overlooking a hundred hectares of wooded canyons and vineyard rows. The food, wine, and place were a symphony for the senses. Fortunately, my conference expenses were covered by the Saintsbury Fellowship, in honour of George Saintsbury (1845–1933). He was a professor of English at the University of Edinburgh and a wine writer. His book *Notes on a Cellar*, published in 1920, is a classic.

One of the fiercest debates was whether wine bloggers were "real writers." Many bloggers were unpaid wine lovers posting reviews on their own sites and on social media. Those with larger followings often had taken wine courses and several had earned advanced diplomas. Some long-time critics who had lost their jobs with the collapse of traditional media resented the incursion of these "amateurs." Bloggers, also at the event, envied the writers' established legitimacy and felt snubbed. The tension between them felt like a third person in the room.

I didn't fit in either camp, having come from tech. I had a website and mobile apps early, unlike the traditionalists. Yet I also wrote for mainstream magazines and had published a book with Random House. I straddled both worlds, an outsider to both. Story of my life.

My approach was personal, conversational, and feminine — also at odds with being taken seriously. The sneering, sometimes vicious, comments on my social media accounts started early in my career. Friends and colleagues would post comments defending

me, but they were often flamed for it, even when they did so anonymously or using a pseudonym. I appreciated their protective
feelings but told them to stop and just block the trolls. When these
nasty posts appeared in the comments section of my site, I deleted
them — an endless round of web whack-a-mole. Some remarks
about my appearance back then remind me of comments now made
about Instagram influencers, many of whom are young women cari-
catured as babes, boobs, and bottles.

Between sessions, I ran back to my hotel room for a call with
Gary Vaynerchuk. He had developed Wine Library TV, a YouTube
channel to promote his family's New Jersey liquor store. He, too,
was a weird hybrid, not having a Master of Wine or another traditional accreditation. He's since created a multi-million-dollar
media agency that helps brands like Kraft Foods, Prudential
Financial, and Unilever with their digital strategies.

"I admire what you've done with your brand," he said.

"That means a lot coming from you, Gary. I'm publishing my
second book this fall. Might you be willing to endorse it with a
short blurb for the cover?"

"Let's do it."

We spoke for a little longer, then hung up. I bounced around the
hotel room for a few minutes before running back to the conference.

I started writing because it gave me joy. I was surprised when
my writing made others happy too, as I didn't think I had the skill
to do it. Reader letters and emails in response to *Red, White, and
Drunk All Over* touched me. One woman quit her corporate job
and moved to wine country to become a sommelier. A man in the
navy wrote that my book was a welcome relief from weeks of grey
days at sea. A depressed young woman highlighted the funny bits
and reread them when she felt down.

Affirmation became my other drug of choice — more addictive
than wine. Adam loved my success. I began to feel like a popular

product line extension of his rather than the other half of a power couple. I had a "Steve Jobs–like obsessiveness" that he admired.

As my website grew, so did my desire for more. I pushed myself harder to create search engine–friendly content that didn't tap into my deepest creative self:

16 Wines to Buy Based on Your Myers-
Briggs Personality Profile

Sure, that headline got lots of clicks, but who cares? I sure as hell didn't. I felt like Google's content rat, hitting the pellet dispenser for eyeballs that didn't really see me. I felt seen on the page when I shared stories about people, but less and less visible within my own marriage.

The Crucible

"Define the word *imminent*," the psychologist said.

"It's gonna happen soon," Cameron, then eight years old, replied.

"Use it in a sentence."

"The destruction of the Death Star is imminent."

The psychologist raised an eyebrow at me. I flushed with pride.

Cameron's grade two teacher had suggested we have him tested academically after he won the math award. Cameron wasn't drawn to sports, so on Saturday mornings he and Adam went to Starbucks to work on increasingly difficult math questions. We learned his math skill was at a grade twelve level. I was secretly pleased that he scored just a little higher on the verbal scale.

Turns out, the Death Star wasn't the only one whose destruction was imminent. Like most couples, Adam and I had our issues over the years. We tried to take corrective action, including the Let's Have a Child Cure, the Move Across Town Tonic, and the Kitchen Renovation Remedy.

Now, after two decades together, we'd done all the hard work with our family and careers. He'd worked his way up to CEO. I'd created a career in wine. We'd raised a remarkable son. I looked forward to the next twenty years — and to the twenty after that.

I assumed that a long-term relationship eventually matured into contented companionship. We had enormous respect for each other's career success. We still had sex, though not as frequently as when we were first together. Does anyone? We didn't argue much, but Adam occasionally yelled at me or Cameron if something broke, or we didn't figure things out as quickly as he expected. I believed I just needed to try harder.

We often hosted dinner parties at home with two or three other couples in tech. I loved the conversation at these meals. I especially loved Adam's confidence. His approach was refreshingly opposite to the small-town question I had grown up with: "What will people think?" Adam didn't care. If he believed something, he said so, and often quite bluntly. Sometimes, those opinions landed hard. But most of our friends were driven types who didn't offend easily. Plus, the wine soaked up any awkward silences.

I admired Adam's candour in contrast to both my relatives and myself, who often didn't say what we felt. I believed he would always be honest with me.

One evening, after several weeks of cold distance, I walked into the bedroom. He had all our financial records spread out on a desk. It was January 21, 2012.

"What are you doing?"

He didn't answer — just stood there staring at the piles of paper.

"What's wrong? Are you upset with me?"

He dropped his head and closed his eyes.

"Have we lost our retirement savings?"

He shook his head.

"Do you feel okay? Do you have ... prostate cancer?" I was panicking at his silence.

He shook his head again.

After a dozen more questions about family, work, and health, I grasped at the unthinkable, just to rule it out. "Do ... do you want a divorce?"

"What if I did?" He sat down on a chair by the bed and rested his forehead in both hands.

"What?" I whispered. I dropped down on the side of the bed, nearly falling off.

He looked at me for a moment, then started talking.

I listened to the emotional content of what he was saying, but not the words. Numb panic. *How could I have missed this?*

His words stung like shrapnel. "Drifted apart ... We've changed ... I can't."

"Is there someone else?" Immediately I regretted asking, ignoring the prickling feeling that prompted the question.

"How can you even *ask* me that?" His face pulled tight.

Guilt torched my cheeks. Here I was accusing some mythical other woman of causing our marital breakdown, rather than asking more painful questions.

What did I do wrong? Was I not loving enough, not sexy enough?

In my mind, I walked through a list of my potential faults like a home inspector. So many cracks. Which one had caused the collapse?

～☜～

Later that evening, after my tears ran dry, I wondered if I should have noticed the warning signs. We'd always loved talking about our careers and long-term aspirations. I realized now that he had stopped asking me about my work more than a year ago. He spent hours each evening reading, yet he'd not finished my second book.

He had also started calling me Mumsy. At first, I took this to be part of his British upbringing. Eventually, I felt desexualized in his eyes. That was a flashing neon billboard and I missed it. When we met in our early twenties, we'd had a lusty relationship. Although that young flame had softened, it wasn't extinguished.

The television show *Sons of Anarchy*, about a criminal motorcycle gang, may be a bizarre source of marriage advice, but as a biker's wife observes, "Only men need to be loved. Women need to be wanted."

I *still* wanted to be desired.

I didn't just feel desexualized, I also felt depersonalized. It seemed he praised me only for my career achievements, how professionally I dressed, and other external factors. He didn't recognize the mental load of keeping the conversation upbeat at dinner, anticipating when his favourite pantry food was running low, or worrying about small vacation details.

I participated in the depersonalizing process, abandoning my body, where I'd lived for years as a dancer, and moving into the cold attic of my mind, where it was all words and work. I saved my strongest emotions for writing, trapped in black type on a white screen. My head wanted to live on without the rest of me. My body just slowed it down.

I loved that Adam respected my skills, and yearned for more of his approval. One way to get it was through professional recognition. While in Australia on assignment for Air Canada's *enRoute* magazine in 2003, I attended the World Food Media Awards. I couldn't resist entering the competition, even though I'd been writing about wine for only four years.

Across the categories, there were more than a thousand entries. In the World's Best Drinks Journalist category, an international panel of magazine and newspaper editors shortlisted fourteen nominees including Gerald Asher (*Gourmet* magazine, U.S.), Tim Atkin (the *Observer*, U.K.), Chris Orr (*Decanter* magazine, U.K.), and Huon Hooke (the *Sydney Morning Herald*, Australia).

That night at the ceremony, they announced my name. I asked Canadian food columnist Lucy Waverman, who was sitting beside me, if I'd heard right. I was convinced it was wishful thinking.

That win gave me the confidence to apply for the James Beard Foundation Awards, the Oscars of food and drink writing in the U.S. In 2004, an article I wrote on my website was shortlisted for the M.F.K. Fisher Award for Excellence in Culinary Writing. This was part of the Beard Foundation's ceremony and given out last, like the Best Picture Award. I was a country mouse sitting in that Manhattan hotel in an audience of three hundred big-city cats: writers and editors from *Bon Appétit*, *Food & Wine*, the *Atlantic*, and others.

By the end of the evening, I had gulped down as much wine as I could. When they made the announcement, I was again sure I hadn't heard right. Adam smiled and nodded. Before I went up to the stage, he gave me one of the most loving kisses I'd ever felt from him. It was better than the medal.

As the winners gathered on stage for a group photograph, I felt dizzy standing beside Bill Buford (the *New Yorker*), Russ Parsons (*Los Angeles Times*), and Melissa Clark (the *New York Times*).

Colman Andrews, editor of *Saveur* magazine, leaned over and said, "This is the first time a piece on the internet has won the M.F.K., congrats."

He shook my hand, and I wanted to say something clever but self-deprecating — like he was shaking my research arm, and the other hand was my editing division. I kept my mouth shut and thanked him.

Jeffrey Steingarten, *Vogue* magazine food columnist, walked up to me afterward and asked with a sly grin, "Who the hell are you and where did you come from?"

Adam smiled broadly in reaction to Steingarten.

The morning after the ceremony, we were on the way back to JFK airport. As the taxi wove through streets banked by skyscrapers, Adam was glued to his phone. Through my headphones, I listened over and over to the Journey song "Don't Stop Believin'."

~⊚~

A sprinkling of New York glitter, then back to the grind. My mind was crammed with tiny details, from picking up the dry cleaning to arranging household repairs. I usually had thirty-two mental browser tabs open. I planned our social calendar, dinner parties, and holiday gatherings. I took our son to his classes, monitored his homework, and attended his school concerts. All of this is often considered "normal mother stuff." In retrospect, not sharing those tasks with Adam was a mistake. It created more distance between us.

Meanwhile, Adam was developing his career, interested in big ideas and networking. When there was something I needed him to do, I felt like a to-do-list nag. I hated it. I didn't know how to dig myself out of the role. As the years went by, my desire for skin-to-skin touch with Adam came only after we had been out for dinner with wine and had a great conversation. I needed the mental bond before wanting the physical one. My synapses for emotional connection gradually shrivelled; those neural pathways in my brain went dark.

I didn't notice. He didn't seem to care.

~⊚~

"What if I did?"

Adam's answer to whether he wanted a divorce was a bomb blast still ringing in my head. I just stared at him, seeing the rubble of our relationship. Under the shock was shame.

I had secretly been a little proud about outlasting my mother's marriage. Mom, the high school prom queen, met my gregarious father in Toronto at a "down-east dance" for Atlantic Canadians. They married two years later. In another nine months, I was born. When I was two, we moved back home to Nova Scotia and lived in a trailer. Mom taught at a small school. My father never gave up his pre-marriage carousing, arriving home in the middle of the night drunk and playing mournful country tunes on the stereo. One night after he had passed out on the sofa, Mom cut the stereo power cord. The next day, she and I moved to another town. I was too young to know what was happening, but I love that story now — Mom's strength and her fierce protection of me.

In the few pictures I have of my father, he always has a beer bottle in hand, except for one where I was sitting on his lap. It's Christmas, just before we moved to that town. As I grew up, I didn't miss him, though I missed the idea of having a father. I told kids at school that he was out at sea, like many of their dads.

I thought I'd improved on Mom's story. She had gone to a local college, lived in a small village, and taught elementary school. I'd finished a graduate degree, lived in the big city, and was the successful author of two books. I had been married for twenty years to my intellectual soulmate versus her two with the life-of-the-party guy. Clearly, I had more smarts to keep my marriage together. Oh, so wrong.

That night, I couldn't sleep. Adam and I had separate bedrooms after Cameron was born. I didn't want to wake Adam when feeding our son several times during the night. We stuck with that arrangement since Adam liked reading late into the night and I woke early to write. I'd read several articles about separate bedrooms becoming common for many reasons, from insomnia to snoring. But was sleeping separately part of the issue, too? Would there have been a stronger emotional bond if Adam also had to sacrifice his sleep or would our marriage have ended sooner?

My mind kept replaying our recent interactions. How could this be happening when I still loved him so much? When did it start? Could I have prevented it? Then my mind raced forward. I was going be a single mother, like Mom. A cold sweat snaked down my spine as I gripped the blanket under my chin.

Where would Cameron and I live? How would I support my seventy-one-year-old mother, who depended on me? What about the freelancers and their families who also relied on my business? Would I have to go back to tech to earn a living? I hated corporate life. How could I start over in a field I had left thirteen years ago that was moving so fast? I'd have to sit in front of young interviewers who'd look at me and then down at the gaping corporate hole in my resumé. I'd likely get rejected for being too old, though they'd position it as my skills were outdated.

Now that I feared losing my wine writing career, it seemed even more precious. The ceiling moved toward me. I couldn't swallow. My breaths became shorter and shorter. I was terrified that my marriage wasn't the only thing about to collapse.

Karma's a Witch

I stood in the bathroom, one hand on the counter for support, the other gripping the toothbrush. The toothpaste fell off. I stared at Adam in the mirror as he got ready for work. He was still handsome, his dark hair now greying at the temples. He picked out a suit. It could have been for my funeral.

He looked at me, looked away, and left.

I curled up in a ball on the bed, sobbing. My head was exploding. *Why? Why now?*

Eventually I got up, took two Aspirin, and grabbed my phone.

"Mom," I whispered.

"What's wrong, Nat?"

Silence.

"What's wrong? You're worrying me, Nat."

"Adam ... Adam wants a divorce."

"Oh, honey. You don't deserve this —"

I burst into tears, rocking back and forth, moaning.

"I'm here, hon. Let it out."

After I calmed down, I recounted the previous night's conversation with Adam. There wasn't much I could share with her other than my shock. She also suffers from anxiety. I didn't want to worry her with my fears about the future.

"Have you told Cameron?"

"Not yet. I need to be able to tell him without breaking down."

"There's no rush, Nat. Take it one day at a time. It took me several weeks before I could tell Grammy and Grampy that we ran away from home."

That's how she still describes leaving my father. This time though, I was the one being left behind. She was trying to make me feel better, but her words chewed me up inside. I couldn't remember what else we talked about until she said, "I'm here for you. Call me anytime, Nat."

After we hung up, I called my family doctor for referrals: a marriage counsellor for us and a psychologist for me to see on my own. I was still clinging to the notion that we were smart enough to work this out with professional help. We weren't those screaming idiots on reality television. I know how horrendously stuck-up that sounds. Pride was the wind in my perfect storm.

A week later, Adam sat beside me in our counsellor's office with his arms crossed over his chest, giving curt answers. During our third session, the counsellor turned to me: "You need to get a lawyer."

Wait, I thought. *Aren't you supposed to help us work things out? Aren't there other options like more counselling or a trial separation? Are you saying we should go straight to divorce?*

As soon as he said it, something inside me knew. I just wouldn't acknowledge it.

∽◈∾

— 54 —

In the days that followed, I slowly accepted that Adam had no interest in working things out. It would have been easier if I wasn't still in love with him. With bone marrow melancholy, I had to face the inevitable. I followed the counsellor's advice and found a lawyer.

While my life was chaos, I controlled the only thing I could: drafting the separation agreement. Why not? I had always done the secretarial duties in the family. Finally, the thankless administrative tasks might be worthwhile. Controlling this one piece of my life put my mind at ease. I was also able to think through all the issues carefully. The most important was Cameron. At fourteen, he was at a vulnerable time in his life, undergoing many emotional and physical changes, yet still a child when it came to adult relationships.

"We need to talk to you about something." Adam sat at the opposite end of the sofa from me. Cameron, in the chair across from us, looked alarmed.

"Your mother and I have decided to get a divorce."

"Oh." Cameron looked from his father to me and back again.

"This is between your father and me. It has nothing to do with you, hon. We both love you … very much. How are you feeling?"

"Okay." Cameron looked blank as he fidgeted with a pencil.

Was he trying to analyze the situation in his head? Had he already disconnected from the conversation? I couldn't tell. "Are you surprised?"

"Yeah, I thought I was … in trouble … for something." Cameron grimaced.

Apparently, Cameron wasn't expecting the news either.

We assured Cameron that he'd stay in our home with me and attend the same school with the same friends. His father would find a place close by. Cameron still wasn't reacting much. Although he wasn't normally highly expressive, I worried about how the separation was hitting him.

The next day, I asked Cameron if he'd like to talk with a counsellor, but he said no. His answer wrenched me, but I decided it was better not to force it. Giving him a hug, I told him he could change his mind or talk to me anytime. I wished I could fix this for him with one of the Bob the Builder bandages he loved when he was two.

Things had been civil between Adam and me. But I felt caught unaware again when a friend said that Adam had told him we'd become "just roommates." Was this sympathy-seeking male code for *he wasn't getting any*? My shoulders slumped as I sat back in my office chair. I felt like this characterized the little sex we still had as obligatory, as though it were on my to-do list:

✓ pick up paper towels
✓ call the roofing company
✓ have sex with Adam
✓ finish chardonnay column

Before I became the Wine Witch, I was the White Witch, from C.S. Lewis's novel *The Lion, The Witch and The Wardrobe*. Plunging Narnia into a one-hundred-year freeze, she also cancelled Christmas. She was frigid — and now, apparently, so was I.

Adam also told friends he'd been pondering leaving me for some time. Ponder all you want, I wanted to say to him — just share those ponderings first with me. But it was already too late for those conversations. I can't remember ever being late or missing a deadline in my life. Now I'd misunderstood the whole point of the marriage assignment. I could pair the most difficult dish with the most obscure wine. Yet I couldn't master the basics to keep my relationship together. The narrative of my life had run off without me.

‿❦‿

"If one person is unhappy in the relationship, it's their unhappy."
My friend Cassie's dark brown eyes were intense. "It's their responsibility to explore what's going on."

We sat on the living room sofa, the cold February sun reflecting
on our glasses of pinot noir. She ran her own successful landscaping
company. We'd known each other for a decade. Her husband had
cheated on her, but they had managed to stay together. We had
shared wine and tears back then, too. I admired her strength.

Cameron was upstairs doing homework. Adam was out at another late business dinner. It had been a month since he'd dropped
the divorce bomb, but he was still living with Cameron and me. I
didn't want him to have to live in a hotel while he searched for a new
house. Still, passing him in the hallway every morning pierced me,
knowing that even though he hadn't moved out, he'd moved on.

"How did you guys stay together?"

"Lots of therapy and books." Cassie laughed. "It's not for everyone — every marriage is different, Nat." She put her hand on mine.

The softness of her skin, her tenderness, cracked something inside me. I started sobbing. Cassie seemed startled. Like most of my
friends, she'd never seen me down, let alone crying.

"No matter what happens, I'm here for you." She hugged me.

"And *this* is here for us." I took deep, shaky breaths and reached for
the bottle to top up our glasses. We laughed, though mine was ragged.

After Cassie left, I dropped back down into the sofa. Therapy
and books were last week's failures. So much was changing so fast,
and I couldn't do anything about it. I used to worry about matching
dinner plates. Now I struggled to get out of bed each morning.

That week Adam kept telling me, "I gave you twenty years," as
if asking what more could I want. I thought, *It feels like you took
twenty years from me ... years that I could have spent building a life
with someone who would have done the challenging emotional work of
talking about issues rather than running away from them. You reached*

forward in time and took away the person I had dreamed of becoming. After twenty years, every relationship needs a reboot, not the boot.

Were these angry thoughts a good thing? Were they even justified? Was I finally moving through the five stages of grief? Even though psychiatrist Elisabeth Kübler-Ross's concept of grieving has since been debunked, I still grasped at it to understand what was happening. Step one: denial with shock and sadness. Check. Step two: pissed off. Check. If so, steps three and four were next: bargaining and depression. What about step five: acceptance? Hoping for that seemed delusional.

I had learned how to water down angry thoughts with unwanted tears. When did that start? Was it when I was a child, unable to fix Mom's grief about her divorce? I didn't know what my father had done to make her so angry with him. Had I modelled my marriage on hers, with a man focused on the world but with little to give emotionally?

I wanted to be angry like the witches I loved in literature — Circe, Hecate, Morgan le Fay. They got mad as hell and didn't give a damn who fried in their fury. That was the opposite of what traditionally "nice" women did. We were supposed to be polite and silent, swallowing our distress with wine. I became a professional at this, crocheting my own 1950s straitjacket.

Somewhere inside me, though, anger was biding its time.

I swung between sadness and anger as we discussed how to divide our assets. We negotiated the dissolution of our marriage like a corporate divestiture, line item by line item. Every piece of furniture had some emotional attachment: where we had purchased it, how it had moved with us from home to home. Even a small knick-knack or a book brought back memories of someone opening it as a Christmas gift or reading it on vacation.

"I think we should sell the house." Adam sat at the opposite end of the kitchen table one morning. "You don't need all this space, and we're going to split custody of Cameron anyway."

My heart sank as I thought of being without Cameron every other week and of losing my home on top of the trauma of divorce.

"Cameron is already dealing with us splitting up. I ... I think we should keep him in the same home, the same school."

"I disagree." Adam's eyes narrowed. "He's young, he's resilient, this will be good for him. What doesn't kill you ..."

"This is our son." I stood up. "Not the car or the retirement fund. You said you didn't want us to fight this in court and give half of what we own to lawyers. Well, I'm ready to give everything I have to my damn lawyer!"

Ah, there you are, anger. You finally showed up when I had to defend my son. Why weren't you there for me?

Adam raised the issue several more times but backed off when I pointed out we had recently purchased the house and made several renovations. We wouldn't recoup the cost by selling it then. I wanted Cameron to have a strong relationship with his father but also made sure I maintained primary custody.

On the icy late-March morning Adam moved out, he carried a box of old wine glasses with dishwasher stains that I had used for tasting events.

"You're taking *those*?" I was thinking of the good Riedel glasses he could take instead.

"Yes, I'm taking these and whatever else!" Adam waved his hand toward the house.

His comment about the glasses hit me hard. They were so connected to my work and identity. Did he think he was responsible for everything, including my career success?

Months later, I gave away many remaining household items to charity. As each box left the house, I felt lighter. I sold a few things, including my wedding dress. In the listing for it on a classified ads site, I added, "Husband included."

Budbreak

Game of Crones

A few days after Adam moved out, I sat in my office staring at the ceiling, still going over clues — his facial expressions, body language, comments — I had overlooked leading up to that eviscerating conversation.

Ding!

A strange email appeared in my inbox from Sean, someone both Adam and I knew from the tech industry.

"There's something you should know," Sean wrote. "I need to speak to you."

I panicked and emailed back immediately. "Please call me now."

The phone rang.

"I'm sorry to disturb you." Sean's voice was deep and hesitant. "But I thought you'd want to know this …"

"What is it?" My voice rasped.

"I think your husband and Mary are together."

Mary was also in the tech industry. I'd always admired her flaming auburn hair and emerald-green eyes.

What? Oh God, no.

"I don't think so. They just know each other from industry events."

Sean had to be wrong. Adam always took the moral high road. His firm ethical stance on many issues was another reason I admired him so much.

"They were shopping for a house together. They picked out furniture at HomeSense last week and they're putting cabinets in their new house. Her parents are joining them Friday for Chinese takeout."

For several long moments I couldn't speak. The week before Adam moved out, he had asked me what I thought of the quality of HomeSense furniture. Yesterday he'd called me from work to get the contacts for California Closets and our painter. This morning he had emailed me to ask for the phone number of our favourite Asian restaurant.

I felt sorry for Adam. He was living on his own, fixing up a new place, and eating takeout on a Friday night alone. I had been as helpful as I could.

My fingernails dug into my fist.

"How ... how do you know that?" I blinked hard, grief overcoming anger.

"It was completely accidental, but I thought you should know."

So this wasn't actually proof of anything.

"Mary's probably just helping him, as a friend," I stammered, defending Adam — or my own pride. "Even if they're dating, he's a free man. We've been separated for two months."

There was no way I would have agreed to keep living under the same roof for two months after our separation discussion if I had believed he had been cheating.

Still, I felt heartbroken over how fast Adam had rebounded.

"That may be true. I just didn't want you to be blindsided," Sean said.

After I said goodbye to Sean, I called Adam. I didn't want to, but I had to.

"Are you dating Mary?"

Silence.

"I have no idea what you're talking about." His voice simmered.

"Were you with her when we were still together?"

"No, I wasn't! You're crazy!"

Waves of burning frustration flooded my body, not just over his potential deception, but also because I felt I was the sole cause of his loneliness. Had it been a dance of three?

"Are you being straight with me?" My voice was rising. Fear, sadness, and even the desire to still protect Adam were there, but where was my anger about this possible betrayal of my trust? Was I afraid to unleash it because I still depended on Adam for child support? There was even a deeper layer of anger about that dependence.

He hung up.

~⊚~

"After working on hundreds of divorce cases, I can tell you that most men don't leave abruptly — unless they have emotional support already lined up. Someone in the wings," Emma said. We sat in her small law office to draft the separation agreement on a blustery April afternoon. The hair on the back of my neck stood up.

In her mid-fifties, with reading glasses on a beaded chain, she had the air of a stern high school English teacher and the street cred of having gone through a divorce herself.

"Most men don't make a hard stop without a soft landing. Separation can be harder on them than on their wives. They're lonelier. They're usually the ones moving out of the family home.

"When there isn't someone waiting for them, they waver. There's a lot of back and forth about re-establishing the relationship. This has nothing to do with how long they were thinking about it. Rather, do they have someone they can talk to? If they do, they move on."

Had I been gullible? Was this what had happened? I still wasn't sure.

On the way home, I thought about how it's far harder to heal on your own first than to jump into another relationship immediately, to feel the pain of loss alone, and to think about what you need to change before starting a new relationship. It's the emotional equivalent of a dislocated shoulder that you never reset. During the first session, our marriage counsellor had talked about how reinvention is necessary in long-term relationships. "You can live many lives with the same person or the same life with different people."

I should know because I had been on the other side of the scenario when I met Adam. He was separated from his first wife, and they were living five hundred kilometres apart. Fair game, I thought. He's a free man.

I wasn't even looking for love at Western. I had just completed a personal finance report projecting my income as a marketing manager. I'd also mapped my life as a single woman, content with living on my own. If I wasn't married by thirty-five, I'd go to a sperm bank, the gold club kind, and have one child. It would be a girl because I'd know what to do with a girl: shopping, mani-pedi, career advice.

I learned from Mom that I didn't need a man to do anything. But as I got to know Adam, I wanted to do everything with him. We were two thoroughbreds racing side by side to success, wherever that was.

In the first few years we lived together, we'd have breakfast at the small café around the corner, then walk to the subway station. He'd go downtown to Citibank. I'd head uptown to Procter & Gamble.

"Do you want to get married?" I asked Adam. The aroma of freshly brewed coffee and warm pastries filled the café as other commuters came in from the rainy October morning.

"Are you proposing?" His eyes twinkled.

"Yes. Should I get down on my knees?" I smiled.

"Why not?" Adam leaned back on his chair.

"The marriage or the knees?"

"Both."

"I'm not getting down on my knees — and I'm not changing my name."

"I might change mine. I'm not attached to it. You have a longer family history."

I loved how enlightened he was.

"Adam MacLean, I like that. Will you wear a kilt at the wedding?"

"Do I have to wear anything under it?" Adam grinned.

"I hope not."

He didn't change his name as we dove into our careers, but he had no issue with Cameron taking my last name. I admired him even more for his open-minded attitude.

I prided myself on being a modern woman who wouldn't crumble with convention. I told Adam diamond rings were an unnecessary expense. He liked that. We bought simple gold bands with Celtic knots engraved on them, the symbol of eternity.

Our marriage was eternal and modern, until it devolved into a 1950s time warp.

Now, I looked down at the slender wedding band still on my finger, felt the weight of it, started tugging. It wouldn't budge. I ran cold water over my hand for five minutes before it finally came off.

The indented ghostly white skin where it had been unexposed to sun was still twenty years younger than the rest of me. The last part of me to let go.

A Marriage of True Vines

—————

Twenty years ago, I had planned a Scottish wedding with bagpipes, dancers, and haggis, the traditional mutton sausage best washed down with a full-bodied Rhône Valley syrah. The French always were sympathetic to the Scots.

Even though Adam was now legally divorced, we discovered we couldn't get married in the Catholic Church unless he got an annulment. Neither of us wanted to go through that lengthy process.

Over the previous month, Mom had hand-calligraphed the invitations to our friends and family. They were neatly stacked in a box on the kitchen table when I told her there wasn't going to be a wedding. I'd never felt such embarrassment. She didn't even know about Adam's first wife.

I was angry with the Catholic Church for turning its back on me and I stopped attending Mass. Looking back now, I recognize my own hypocrisy. But all I could think then was that, for years, I had taught Sunday school, read the Scripture at Mass, and organized the children's liturgical dance group. I was also angry for Mom, who, despite the stigma of being a divorced single mother, served the Church for decades, spending her evenings on various committees.

Adam and I eloped, with Mom in tow, to the Villa Eyrie Resort on Vancouver Island. A justice of the peace performed the ceremony atop Malahat Mountain overlooking the Finlayson Arm waterway. It was fairy-tale beautiful. The world was spinning just for us. But I felt as if I were hiding from my friends and relatives ... and the Church. Was it shame about marrying a previously married man that first started eating away at me? All I knew was some nameless loss I couldn't identify was creeping through me.

A few years later, as Adam's career took off, we decided to have a child. My career at the supercomputer company was solid, though not anywhere near Adam's trajectory. We'd both always wanted children. Now we could afford for me to leave my job and stay home with our son. There was no question Adam would continue working because he earned so much more than I did.

I transitioned to writing about wine while at home with Cameron. The job was glamorous but paid almost nothing. At first, Adam and I discussed all major purchases, but over time, I felt like I was asking permission. He controlled our finances and questioned me on each request.

After a few years, I dreaded when the monthly credit card bill came in the mail. I wanted to hide it so I wouldn't be called to the principal's office to explain what I'd done with his money. For twenty years, my confidence slowly leaked from me. I had become so dependent on Adam that I couldn't imagine life without him. I couldn't remember the young, confident woman who'd met him in business school and then proposed.

Adam had been more excited than I was about my magazine bylines, publishing deals, and professional recognition. I doubled down on this pocket of support with more columns, more books, more awards.

Now, with my separation, I felt an icy prickle at the back of my neck.

Who am I if I'm not Adam's wife? Not the wife of a successful CEO who organized the best dinner parties for the city's tech high flyers?

Thank God I still had confidence in my writing. My thoughts were fuzzy or frozen, so I punched out my magazine columns mechanically. Every night, I wrote in my journal, now a shopping list of sorrow.

I was more thankful than ever that I had kept my name, even though I'd lost my identity. As a writer, and now as a divorced woman, my name meant even more to me.

One afternoon, as I was tasting a dozen cabernets, I realized I couldn't detect the aromas. Had I lost my sense of smell? I googled to discover that the size of the brain is smaller when depressed, according to a 2019 article by Jessica Hamzelou in *New Scientist* magazine. That can diminish or eliminate the sense of smell.

Was depression the smell of nothing? I panicked and went to see my doctor. She prescribed the antidepressant Zoloft, warning me about mixing it with alcohol.

When I came home that evening, I crumpled onto the bathroom floor. Despite my modern career, I couldn't pull myself together. I had resorted to a common 1950s method for housewives who couldn't cope. Drug yourself. Slow tears slid back into my eyes as I lay on the cold tiled floor, looking up at the blurry ceiling fan.

The stigma associated with antidepressants is a double whammy for those already anxious or depressed. Now I realize they can be as necessary for a mind needing to heal as a cast is for a broken arm.

Cameron was still doing well in school and seemed content. I didn't want him to feel my anxiety. At fourteen, he was too young for me to share exactly what was happening. Yet I didn't want to teach him to bottle up his feelings. I had to pull myself together for him.

It took me a decade before I could share with Cameron how I felt at that time. When I asked him if he had noticed anything unusual during the separation, he said, "All I remember is that you kept playing the same song over and over again in your office ... something about you losing your husband but not knowing where he went."

P!nk's song "So What" had become my anthem as I danced it out in my office. Years later, I discovered that the singer also owns a California winery where she helps make the wine. What I love most is that her name isn't splashed over the label of her Two Wolves Wine, unlike some celebrities who have nothing to do with the wine they endorse.

Two Wolves is named in honour of what was previously thought to be an ancient Cherokee legend. Abraham Bearpaw, Special Projects Officer with Cherokee Nation Community and Cultural Outreach, told me that the story actually originated with one of several American pastors, who in turn attributed it to the Cherokee Nation:

> "A fight is raging inside me," an elderly man said to his young grandson. "It's an awful battle between two wolves. One is evil and filled with anger, greed, envy, self-pity, regret, resentment, arrogance, and false pride.
>
> "The other is good and filled with love, joy, peace, hope, humility, kindness, empathy, compassion, and generosity. That fight is going on inside you and every other person."
>
> The grandson paused, then asked his grandfather, "Which wolf will win?"
>
> The old man replied, "The one you feed."

❧

"How did he get over a twenty-year marriage so quickly?" I sat on the sofa opposite my therapist, Miranda.

"I know this is hard for you, Natalie." Miranda was my age and had a warm smile that made her eyes crinkle.

"I keep wondering if they were together before we separated? Was she the first, or had there been others? Had I wilfully ignored them all, wanting my marriage to be perfect? Then I feel like I'm just being paranoid."

"Those feelings are valid, as is the pain of questioning your assumptions about reality." Miranda suggested I watch the movie *Gaslight*. Ingrid Bergman's husband, played by Charles Boyer, questions what she thinks is true, eroding her confidence.

As I watched Bergman slowly unravel, I thought, *That's it!* That's how I felt when Adam didn't answer my initial question about being with someone else. Instead, he deflected by demanding, "How can you even *ask* me that?" Had I ignored what I'd known before I knew?

The film was released in 1944, when this pattern of manipulation, especially from the spouse with economic power, wasn't acknowledged. The victim's self-esteem and trust in her own intuition is shattered, particularly if she's missed many clues. It's insidious in a marriage in which both partners are expected to open up to each other with complete vulnerability. Twenty years is a long time to let your guard down, to stop wondering if it'll work out, because obviously it has. Until it doesn't.

I wondered what kind of pathetic woman is attracted to that kind of man. I wasn't the type who fell to her knees, weeping on the sidewalk. Or was that just the story I told myself?

I was confident when we met. Was it a slow erosion over time I didn't notice? I even doubted myself about doubting myself.

"Why didn't I see the divorce coming?" I shook my head. "I asked him if he had prostate cancer, for God's sake! Really? I'm so naive."

"Try not to kick yourself. You're not naive. You're trusting. You can't imagine anyone else doing what you're not capable of doing yourself. It's a more optimistic way to live.

"Infidelity isn't just physical, it's also emotional," Miranda added. "That's often where it starts, being unavailable to the one you're with, because someone else is filling that need. The person doing this may not even realize it's happening."

"I think that old line, 'We were just friends and then it developed into something more,' is bullshit," I said. Did he tell her the things he should have told me, discussed issues with her that we should have tackled together? Then I'm the only one surprised when he's made a sudden decision to separate and there's no room for discussion. "Real men talk to their spouses first."

I was speeding my way up that grieving curve.

Tempest in a Wine Glass

———

"How's the essay going?" I walked past Cameron in the kitchen to get another green tea. He sat at the island staring at his laptop. May sunlight streamed in through the windows. I was the head of our English department in the family. Adam oversaw math and science.

"I wish Zeus would hit me with a lightning bolt." Cameron was a fan of Rick Riordan's *Percy Jackson* novels, about a teenage boy who's the son of a mortal mother and the god Poseidon. However, Cameron didn't like writing assignments any more than Brussels sprouts.

He was applying for the International Baccalaureate, an enriched academic program at the city's only public high school offering it. The entrance process required a long essay, several gruelling exams, and academic and character reference letters.

"Don't forget you have extraordinary powers if you use them." I smiled.

He frowned at me and started typing.

The program offered the quality of a private school education without the private school fees. I liked that it drew kids from across the city who were serious about learning and came from diverse backgrounds. I was a proud mama when, weeks later, he was accepted.

I also took it as a sign that Cameron was coping well with the separation, at least outwardly. He remained stoic. I kept asking him if he wanted to talk. He didn't. I couldn't keep nagging him. I didn't want to drive my son away, too.

Life settled into a new pattern, like dust that coats everything after a tornado. I was busy working with developers to create mobile apps that scanned wine bottles to access my reviews and pairings. Cameron and work filled my life, and so did wine. I reviewed more and more wines. Sure, I spat out the samples, but there was always that small amount of alcohol that gets absorbed through the soft palate of your mouth. Then there was that tiny trickle that goes down your throat when you want to be *extra* sure the wine has a long finish. If you're tasting thirty wines, it adds up. When it's 11:00 p.m. at another tasting dinner and you're trapped with a winemaker who's confident that you're as fascinated with his new stainless-steel tanks as he is, you swallow the wine.

Before you play that tiny violin for me, I did — and still — love what I do. It's a great privilege. I taste the most amazing wines, often paired with sumptuous meals. I've travelled to the most beautiful places on this planet and felt the kindness of people who want to give me something to drink that they made themselves. My career is a choice — and I'd make the same choice again.

Still, there was constant professional pressure to drink wine. As a woman in a man's world, I kept up with (and drank as much as) the men. Not exactly the kind of equality I was hoping for. I couldn't cut out early from an event, even when my body was groaning with exhaustion. Forget dry January, when even a single detox day was difficult.

My liver for the people.

Before the separation, I'd head to Tasting Alley around 5:00 p.m. Since the conversation with Adam in January, my personal cocktail hour had crept stealthily up to 4:00 p.m. I'd drink a glass of wine as my reward to keep working another hour. Glass two kept me going for one more. By glass three, I'd be watching Tina Fey videos.

My daily ritual numbed the pain of the separation during the "arsenic hour," the end of the workday when you're tired and hungry — and want to either take arsenic or give it to those around you. When I worried about how much I was drinking, I'd have another glass to calm my anxiety. Wine blanketed my screaming thoughts about the future.

Cameron usually arrived home from school and went up to his bedroom to start homework as I was starting on my first glass. When I asked him a decade later about my drinking, he said he didn't notice the increase. He'd grown up seeing his mother with a wineglass in hand, a maternal prosthesis. There was no difference to him between my "work wine" and "personal wine." Increasingly, that was true for me as well.

I still met magazine deadlines, paid the bills, monitored Cameron's homework, attended his school events. But wine wrecked my sleep. I'd wake up with a headache and pulsing regret at 3:00 a.m. — the witching hour.

∽◉◇

"May I ask you a really personal question?" My friend Nina leaned toward me, over the restaurant table, wishing to be discreet. The tea light cast a soft glow on her pale skin and hair. I'd known Nina for years. We'd both taken the same public relations degree in Nova Scotia and now both lived in Ottawa. A warm June breeze, laden with the scent of lilacs, wafted in through the open window. "Do you drink more wine when you're sad or stressed?"

"Yes and yes."

"Do you think you drink too much?"

"Yes and yes." I sighed.

"I didn't have wine last night." Her hazel eyes looked at me for affirmation.

"Was that your first night?"

"In years."

"You should wear a button that says 'Ask me about last night.'"

Nina smiled sadly, puncturing my favourite emotional armour of the reflexive quip.

I had made a career out of boozy slapstick jokes — my way of deflecting serious topics and real feelings.

My first book, *Red, White, and Drunk All Over*, was an irreverent poke at the stuffiness of wine. Now these little asides seemed to pepper my writing. Beneath the jokes was a real question: How much was too much?

On social media, women often sent me private messages asking if they needed to worry about having a couple of glasses a night … or maybe a *little* more than that. They wanted to know if they were over the limit. Traditional guidelines suggested one to two glasses of wine for women per day, two to three for men, with a maximum of ten and fifteen per week, respectively. As of 2023, the Canadian Centre on Substance Use and Addiction advises that anything over two drinks a week for both women and men could have negative health risks and that the risk increases the more you drink.

One serving is a five-ounce pour, which can look stingy in fishbowl-sized glasses. This is based on wine with 12 percent alcohol, not the 14–16 percent of some warmer climate wines, such as a shiraz from the Barossa Valley, Australia, or a malbec from Mendoza, Argentina. Also, the alcohol content on the wine label may not be accurate. Canadian and U.S. governments allow producers of wines of less than 14 percent alcohol to indicate a level that's up to 1.5 percent higher or lower than the actual figure. So a wine labelled 14 percent might really be 15.5 percent.

Of course, I read all the reports that promoted the health benefits of wine. These included reduced risk of heart attack, dementia, and Alzheimer's. I matched these up in my mind as slugfests against studies citing the increased risks of weight gain, drunk driving, liver disease, diabetes, and breast cancer.

I even interviewed pro-wine health professionals, including a doctor who told me exactly what I wanted to hear. But my own doctor was blunt: "Alcohol increases your risk of breast cancer, period. It's a linear relationship." I tried to get her to admit to some wiggle room, but she wouldn't budge. I thought about switching doctors.

When I started drinking wine, it was for pleasure. Then I started drinking more wine for more pleasure. Just thinking about my first glass of wine made me feel better. That's not surprising. Ten times more of the hormone dopamine is released in anticipation of pleasure than while actually enjoying it. We're wired for desire, not satisfaction. That's why more dopamine is released at the thought of having a glass of wine than when we're drinking it. That mechanism served us well in the cave days when we always had to be hunting for food to survive. It's not so great when you're polishing off that bottle of rosé.

The first bite of food or sip of wine is the best. The second is *almost* as good. It's a gastronomic law of diminishing returns. You're already adapting to the flavours. They don't light up your brain's dendrites, the branches carrying signals between neurons, as much as they did on the first taste. We're thirsting for something much more than relaxation from alcohol. The opposite of addiction isn't sobriety, it's connection. Too much alcohol takes us out of the moment when we're trying to connect with someone over a glass of wine.

I didn't start drinking wine until after graduate school, when I had the funds to get fancy. I wrote in *Red, White, and Drunk All Over* about the taste of my first great wine:

> As I raised the glass to my lips, I stopped. The aroma of the wine rushed out to meet me, and all the smells that I had ever known fell away. I didn't know how to describe it, but I knew how it made me feel.
>
> I moistened my lips with the wine and drank it slowly, letting it coat my tongue and slide from one side of my mouth to the other. The brunello trickled down my throat and out along a thousand fault lines through my body, dissolving them.
>
> My second glass tasted like a sigh at the end of a long day: a gathering in, and a letting go. I felt the fingers of alcoholic warmth relax the muscles at the back of my jaw and curl under my ears. The wine flushed warmth up into my cheeks, down through my shoulders and across my thighs. My mind was as calm as a black ocean. The wine gently stirred the silt of memories on the bottom, helping me recall childhood moments of wordless abandon.

I still yearn for that first taste again.

I love wine because every vintage and every bottle is different, unlike the packaged food I used to market at Procter & Gamble. Wine is an agricultural product celebrated for diversity and unpredictability. It's like going to a ballet versus watching an edited version on television. That live-in-the-moment risk is thrilling. A dancer could fall flat on her face or soar weightless in the air.

Wine is more an experience than a thing in the way it accesses memories and emotions. I can float from place to place in my mind on the magic carpet of scent.

I also love wine because it's fleeting — not like a painting that'll exist for centuries. This glass of wine in front of me has one chance, one moment.

Now my unquenchable desire for pleasure was bringing me pain. It dulled my senses and feelings. It zapped my energy and sleep. I was on airplane mode: still operating, just not open to the richness of life and ignoring the warning signals.

I'd always made my personal wine habits fodder for public consumption. Had I become an enabler for Nina, Cassie, and others who read my work? They seemed reassured that they didn't have a problem compared to my consumption. Had I become a collaborator with the wine industry in reassuring women that drinking wine was their just reward, even after that drinking became toxic? Was my contribution to the world more pleasure or pain?

Good Witch Hunting

Post-separation, I was Alice in Wineland, falling down the tunnel of my loneliness. Every bottle seemed to be labelled *Drink me.*

I started reading alcohol addiction memoirs by women to see if I identified with them: *Lit*, by Mary Karr; *Blackout: Remembering the Things I Drank to Forget*, by Sarah Hepola; and *Drinking: A Love Story*, by Caroline Knapp.

Their extreme stories falsely reassured me because they drank so much more than I did. They drank in the morning. They hid bottles of vodka in the baby's diaper bag, for God's sake. I did none of that.

What resonated in these memoirs was their desire to be released from anxiety. Looking at the world was exhausting. I took in too much sensory detail, noticed every faint smell, every change in light or sound: it all came in too bright and loud. To paraphrase William Wordsworth, the world was too much with me.

Wine turned down my sensory stereo. As novelist F. Scott Fitzgerald said, "First you take a drink, then the drink takes a drink, then the drink takes you." Wine seeped into each crevice, untying my muscles, slowing my synaptic firing. The ecstatic surrender of wine — church for the unchurched. Without the drinker, wine is an unplayed instrument. Together we create the experience.

I wrote about how wine — and alcohol — made me feel, but did that make me an addict? If you look at the history of those who've suffered from addiction, they often started with anxiety or depression. A drug was a way of alleviating the symptoms. As children they felt anxiety without an outlet, but most didn't say, *Hey, I just want to get smashed this evening.* As adults, though, we can self-medicate.

Panic attacks, anxiety, and depression run in my family. My parents' divorce sparked childhood fears of not being enough to ease Mom's grief and anger. I remember only three things she ever said about my father when I was a child: he had dead eyes; he had accidentally shot himself while hunting and nearly died; and just once, when my behaviour had upset her: "You're just like your father."

That last comment felt the most damning of her criticisms, since I didn't know this stranger who had hurt her so much. I didn't see my father until I was sixteen. Mom hadn't prevented him from contacting me. He just hadn't bothered.

"I wouldn't know ya if I tripped over ya," he said, as we sat in my grandparents' kitchen in Baddeck, Nova Scotia. He was tall and handsome, with watery, red-rimmed blue eyes.

At sixteen, I longed to connect with him, to find some piece of my missing identity, to have one of those TV dads who'd grill a new boyfriend before a date. I didn't know what to say. I felt embarrassed and shy. It didn't matter, though. I didn't see him again until I was eighteen, and after that, received only a few phone calls apologizing for missing my birthdays.

It would be a decade before he got sober, though he was still gambling everything away at the racetrack. Years later, I gave him cash to buy furniture for his apartment. He also lost that on the ponies.

~~✦~~

As a child, I couldn't drown my feelings in drink, but I could be obsessive in other ways. When I was eight, I stood transfixed in the local mall in front of a wall covered with colouring contest entries to win tickets to *The Jungle Book* movie. I had dragged Mom over to look at them, some carefully coloured within the lines, others not so much. One kid had glued a cotton ball on the cloud above Mowgli's head.

"I want to enter." My eyes narrowed as I thought about how to win.

We took home a sheet that I coloured, then added cotton balls on the clouds. My secret weapon? Glitter glue. I sprinkled it on the pond beside Mowgli. A week later, I pulsed with pride when I took Mom to the movie.

The next year, my school announced a fundraiser with a local grocery store that had agreed to donate funds based on cash register receipts students gathered. As Mom and I stood in the checkout line, I noticed some people didn't take their receipts. I walked past the cashier and picked up those lying among the plastic bags. Then I moved to the end of the checkout line next to ours, asking a woman if I could have her receipt. She smiled and gave it to me. I moved from line to line, until Mom dragged me out of the store.

When we went to the store again, I stayed at the ends of the checkout lines while she shopped. I was giddy with a roll of receipts as thick as a large roll of duct tape. In class the next day, the teacher created a chart showing sixty stars beside my name compared to two or three for most of the kids. I pestered Mom to go back to that grocery store every day. Was this the beginning of never enough?

My separation unnerved me, shook loose my confidence in keeping another important man in my life. There had never been enough glitter glue, grocery receipts, or gold stars to fill the hole my father had left. Now there wasn't enough wine to fill the crater where Adam had been.

∿☙∿

I opened my office window. The pre-dawn, pine-scented June air enveloped me, along with a chorus of crickets. Five months after the separation, I was using my best brain for writing early in the day and delaying tedious administrative tasks until the evening. I couldn't face doing them without a glass in hand.

Each day, I depleted myself to the point of needing wine to transition from work to home life — a particular challenge when they were under the same roof. Having that first glass of wine softened my steel edge so I didn't snap at Cameron over dinner. If I called Mom with a drink in hand, we'd talk for forty-five minutes instead of ten. I met friends only for dinner with wine, never for lunch or coffee.

I told myself I deserved that glass, or four, at the end of the day. The phrase *I deserve it* implies that you've worked hard, maybe a little too hard, for your reward. Somebody owes you — your husband, your kids, your boss. Since no one else is going to even the score, you'll do it yourself. Everyone else be damned.

I deserve it is mentioned in addiction literature as a rationale for destructive behaviour. We know emotional needs can't be satisfied by stuff, though we keep trying. That explains my obsession with shoes. Friends and strangers frequently compliment me on them. It's just another socially approved addiction.

One day, I was listening to a radio show about how consumers use purchases to close the gap between the real and ideal self. *If I buy this dress, I'll look slimmer, prettier.* I thought, *Oh hell, that's what I'm doing with wine.* If I have this glass of wine, I'll be calmer, happier, better able to handle everything with a smile.

There's also the concept of laddering up: I'm already in for this dress, so why not get the shoes as well. The wine equivalent? I've already opened this expensive bottle that won't taste as good tomorrow. May as well have another glass and finish it.

Compulsive behaviour is a quicksand of not enough — not enough work done today, not enough drinks consumed, not enough shoes purchased. Ultimately, I'm not enough.

What's wrong with treating myself? If I can afford it and no one else is hurt, what's the problem? There's nothing wrong with rewards. It was my mindset that mattered when I had that drink. Did I feel owed or thankful?

I knew I had to ease off wine, but I couldn't bear the thought of quitting completely. My work depended on it. I didn't want to give up something that gave me so much pleasure. I needed more tools and help to manage it.

"Zoloft helps, but I need more." I sat on my doctor's cold exam table.

"Okay, tell me what's happening." Her eyes softened.

"It doesn't make me feel happy. It just unties the knot. I'm worried that when it's not enough, I'll drink more wine."

We chatted more about my anxiety.

"I'll increase your dose, but make sure you continue the sessions with Miranda. The medication and therapy work together. And watch your drinking. Alcohol increases the side effects of Zoloft and reduces its effectiveness."

Two days later, Miranda said, "You have an orchid brain."

"A what?"

"It's delicate, hypersensitive, acutely self-aware."

"What's the opposite?"

"Dandelion brain. Grows anywhere, very resilient."

"I wish I had a cactus brain."

"That orchid brain makes you a better writer."

"And a lousy socializer. Should I quit drinking?"

"That would be punitive."

"But if I ask about quitting, doesn't that mean I have a problem?"

"It doesn't have to be all or nothing for some people. In my experience, telling someone to quit often doesn't work. It's about reducing the harm. Try to coast longer on each glass, each sip. Don't drink it like water. Take just enough to wet your tongue or moisten your lips. Think of it like chocolate cake. You take small bites for the prolonged pleasure."

"I want to inhale the whole cake."

Pruning

Labelling Luna

I had been thinking more about labels ever since I felt that Adam had labelled me frigid. My day job was decoding labels, so I should be an expert in deciphering their meaning.

As I noted in *Red, White, and Drunk All Over*, wine depends on labels more than most products. You can read the first chapter of a book or try on a dress, but you can't taste most wines before you buy them in stores — at least not legally. You're left choosing between a label with a castle in the middle distance or one with a fluffy squirrel.

Labels took on a larger meaning after my separation. A divorced woman sometimes gets the cringey label of *starter wife*, especially when replaced with a younger woman. I had labelled myself as a failure when I couldn't keep my man. I didn't want Cameron labelling me a nag.

Friends created labels when they took sides between Adam and me. I was cold; he was domineering. A label justified cutting off contact with one over the other. But no one is ever only one thing or one label.

Increasingly, though, wine labels don't give women much credit. The message on some bottles is that women belong in a particular category. We're vixens drawn to brands like Little Black Dress and Stiletto, with their labels featuring short dresses, high heels, and red lips. Or we're exhausted mothers buying wines such as Mommy Juice and Mommy's Time Out to obliviate the stress of motherhood.

If we're not babes, we're battle-axes reaching for wine labels such as Mad Housewife, with taglines like "Award thyself," "The dishes can wait," and "Dinner be damned." These labels felt so out of touch with what I was going through. It seemed to me that antiquated societal beliefs about women had been turned into slogans. Should we be laughing or raging at jokes that demean women?

The marketing message is that women need to have a reason to drink, whether it's girls' night, a fancy occasion, or just getting through another day of exhaustion. It's implied that we need permission to drink, as we do when we buy things. There's even a wine for sneaky shopping called White Lie, with little lines stamped on the corks like "This old thing?" and "I got it on sale."

We're wallets, not women. We drink cutesy, crappy wines that subsidize the good stuff men drink. Wine was, and still is, the culturally accepted, modern-day Valium for women stressed out with our faces, bodies, spouses, kids, careers, and housework. It's all over Instagram. Vino is the ultimate soft filter to blunt all of those feels. Don't have time for meditation and yoga? Calm your central nervous system with this cabernet. Wineries offer Vino Vinyasa yoga classes: detox then retox. There's a colouring book called *My Mommy Drinks Wine*, and a women's wine bar with a play space for children. All fun and games until it's time to drive the kiddos home.

I had internalized all those social media slogans:

"Mommy drinks wine because you cry."

"Wine is to women as duct tape is to men — it fixes everything!"

"Well, actually, it's only mansplaining if it comes from the Mansplain region of France. Otherwise, it's just sparkling misogyny."

Wine is positioned as less candied and more sophisticated than the cosmopolitans featured in *Sex and the City*. You can cloak your overindulgence with connoisseurship of artisanal, dry-farmed, old vine, natural wines in a way you could never do with that third cosmo. Several of my other favourite television shows, like *Scandal*, *The Good Wife*, *Dead to Me*, and *Cougar Town*, showcased professional women who rewarded themselves with a glass of wine, or three. Their oversized stemware reminded me of Virginia Slims cigarette ads from the 1960s, positioning them as torches of freedom for liberated women.

The difference today is that cigarette packages have large health warnings on them, and often pictures of blackened lungs. Alcohol labels usually don't have photos of liver cirrhosis. That may come if there's a backlash from the marketing push for "clean wines" and other "self-care" brands that avoid the fact that alcohol is a drug and can be toxic. The Canadian Centre on Substance Use and Addiction, a national advisory organization, would like to see cancer warnings and the number of standard drinks on all alcohol labels.

Conversely, wine is marketed to men as sophisticated and artisanal. No one asks a man why he wants a drink. He has one because he wants one. Several studies have revealed that many men embellish their wine expertise to impress others. British wine writer Hugh Johnson put it best, "Wine is like sex in that few men will admit not knowing all about it."

According to a ridiculous stereotype, Bordeaux wine bottles with their square shoulders remind French winemakers of their stout wives. The slender-sloped Burgundy bottles bring to mind their mistresses. Wink, wink.

I had always laughed off these narratives, just as I did with my boozy quips about drinking too much. Now the jokes fell flat. Both the wine labels targeting women and the labels we slap on women themselves profit from powerlessness. As the frigid wife, I had been painted onto another worn-out label. It was time to create my own design.

～ॐ～

"How are you?" Nina asked. We were sitting at our favourite wine bar. The lights behind the bottles on the back wall made them glow like candy-coloured lipsticks.

I'd told her and other friends about the separation but not my suspicions as to why it happened. My marriage crumbling after two decades was failure enough, especially when my friends were all still married.

"I'm great, thanks! Busier than ever." I forced the words out through my happy screen.

"Well, you're all over the liquor store."

"What do you mean?"

"Your wine reviews … I saw at least five of them on those little cards today."

"Ah, shelf talkers. Yes, I've been busy."

"I bought Vince the Rhône you recommended. Loved your description of it."

"I hope he likes it."

"Well, you gave it a 92, so I'm sure he will … he won't buy anything under 90."

"Most men love scores, but women like to please. Which wine would please you most right now?" I looked at the restaurant list.

She smiled. "The one you like, of course."

"Let's try the Catena Appellation Lunlunta Old Vines Malbec."

"There must be a story behind it if you're not going with pinot."

"You're right! Dr. Laura Catena graduated magna cum laude from Harvard University and has a medical degree from Stanford. In 1995, she joined her father, Nicolás, at the family winery in Argentina. She's now managing director of Bodega Catena Zapata and founder of her own winery, Luca Wines. She and her husband have four children and live in San Francisco. She's an emergency room physician ... I wonder what she does in her spare time?"

"I thought *I* was a busy mom," Nina said. "She has a schedule that would tire a horse."

I ordered our wine. "What do you think of wines marketed to women?" We loved chatting about branding because she ran a successful public relations company. Marketing had been my beat before wine.

"You mean the ones with pink labels?" she asked.

"Yep. Personally, I can't resist a *hey, girrrrl* label or an adorable iguana. I guess I'm at the mercy of those intrepid marketing teams. They somehow read my mind after I drank too much of Gnarly Dudes Shiraz."

Nina laughed as we sipped on the Catena Malbec with its berry and savoury spice flavours. It was perfect with our meat lover's pizza.

Wine labels increasingly target women because we're still mostly the ones who plan family meals and social get-togethers. We also still purchase most things for our households, including 80 percent of wine.

I wasn't a bystander in the labelling game. I was team captain. In magazine articles, I had often described my glass of wine at 5:00 p.m. as "Mommy's little helper." That's how I marketed wine to myself. It was also my way of fitting in with other "wine moms." It sounded lighthearted, but it had the bitter edge of resentment. By that time of the day, I was exhausted. No one was helping Mommy, so Mommy helped herself — to a drink.

Even when nobody was asking me to plough through more emails at the end of the day, I'd do it as long as I had my first glass of wine for the evening. I created my own reward to extend my "productive day" another hour. How does she do it all? With wine. There's no internal reward for cleaning out your inbox, which someone once characterized as an organized list of other people's priorities. But my sense of thankless depletion was never soothed by a drink. It dulled the roar, but not the whimper.

The sexist narrative was also embedded in industry tasting notes, including some of my own. Wines were described as either feminine (light-bodied, smooth, supple, easy-drinking) or masculine (full-bodied, muscular, complex). Even the assumption that *feminine* means something lighter than *masculine* is problematic. While chardonnay has often been described as blowsy or slutty, I've never seen those same descriptors for a full-bodied red wine, like cabernet or shiraz. Of course, wine doesn't have exclusive domain over sexist tasting notes among alcoholic drinks.

"Have I had this much fun with a sexy 41-year-old Canadian before?" Jim Murray, author of the *Whisky Bible*, wrote in his review of the Canadian Club brand. "Well, yes I have. But it was a few years back now and it wasn't a whisky … [T]his whisky simply seduces you with the lightness and knowledgeable meaning of its touch, butterfly kissing your taste buds, finding time after time your whisky erogenous zone or g spots … and then surrendering itself with tender and total submission."

In his book that's sold more than a million copies, Murray described the Highland Park 40-Year-Old "[l]ike a 40-year-old woman who has kept her figure and looks, and now only satin stands in the way between you and so much beauty and experience … and believe me: she's spicy."

In her *Toronto Star* article, Christine Sismondo interviewed whisky journalist Becky Paskin, who commented on Murray's book: "In the 2020 edition there are 34 references to whisky being 'sexy' and many more crudely comparing drinking whisky to having sex with women.

"Much of the industry has been working hard to change whisky's reputation as a 'man's drink,' but condoning, even celebrating, a book that contains language like this erases much of that progress and allows the objectification of women in whisky." Paskin added, "The explicit, lurid, and sexist way Murray chooses to review whiskies in his 'Bible' is prehistoric, and frankly vile. Whisky reviews are no place to boast the gross details of sexual conquests, or compare a drink to a woman's body shape."

Murray named Alberta Premium Cask Strength rye whisky as the best in the world. In response to his sexist language, Sismondo reported that the owner of Alberta Distillers, the Beam Suntory company, reversed plans to reference his review in promotional materials.

Murray rebutted that he was being denied his freedom of speech. I don't know if Murray has a daughter, but I wonder how he'd feel if she were described using his tasting notes. The 2022 edition of *Jim Murray's Whisky Bible* has sold quicker than any other, requiring multiple print runs.

As much as these sexist tasting notes repulsed me, they made me think of my role in promoting gendered wine messages to women and to myself. Was I part of the industry's marketing machine frequently touting the statistics about how important women are to the wine industry without talking much about the dangers? I wrote about women winemakers as though they represented a new breakthrough in equality when few owned their wineries and many faced workplace harassment.

My culpability in these narratives has now become clear to me, but in 2012 I couldn't see it. I wondered if there was a way out. It's hard to read the label from inside the bottle.

Under His Eye

—————

The power of words and labels reminds me of my favourite high school English teacher. We nicknamed her Mad Dog Mackenzie, because she was fierce in critiquing our essays, but we loved her caustic wit and brilliance.

I was part of an advanced English class of thirteen odd ducks swimming in a student pond of two thousand. We could choose most of the books we studied, rather than follow the standard curriculum. For my report on a Canadian author, I'd chosen Margaret Atwood's *The Handmaid's Tale*. Atwood was born in Ottawa, but her parents were from Nova Scotia, so I was curious to see if I could detect her Maritime roots.

"Do you know what this story is about?" Ms. Mackenzie asked me one day after class.

"A dystopian novel about a fascist theocracy previously known as the United States."

"There are some serious and disturbing issues in this book, Natalie." She looked at me above her glasses. "Women are violently oppressed and systematically raped. Are you comfortable reading that?"

"Yes, I am." My sarcastic tone was gone. "Margaret Atwood is our country's best writer. She may be hard to read, but I can learn a lot from her."

Ms. Mackenzie held my gaze for a few moments.

"All right," she said softly. "It's an excellent novel, but I want you to come to me if there's anything in this book you'd like to talk about."

My view of Ms. Mackenzie changed that day. She may have been fierce, but she was also protective.

The disturbing themes in the book came back to me in 2018 when a U.S. retailer launched wines to capitalize on the novel's blockbuster television series.

The character, Offred, adorns the label of a French pinot noir described as having "lush, fruit flavors of cherry and cassis complemented by earthy flavors of mushroom and forest floor. We honor Offred with a wine that will stay with you long after you've finished your glass and a powerful experience you will never forget."

This description reminds me of the scene where Offred is in the forest fleeing from armed guards who are rounding up fertile women as breeding chattel for the elite. She's clubbed over the head and dragged off to sex submission school, separated from her young daughter, who is sent to live with regime-approved parents.

The Offred Pinot is "so beguiling it seems almost forbidden to taste. It's useless to resist the wine's smooth and appealingly earthy profile, so you may as well give in."

In what warped mind is Offred, the embodiment of this wine, able to seduce men with her charms when in fact she's a sex slave? Why choose thin-skinned pinot noir? If Offred is any type of wine, she's an amarone, strong enough to endure a bitter finish.

When the character Ofglen is uncooperative, she undergoes female genital mutilation. She rebels and is brutally beaten before being sent to a nuclear waste labour camp. She is "the inspiration for a bold cabernet sauvignon — which, aptly, hails from the Rogue Valley." The wine, made for "Gilead's most rebellious Handmaid," promises to deliver much "pleasure and enjoyment."

Blessed is the fruit indeed.

Then there's Serena Joy, former activist lawyer, now housebound trophy wife of Commander Fred. Her character is represented as a Bordeaux white wine blend that's "sophisticated, traditional, and austere." While the "wine may initially come off as restrained, a few sips reveal it to be hiding layers of approachable white grapefruit and lemongrass, backed by weight and concentration." The retailer's website advised not to judge her too quickly, "lest you miss out on a sublime experience." This wine pairs best, presumably, with a woman who supports a misogynistic culture, encouraged by the fact her husband whips her and has her finger cut off.

Now, now, forget about all that. Drink up, ladies! Oops, sorry, you can't. Women in Gilead aren't allowed to consume alcohol.

How did anyone find women-empowerment branding opportunities based on these characters? Why name the wines Offred and Ofglen, the possessive slave names of their commanders Fred and Glen, rather than their real names, June and Emily? I assume that would be Offbrand.

I can't think of a product category today where such blatant sexism gets past the concept development and focus groups, let alone bottled, labelled, and launched with a full marketing campaign.

Spinoff merchandise included more than wine. The phrase *Nolite te bastardes carborundorum* (don't let the bastards grind you down) that a Handmaid scratched into the wall before she hanged herself is printed across the front of a red hoodie in the style of the pasted newspaper letters from a ransom note.

There was also red silk lingerie. Apparently, you can wear your convictions on your chest, and you've done your part. Clearly, there are several missed tie-ins. How about Handmaid's Tale Tasers or Power Pink Pepper Spray?

Meanwhile, unrelated to the wines, a women's co-working space in New York City hosted a book club event focused on *The Handmaid's Tale* called "Dystopia & Rosé."

Pink-washed reminiscing can be just as dangerous as modern misogyny, as Margaret Atwood observed in a pre-recorded video for attendees. "People have a nostalgia for what they think of as the good old days. Some people think they would like to move back to those good old days, without knowing — or possibly caring — what those days were actually like, and why people wanted to change those situations in the first place."

The book still resonates with me today. I had longed for an old-fashioned ideal of the perfect marriage while ignoring its darker underside. To paraphrase the character June in *The Handmaid's Tale*, I was asleep. I'm awake now.

After only one day on the market — and a huge social media backlash — the U.S. retailer withdrew the Handmaid wines for sale.

Praise be.

Glinda Gets Her Groove Back

"You need to go out with friends for a drink and talk dirt about him." Emma, my lawyer, had an impish glint in her eyes. We had just finalized the separation agreement.

Really? The Catholic in me thought of Mary, Our Lady of Perpetual Sorrow, who pondered things in her heart. She didn't run off at the mouth about them.

"Isn't that slander?"

"It's not slanderous to tell your friends what happened."

"What about writing a book?" I was joking.

"You can do that as long as it's your opinion about what happened. Tell your story from your perspective. It's also not slander or libel when something is true."

As I drove home, my thoughts were a swarm of blue butterflies. I wanted them to fold their wings and settle along one long exhale. Would telling friends be an unhealthy rehash of events? Back in January, I had told them Adam and I were separating, but I hadn't gone into detail. Would they think I was a psychological exhibitionist? For me, opening up was akin to filming my own reality show, *The Hopelessly Naive Housewife of Canada's Capital.*

I had already shared everything with Miranda, Emma, and Mom. Shouldn't I just move on? I longed for the gift of forgetting.

~~◎~~

That Friday night, I invited my friends over for drinks at my place.

"Something's missing," Nina said, looking around the kitchen, as she and Cassie sat down at the island.

"Yes, a husband."

They laughed.

"How are you really?" Cassie asked.

"Fine, awful ... Adam, the way he was behaving ... the things I've learned since then ... I think he may have been with someone."

They looked at me, stunned.

"What?" Nina asked.

"Yeah, it threw me, too." I poured the pinot into the glasses.

"I'm so sorry, Nat." Nina came over to hug me.

"It's okay, three's a crowd anyway. There's a wine for that — Ménage à Trois." Then the tears came. Cassie joined the hug and sniffles.

"You know, Nat," Nina said as we all sat down, "I remember dinner parties where Adam would go off on a tangent about tech or something. Then you'd say something lighthearted and bring us back to something less intense."

"Or I just poured more wine."

Their eyes were warm and sympathetic.

"You've got so much going for you," Cassie said. "You're smart, you have your own career, you have a great son, you're a warrior. Adam can't take any of that away from you."

It turned out that telling friends made it better, not worse. It was a vacation from my mind, going back and forth over my own thoughts. They said things that countered my dark thoughts: *I failed the wife test. I'll end up alone, eating cat food.*

It was surprising, even shocking, what they revealed about their own relationship struggles after I told them what was happening. The floodgates opened, taking our friendship to a deeper, more satisfying level than just talking about our kids and the latest episode of whatever show we were binge-watching. My marital disaster gave them permission to share from the heart. Even though we were divulging painful stories, it was pure joy to connect soul to soul.

"This is an exciting new opportunity for you," Nina said, her hand on my forearm. "You deserve someone who loves you."

"Guess I'll have to get back on the dating scene. Has anything changed in the last twenty years that I should know about?"

Nina smiled, but she had no advice as she, too, hadn't dated for twenty years. I actually didn't feel like I needed a man with these wonderful women supporting me. Then I looked down and noticed I hadn't even finished my first glass of wine — I had been drinking it slowly.

I had thought that independence meant holding it all in, not needing anyone. Now that I was truly on my own, I felt the healing, restorative power of wide-open friendship. I thirsted for it, a dehydrated plant finally receiving the life-giving water she needed.

This reminded me of the intense female friendship in my favourite movie, *Thelma & Louise*. In this roadie pic, two strong working-class women are on the run from an abusive husband, a noncommittal boyfriend, and the police. Thelma tells Louise that she's never felt more awake, that everything looks different. Rather than be captured, they drive their 1966 Thunderbird off the cliff into the Grand Canyon — together to the end.

～◎～

I was learning that I could mourn the loss of my family without wanting Adam back. I could miss the things we used to do together even though I didn't miss him. Independence and loneliness were no longer the same thing.

Some worries, however, remained. One day I was polishing a wineglass at the kitchen sink. Rain pelted the window.

I can't lose Cameron.

Cameron seemed to be adjusting to our new life. But I didn't want him to view weekends as an escape to Dad's Den of Decadence, featuring chocolate, video games, and late nights. Then he'd return on Sundays to Mom's Manor of Misery with homework, vegetables, and sensible bedtimes.

The side of my finger was stinging. I looked down at the blood. I'd rubbed so hard on the bowl of the glass that it had snapped off from the stem. My Chill Mamma persona needed a little buffing. So I launched a Stealth Mother PR campaign to change my image from nag to someone who cares. Instead of bugging Cameron about studying for exams, I reframed it: I'm organized, and I can share those skills with you to help you succeed. Reminding you about this doesn't make me a nag, it shows how much I love you.

Years later, he thanked me, but at the time, scowls alternated with eye rolls. I had to let go so I could hang on. Instead of grilling Cameron with questions about life at his father's house, I backed off and let him know I was available to talk any time about anything.

I never spoke ill of his father to him. I did the opposite, talking about his father's intelligence and business success. I reminded Cameron about Father's Day and took him shopping for gifts, often a bottle of his dad's favourite Bordeaux. I had to swallow my grief so Cameron wasn't left with a bitter aftertaste. At fourteen, he still thought of his father as his hero. I wanted to honour that. I still do.

Mom and I were sitting at the kitchen island after dinner on a Sunday evening when Cameron joined us. He was quiet, as usual. Adam had just dropped him off.

"So how was your weekend, Cameron?" Mom asked. "What did you get up to?"

"None of your damn business," he muttered.

Oh God. Was the impact of the separation finally hitting him?

"Cameron," I gasped. "Do not talk to your grandmother that way. Apologize now!"

"No." He got up.

"Go to your room *now*."

"Already going." He marched off.

"I'm so sorry, Mom. I don't know what's got into him."

"It's okay, hon. The separation has been hard on him, too. Everyone has their bad days."

"Sure, but that's no excuse to talk to you like that."

Later that evening, a family member emailed me to see if Cameron was still upset. Apparently, Cameron had been with Adam as Adam's mother was dying at the hospice. Cameron had been weeping.

What? Why on earth hadn't Adam told me?

I went upstairs and knocked on Cameron's door.

"Come in. Mom, I'm sorry. I'll apologize to Grammy."

"That would be great, Cam." I sat on the edge of his bed. "Your father's sister-in-law told me what happened this weekend. That must have been hard for you."

Cameron sniffed, trying to hold back the tears.

"Yeah. It was pretty intense. Everyone was crying."

We talked for almost an hour about life, death, homework, and snacks. While I was still upset he went through such a traumatic experience, I was glad we could talk about it.

"Would you like to chat with a counsellor about this?"

"No, I'll be fine."

I pulled him in gently for a hug. He wrapped his spindly arms around my shoulders and squeezed me like when he was a toddler.

Still, as I held him, I wondered, will he be fine? Will I?

~⊙~

My next challenge was establishing my own finances as Adam had managed them all. The American Express agent told me I wasn't eligible to get my own card. I had no credit history as I'd only had a co-holder card in his name.

I'd never had a student loan because I paid for university through scholarships and the Highland dance school that I started when I was fifteen. One of my youngest students, Catherine, had won the category for six-year-olds in a local competition. With her parents' permission, I used a picture of her in her kilt with her trophy in a one-page flyer with details about the MacLean School of Dance. It was my first customer testimonial, though I didn't know to call it that.

I asked Mom to drive to each of the six elementary schools in our town. While she waited in the car, I went in to speak to the principals to get permission to give out the flyers to the classes. I told them this job would pay for my university. That fall, thirty-six students registered with the MacLean School of Dance. My business never required a line of credit because I bootstrapped it using the cash parents paid me and taught lessons in our basement.

In my final year of high school, my guidance counsellor asked if I had applied for the Terry Fox Humanitarian Award. The scholarship was created in memory of the young man, an amputee, who ran across Canada to raise funds for cancer as he was dying. It was based on academics, community service, and courage in overcoming obstacles. I told him, "No. I don't have any obstacles."

It didn't occur to me that being the daughter of an alcoholic father and a single mother on a limited income might be an obstacle to anything. That's because Mom instilled in me both gratitude for what we had and confidence in what I could accomplish. She posted sticky notes on the bathroom and bedroom mirrors that read *All things are possible* and *What you believe, you can achieve* and other quotes from the psychologist Norman Vincent Peale, whose books she read to me.

With the counsellor's urging, I applied and won. It covered tuition, books, and room and board for four years so I could continue my community service. I'd been spending my Friday nights volunteering at a women's shelter in a crime-ridden part of Halifax and Wednesdays teaching literacy to adults. Both were perfect for an introvert who never went to parties in high school or university.

Now the American Express customer service representative suggested that I establish a credit history by getting a phone line in my name. Then, after six months of paying the bills, I could call back and apply for a card. When I called the phone company, I couldn't get our account switched to my name without Adam's permission. I'd have to have him on the same call with me to do this. Still stuck in that 1950s time warp.

Adam and I sat on hold for close to an hour at the end of separate phone lines waiting for the agent to grant me the privilege of someone half my age — my own phone account. It was mostly typing, with occasional dead air as she went through the process.

We'd hardly spoken since I'd called him about Mary.

During one of those silences, Adam asked me, "Am I still on your wine newsletter?"

"Yes." I made a mental note to unsubscribe him.

"Do I have access to your wine reviews, the paid part, for twenty-five dollars?"

"Are you asking me for a free subscription?"

"Yes, if you still want free financial advice. I want to buy some good Bordeaux."

"So your financial advice is worth twenty-five dollars?"

Silence.

Although it'd been several months since he'd moved out, this felt so cold and transactional. Some part of me still hoped we could get back together and another part knew it would never happen. I got the phone line but felt disconnected.

❧

Friendship was never my strong suit before Nina and Cassie. All my life I'd been perfecting the art of the outsider — great for writing but lousy for birthday parties, which were mostly just Mom and me. My childhood wasn't unhappy, but it was isolated. Mom and I moved fourteen times before I turned ten. Eventually I stopped answering the door when the new kids knocked. It wasn't worth starting over.

Instead, I turned to Mom. We did everything together, from school work and dance lessons on the weekdays to competitions and workshops on weekends. I was too busy to play.

My idol was fourteen-year-old Nadia Comăneci, the Romanian five-time Olympic gold medallist and the first gymnast to achieve a perfect score of ten. I'd listen to "Nadia's Theme" in bed at night, mentally going over every step in every dance, imagining myself in competition, executing moves perfectly. I was determined to be perfect by the time I was fourteen — in dance and in life.

Mom and I lived in rented trailers and basement apartments and bought used clothes and furniture. I wore plastic bread bags in my leaking winter boots. At night we'd joke it was time to "go to mattress," since our bed didn't have a box spring or legs.

As the only single parent among her colleagues of elementary schoolteachers, Mom often hosted parties on Friday nights so she didn't have to hire a babysitter. I remember at age six sitting in the trailer hallway, outside the bathroom, listening to the laughter, clinking glasses, and mostly female voices in the living room. Often they sang along with Helen Reddy's "I Am Woman." It was their anthem. I heard the bits they belted out the loudest. Why did they roar about being down there on the floor?

Helen would have been proud of my entrepreneurial spirit. I charged each teacher a quarter to use the bathroom. One evening, one of the few male teachers told me he only had a dollar. I said, "That's okay, you have three credits now."

◦৩◦

When I was nine, we moved to Antigonish, a small town in the middle of Nova Scotia, so that Mom could complete her degree at St. Francis Xavier University. The budget was tight. She wasn't working and had to pay for her tuition and textbooks, as well as our food, rent, and my dance lessons.

We lived in a basement apartment a few doors down from an old tavern. On Sunday mornings, I got up early to look for coins that drunken patrons had dropped on the sidewalk the previous night. They were often sticky with beer and urine. Mom didn't know I did this. I tried to minimize how often I had to ask her for money for something at school.

Given we moved around so much, my only constant was competition: a way of proving myself based on what I could do rather than being validated for who I was. I learned to keep comparing my performance to others. I learned to keep score.

Highland dancing is unlike most sports in that men and women compete together. It was developed in the nineteenth century by clan chiefs to select the best soldiers based on their stamina, strength, and agility to perform the dances at Highland games. At seventeen, I placed fifth in the Highland Reel event at the world championships in Scotland. The first three places went to Scottish men and the fourth to a woman from the U.S. I also performed in stadium concerts, like the Royal Nova Scotia International Tattoo, with thousands of spectators.

I became all-or-nothing socially: on my own or else performing in front of large anonymous crowds. That's why I don't get frazzled on television. Celebrity hosts, a dozen roving cameras moving in and out, bright lights, live audience, national viewership of millions — bring it on.

Put me in a group of a few people, and my emotional battery drains quickly. They can be the nicest people on the planet. Doesn't matter. The cool blue light of calm drains from my fingers, and red-hot anxiety seeps up my core. Afterward, I need to find a quiet, dark place to recharge.

⟋◉⟍

"I'm so proud of you, hon," Mom told me over dinner during a visit in June. We sat out back in the blue dusk. "Look at how you've come out of this. You've created a stable home for Cameron, you're back on your feet."

"I had a great role model." I squeezed her hand.

The smoke from the grilled chicken blended with our Corison Kronos Vineyard Cabernet Sauvignon. Napa Valley winemaker Cathy Corison is renowned for her cabernets in a region famous for them. Her Kronos Cab is named for the Greek Titan born of the earth and sky. Kronos also refers to time and to the age of these vines, planted in 1971. They're so deeply rooted, reaching down into the earth for small reservoirs of water, that the vineyard can be dry-farmed without irrigation. The vines produce tiny grapes, so the ratio of skin to grape flesh is high. Flavour and colour in the skins translate to concentrated, delicious wine with aromas of blackcurrant, dark plum, and smoke.

Corison is interested in the intersection of wine's power and elegance. If Mom were a wine, it would be this one. She was visiting more frequently now, and between visits we spoke by phone more often. She was, and is, a remarkable woman.

Educating the Whole Witch

T he envelope I pulled from the mailbox had no return address. I unwrapped it, worried about another bill.

As I unfolded the papers, my new credit card glinted in the sunlight. I was as proud as a Girl Guide who'd just earned her merit badge for shopping.

Years later, when Cameron turned eighteen, I suggested he get his own card.

"I use cash. I don't need one."

"Right. That's the best time to get it."

We set up payments for his phone on the card and then for his card to be automatically paid every month from his bank account. I did for Cameron what I wished I'd done for myself.

I also did for Mom what she couldn't do for herself. She had grown up in a rural family of eight children, one of only two daughters. Black-and-white photographs of the boys playing hockey hung on the walls of their home. There were no pictures of the girls.

Mom had asked her mother if she could take Highland dancing lessons but was told there was no money. She and her sister were expected to clean the house, cook dinner, and clean up afterward, while the boys went outside to play. When Mom asked why the boys weren't helping with the dishes, she was told that they had had to do them until the girls came along. But her younger brother was also playing outside.

How different that was from my childhood. While I may not have gone outside to play either, I still had the freedom to choose what I wanted to do, even if that was practising Highland dancing for hours alone. I won the trophies for Mom, who couldn't take dance lessons. I got the graduate degree she gave up for me.

That driving force first propelled me to choose a practical undergraduate degree in public relations rather than in my first love, English. The program at Mount Saint Vincent University, in Halifax, was excellent, but one that I thought might pigeonhole me in a touchy-feely career. Once I had graduated, I wanted to follow it with an MBA. Then I'd never have to worry about paying for dance lessons or whatever my family wanted. I sought advice from a marketing professor in the Mount's business program. He didn't think I'd get in because I hadn't taken courses in finance. I also didn't have the usual seven years' work experience. I hadn't made Western University's cut-off score of the top one percentile on the Graduate Management Admission Test (GMAT). My brain froze (and still does) with math.

In grade one, a well-intentioned teacher had moved me into the grade two class in September. Therefore, I missed memorizing multiplication tables and felt like an idiot still counting numbers on my fingers. Every night, I cried myself to sleep. Blackboard calculations haunted my dreams. Numbers became the enemy, and words, my friends. I discovered the beautiful geometry of language and the mathematical precision of the right word. After several weeks,

Mom realized I wasn't adjusting and asked that I be moved back to the grade one class.

Years later, I wasn't going to let a little math stop me. The marketing professor's comments fuelled my fire. I applied anyway. It felt like strength, but was it? Every time a man said no, I leaned into a harder yes. Sometimes I think that had I talked to a faintly encouraging woman, I might have given up.

For kicks, I also took the Law School Admission Test and did far better on it than the GMAT. After I was accepted into Western's joint MBA-Bachelor of Law program, I found out the selection committee liked my entrepreneurial spirit in starting the dance school. By the time I applied, I had over three hundred students and employed four teachers in three locations.

It never occurred to me that founding and running my dance school for eight years counted. I had learned much about marketing, finance, staffing, and operations. Before I left for Western, I referred my students to another teacher. I didn't sell the school or ask for a percentage of profits. I had the work ethic but not the business savvy. Undervaluing my work started early, as did the constant need to prove myself. I didn't appreciate what I'd already accomplished so I always needed the next gold star.

I deferred starting the four-year program for a year so I could save more money, especially as I'd no longer have the dance school income. I worked in Mount Saint Vincent's alumni relations department.

"You're not twenty-three yet, are you?" the director of alumni relations asked me one morning over coffee in the staff lounge.

"No, why?"

"Why don't you apply for the Rhodes Scholarship?"

"Thanks, but that's for brainiacs."

"It's actually for well-rounded people. I think you'd have a solid chance." She smiled.

Later that day, I thought, *Why not?*

I welcomed another excuse to defer Western, even if I had a 0.7 percent chance of winning a scholarship. British imperialist Cecil Rhodes, who founded the De Beers diamond mining empire in South Africa, established the program in 1903. The prestigious scholarship to Oxford University, in England, was described as the only thing a man can do at age twenty-one that would be in his obituary. It wasn't until 1977 that women were even permitted to apply, and not until 2018 that the criteria describing successful candidates, such as the "qualities of his manhood," were updated to be gender neutral. Today, the scholarship's association with Rhodes also raises issues of colonialism and racism.

Back then all I could think was … *Is that another man I see shaking his head at me?*

The application required writing an essay, getting academic and character references, your alma mater's nomination, and facing several rounds of interviews with scary smart people. Two scholarships for Atlantic Canada were open to those under twenty-four years of age who were either residents of Atlantic Canada or born there but living elsewhere. Somehow, I made it to the final round.

"Don't they call your alma mater 'Pill Hill'?" the grizzled Rhodes judge asked, leaning in toward me.

He sat opposite me in one of Halifax's posh restaurants. The two young men at the table, also candidates, smirked. The judge was referring to the fact that Mount Saint Vincent University was built on a hill and that its student population was about 85 percent women (who may or may not have been on birth control pills). I didn't know if the judge was baiting me with the "Pill Hill" jab, or if it was just plain sexist. I felt myself flushing.

"Highland dancing … that isn't a real competitive sport," he added, when I hadn't answered his first question.

Cecil Rhodes wanted the scholarships to go to young men who weren't "merely bookworms" but who also had "success in manly outdoor sports such as cricket, football, and the like."

"Men — the Scots," I said slowly, "used to do the sword dance as a stamina drill to train for battle. Then they'd use those blades to eviscerate the English. I'd say that's pretty competitive."

He harrumphed.

I got the call the next day from the head of the committee telling me they were very impressed, however, blah, blah, blah. One winner was studying medicine at McGill University and a competitive rower. The other was in biosciences at McMaster University and a champion fencer.

I went to Oxford anyway through my university's English department. Spending a semester studying the Romantic poets with Jonathan Wordsworth, a descendant of William Wordsworth's brother, was a dream. Much to his irritation, my focus was on Keats. While there, I visited The Eagle and Child pub where C.S. Lewis shared an early draft of *The Lion, The Witch and The Wardrobe* with J.R.R. Tolkien. I didn't drink alcohol then, so I walked down the street to the Nosegay tea shop, where I developed a passion for tea.

Then on to Western.

The Ivey Business School, at Western University, uses the case-study method of complex, real-world business problems. Students defend their plans in a classroom of sixty students seated amphitheatre-style, like the rounded rows of the Roman Colosseum where gladiators fought to the death. Even with the deferral year, I was one of the youngest in the program and one of the few women who comprised 18 percent of the class that year. Our human resources professor told a small group of us after one class that several years earlier, the school had admitted more women to increase their percentage in the program. The women who wouldn't have got in without the provision failed, so the school did away with it. In retrospect, this sounds like the excuse used to rationalize why more women aren't corporate executives: not enough of them in the pipeline who merit promotion. But where were the support programs to help them succeed? I wasn't aware of any during my time at Western. Today the university offers several groups to support women, people of colour, and people who identify as LGBTQIA2S+. Thirty-two percent of the 2023 class were women.

I was both pleased and terrified to be at Western, surrounded by mostly male engineers, computer scientists, and accountants. In the auditorium on the first day, the dean made that standard scary declaration: "Look to your right and look to your left. One of you won't graduate."

Thanks for the pep talk.

I slugged my way through the program, waking up in the night with math sweats and asphyxiating on finance by day. I couldn't keep up with all the calculations that the professors scrawled across the blackboards. The engineers just nodded their heads and twirled their pens, mini batons between their fingers. Even as I remember this now, my breathing tightens.

Writing was my saving grace. On exams, I'd write my recommendations for the case study and describe the calculations I'd do if only I had more time (ha). I focused on strategy and making decisions with incomplete information. Isn't that life?

It worked. I was one of two women in the graduating class who made the Dean's List both years. I'll never forget the snide question from a male classmate asking whom I'd slept with to get on the list. *Someday*, I thought, *you'll work for me — or someone who reports to me.*

My grades got me to the final round of interviews with the consulting firm McKinsey & Company. The firm had an "up or out" system: if you didn't get promoted, you were asked to leave. I was a moth to any competitive flame.

At the interview dinner in Toronto, I sat across from a senior partner. He shook his wrist every few minutes to expose the gold Rolex watch from under his starched Hugo Boss shirt sleeve fastened with diamond Mulberry cufflinks. I kept my hands clenched under the table.

He handed me the wine list. "Why don't you choose something."

I took it with sweaty hands and scanned frantically down rows of names I didn't recognize. My only wine experience until then was with Baby Duck bubbly in high school. I suggested something I could at least pronounce and that seemed fancy to me.

"How about the Mondavi Reserve Cabernet?"

"That'll be an interesting match with my Dover sole," he sniffed, taking back the list.

I didn't get the job, but I resolved never again to feel embarrassed about a lack of wine savvy. My desire — need — to prove myself has driven me to do all sorts of productive things. It's also been the destructive force behind the things I've done that make me most ashamed.

Calypso Credit

"**Y**OUR ACCOUNT IS OVERDUE AS THE RESULT OF A FAILED PAYMENT. PLEASE MAKE YOUR PAYMENT NOW OR SERVICE MAY BE SUSPENDED," the email from the gas company read in late July.

How did I mess this up? I felt like antifreeze was running through my veins.

Checking my bank online, I discovered there were insufficient funds to cover the gas bill, let alone water, electric, and others. I scanned down the list of transactions and realized that Adam's monthly child support payment hadn't been deposited. Cameron was with me most of the time, so I was now covering the cost of our family home, from repairs to property taxes, as well as his clothing, food, school trips, and other expenses. I had decided to forgo alimony, the financial support for the spouse whose income is less than the partner's. This is separate from child support, which ends when the child becomes an adult. Alimony can continue for many years afterward. I had no desire to stay entangled with Adam, financially or otherwise.

The child support payments had been set up as automatic deposits from Adam's account to mine. I assumed there had been a technical issue and contacted my bank. When I was told it wasn't an error, I emailed Adam to let him know, still assuming it was a mistake.

Several days went by. Nothing.

I contacted Adam again, asking him to send the latest child support payment as soon as possible please. Still nothing, even though I could see he had opened my emails. Now the small panic in my stomach was twisting into a tornado.

After a week of silence, I wrote to Adam again, saying that if he didn't send the payment, I'd have to take him to court to enforce our separation agreement. The agreement, which stipulated the child support terms, was a legal contract.

Later that day, Adam emailed me, saying that he had discussed the child support payments with Cameron. They'd agreed that since it was "Cameron's money," Adam would start depositing the funds into Cameron's bank account instead of mine. Although we had split our assets, did Adam think there would be no additional costs in raising our son?

The braided towel rug had just been pulled out from under me. I was down on the 1950s linoleum floor again.

"How am I supposed to pay the gas, hydro, electric and other bills?" I wrote.

Adam responded that I should ask Cameron to write me a cheque for those each month.

"So you want me — his mother — to ask my teenage son for money to pay the bills? What happens when I have to discipline him and have to ask him for money at the same time? He's a minor. Our agreement specifies that the child support is deposited into my account, not his. This isn't spending money for Cameron; it's how I pay the bills."

A day went by with no response. I felt Adam was undermining my authority with Cameron and teaching him that women can't be trusted to handle money — they should give this over to the man in the family, even if he was still a child. The first stirrings of anger started deep inside me. I emailed Adam to say I was meeting with my lawyer the following week to discuss taking him to court.

Still nothing.

I called Emma, my lawyer, who sent Adam a letter via courier, reminding him of the terms in our separation agreement and that failure to comply would require us to file with the court. On the day he received it, Adam emailed me saying that he'd changed the deposits back to my account. He wondered why I was so upset. Just another Monday night special at the Gaslight Diner.

I closed my eyes and took a deep breath.

That evening, I let Cameron know that there had been a mistake with the child support payments and that they'd be going back into my account. At first Cameron seemed to be fine with this, but a week later, I knew something was bothering him.

"What's wrong?" I asked him, after we'd finished watching *The Simpsons*.

"You can be vicious," he said.

Vicious. A dagger word.

"What … what do you mean?" I was stunned.

"Dad sent me your email — you threatened to take him to court."

Vicious. The label for the cruellest witch.

Vicious. The label my son now had for me.

I bit my lip hard, then explained, struggling to keep my tone neutral, how the child support covered our household bills. It wasn't his allowance. Cameron seemed to understand this, but I knew his impression of me had changed drastically. I tasted blood in my mouth.

I wasn't willing to share the adult issues with him until he was an adult himself. He deserved to enjoy fourteen-year-old thoughts. A decade later, when he asked me about it as we chatted on the phone, I shared more details.

"I'm sorry you had to go through that," Cameron said.

"Oh, we got the support payments straightened out eventually," I said.

"No, I mean, the rest of it, how you felt … so alone."

He couldn't see me smiling or that my face was wet.

～◎～

One morning, after Cameron left for school, I was washing the dishes and accidentally dropped a spoon on the kitchen floor. I held my breath and waited.

Silence. Sweet silence.

No bellowed accusation, *What did you break now?!*

I dropped a few more spoons on purpose for the satisfaction of hearing the sound without repercussions. Serenity. I was no longer walking on eggshells around the house, afraid of making noise. I remembered the small things I used to enjoy when I was on my own. It gave me great delight one day to let rip a loud burp without even trying to swallow it.

This profound release of everyday tension, of constant worrying about saying the wrong thing, made me realize how abnormal my life had become. The more I read, talked with friends, and discussed these issues with my therapist, Miranda, the more I recognized the distortions in my marriage. At first, I blamed myself for being naive or, worse, for being drawn to this type of relationship.

It hadn't always been like that. We met as penniless grad students and loved talking late into the night. I admired Adam's passion and strength. Somewhere along the line, darker patterns had developed between us.

Perhaps it started with Cameron's birth, though at the time I didn't acknowledge it. I remember after five hours of pushing at the hospital, a specialist came in and used forceps. Cameron was almost nine and a half pounds, with a large head. My family doctor told me that I was torn from "stem to stern." I still cringe thinking about those fourth-degree tears.

After they stitched me up, I had to stay in the hospital for three days of monitoring. On the first night, I sat on a large, blood-stained incontinence pad at the edge of the hospital bed. My swollen legs dangled over the side. I tried to breastfeed Cameron, who was wailing red-faced.

Dried up, unfeminine, unmotherly, unable to give my child what he needed to survive.

"You're not holding him right," Adam said, irritation creeping into his voice. "Bring him closer to your breast."

In obedience, I shifted Cameron around and felt his small blanket getting wet from my tears.

"Sit him up and burp him," Adam snapped.

The nurse came into the room. "Everything okay?" she asked.

"He's hungry," Adam said curtly. He took Cameron from me and went for a walk down the hall.

"Could I please get the pump?" I asked her.

"Of course," she said gently, putting her hand on my shoulder. "It's not my position to say this, but do you need help?"

"I'm just slow getting started," I replied, the tears flowing.

"I mean, would you like to talk to someone?"

It dawned on me then that she thought I was in a troubled relationship. I felt the heat of embarrassment.

"No, no, it's nothing like that," I said. "We're both just exhausted."

She smiled grimly. "Okay, but if you change your mind, just let me know."

Shame swallowed me whole. I insisted that she was mistaken in her impression.

In retrospect, I recognize how differently Adam and I responded to stress. I retreated and became despondent. He took charge and gave orders. Neither approach was effective in a maternity ward, but we didn't know it at the time. The nurse had a brief glimpse of our marriage from the outside, but no one really knows what happens within the walls of a relationship. To most people, our marriage had great curb appeal.

❧

Now that Adam had left, I was changing light bulbs, fixing computers, and dealing with the plumber. Like most couples, we had defaulted to each other's strengths and traditional roles. It was time for me to be whole again.

Mom helped me begin to forgive myself for failing the marriage test. "We were the first generation who had to endure long marriages. Previous generations lost their husbands to war or illness. Men lost their wives in childbirth. Maybe we weren't meant to be married to one person for so long."

That knocked me back. Her words made me realize just how courageous she was to leave her husband and raise me on her own back in the 1970s. Her strength was flowing through me now. I wasn't alone in this. I had a ferociously strong mother, supportive friends, a son I adored. As I leaned on them more, I leaned on wine less. I could stop after a glass or two most nights, and most weeks I took a couple of nights off from wine altogether.

I remembered my strength and confidence before I met Adam. Those naysayers had been kindling to my fire. I had sat watching the dying embers of my own life long enough.

For the first time in twenty years, I was looking forward to living life without fear, without undermining my sanity and suffocating my feelings. I was ready to rise from my own ashes.

Harvest

The Lying, the Witch, and Her Wardrobe

———

We were walking down the aisle of the liquor store when Cameron, his bright blue eyes puzzled, asked, "Why do you wear so much see-through clothing now?" He was referring to my sheer dress, which needed a camisole to stay just this side of decent. It was an innocent question.

I wanted to say, *Because, honey, Mama's back on the market.*

But that's not what your fourteen-year-old son wants to hear.

"I just find these clothes cooler in August."

For months after my marriage to Adam imploded, my wardrobe had consisted of baggy clothes that an eighteenth-century nun would find frumpy, including full-coverage underwear (a.k.a. the enormous granny panties in the movie *Bridget Jones's Diary*). Sexual desire had been stirring in me like daffodils pushing up under the spring thaw. I realized that unless I wanted to date an equally frumpy man, something had to change. So my necklines headed south. My hemlines rose faster than the tides in the Bay of Fundy.

I wanted to merchandise a little. Beyond that, I loved dressing this way and felt more connected with my own body. Now when I went out for dinner with girlfriends, I'd wear every sparkly piece of jewellery I owned. In retrospect, I looked like a human Christmas tree.

I'd been twenty years off the dating scene, with a high-school health-class understanding of female sexuality. While human bodies hadn't changed, what we could do sexually with social approval had. Writing about wine may look like one of the most sociable jobs on the planet, but in reality, it's solitary, especially if you're serious about the writing part. The challenge was how to meet someone when I worked alone at home. I was excited about the prospect of meeting new men. I didn't need to fall in love. I just wanted to dance with several princes at the ball, then head home in my carriage and call it a night. Well, okay, he could come home with me, but no sleeping over. It isn't charming dealing with most princes the next morning. Better to satisfy lusty desires before midnight, when he'd turn into a pumpkin.

"Women in their twenties and thirties have high estrogen, the fertility hormone that drives us to have children," my doctor said during my next Pap test. "Oxytocin, the 'cuddle chemical' that drives us to care for them."

I had told her about my separation. My feet squirmed in the metal stirrups, but her explanation was more chilling.

"Men have lots of testosterone, the hormone that makes them want to have sex but not to stick around. In our forties, estrogen declines, but women's baseline of testosterone remains the same. It becomes an increasingly important part of the female hormonal mix. Et voilà, we get the stereotype of mature women as 'cougars' on the prowl for sex but not reproduction."

Oh my God, she was right!

One of the UPS delivery guys was a strapping young man. His biceps curved deliciously out from his short-sleeved shirt in the August heat. He'd jokingly asked a few times if he could come in and "try the wine" with me. He was the only man I saw almost daily, but what was the attraction? His military-like uniform? The thoughtful gifts he brought me from Amazon? His teasing phone number: 1-800-PICK-UPS? He was always on the run and unattainable. Dependably there, then dependably gone. I mused about having the wine equivalent of a pool boy: vinous cougar seeks spittoon stud. But alas, what would we have in common, other than he delivered the wine and I drank it? It wouldn't last much beyond a few urgent deliveries.

I started thinking of what, and who, I really wanted in a relationship. Even if I were ready, could I find someone so late in life? Weren't all the princes married by now?

~⊚~

"If you do the real work of becoming whole, you won't feel so alone," Miranda said at our next counselling session.

I sank further into her sofa among the throw cushions, holding one to my chest.

"But what if I end up with another version of Adam?"

"You won't attract the same person as Adam because *you're* not the same person.

"Think about how you want to present yourself. They won't have the background on you or get to know you slowly through friends and family the way Adam did."

"Why did I pick him in the first place?" I sighed.

"He was right for you at that time of your life. He was what you needed or felt you needed. You had to get him — the dynamic of that relationship — out of your system."

She was right. Adam had seemed like the antidote to my small-town worries about what others thought of me (he blissfully didn't seem to care) and to my Catholic guilt about everything. I realize now how important the support of small towns and family are, even if they're judgmental.

She paused, then asked, "What kind of man are you looking for?"

I retreated into the tech jargon from my pre–wine writing days. "A feature-rich boyfriend, with great source code."

"Meaning?"

"A multi-talented man with a loving family history."

"Meaning?"

"I want someone who has interests and friends outside of work, who's connected with his family. I wonder if I had married one of those nice Nova Scotia boys with seven siblings and thirty-eight cousins, things might have turned out better. Then again, I probably would have left him. I was such a little snob."

Still, my notion of the ideal mate was shifting into something beyond career success.

After my appointment, I bought lipstick at the cosmetics store so I could get free tips on updating "my look."

"You don't want to bunny," the makeup artist told me, as I sat on a stool at the counter.

Bunny?

"What's that?"

"Right here." She pointed to the tiny wrinkles on either side of her nose as she sniffed.

Great, a new wrinkle verb.

Then she added, "But the 11 is worse."

The 11?

"Those two lines between your eyebrows when you frown." She mentioned she was due for Botox.

"Isn't that poison, like a toxin?"

"Yes and no," she said. "Botox has been around for over thirty years. My doc thinks it's safe. It just relaxes the muscles that cause those wrinkles."

I got the treatment but told no one except Mom. Why do so many people think of Botox as the equivalent of doping in the sports world? It's viewed as cheating, especially for women who should be "natural" beauties. When that natural beauty fades, we lose our currency. We go from Snow White to the wrinkled, warty stepmother who was, of course, a witch.

The needle stung, but I was pleased that I liked the result for me, rather than to please someone else. For the first time in months, my facial muscles relaxed from constant worry.

∽⊚⌀

I hadn't met a potential date in the last six months and still hadn't used online sites. It was time to stop waiting for a prince to find me. The next morning at Starbucks, with a magnum-sized tea, I posted on Facebook: "The Top 10 Wines for the Newly Single Woman." It was a subtle cue for particularly perceptive men, the ones I wanted to date.

Silence. No one got it. Did no one read between the wines anymore?

On Instagram, I asked if someone could recommend a successful gentleman who owned a large, well-stocked wine cellar. This was for a magazine article, of course.

One woman replied, "If you find more than one, darlin', please send him my way."

I wondered if I could organize an informal wine tasting with friends, but instead of everyone bringing bottles, they could bring me potential boyfriends — BYOPB. They didn't know any eligible men, let alone those with big cellars.

I was glad to be sexually interested again, even if I wasn't ready for a lifelong partner. A muscular handyman in tight jeans was now sprawled out on my kitchen floor fixing under the sink. I commented on how many screws it required to do the job.

He responded with a husky French accent, "A man without a large tool box is not a man."

I nearly jumped him.

I began scanning newspaper articles such as "The Top 30 Worthy Bachelors," settling on a forty-three-year-old, pinot-loving pediatrician. How to meet him without being creepy? Should I send him a very *direct* message on Instagram?

Abandoning that idea, I turned to online dating sites. My biggest issue was the lack of anonymity, since I was on television so often. I wasn't willing to post a detailed profile publicly and have one of several nut jobs who stalked me on social media find me there. That ruled out apps like Tinder. There were also niche dating sites for farmers, book lovers, vegetarians, and Star Trek fans. I glanced at a couple of sites for wine lovers, but a relationship based on tannin structure wasn't enough for me — though I did like a long finish.

Even when someone filled in details, there was no guarantee of authenticity with these sites. I registered on one with the handle "SingleandHappy." I didn't answer any of the seventy-five questions or add a picture. I just wanted to see how the site worked.

The next morning, I discovered seventeen messages in my inbox with the subject line: "He checked you out!"

I opened the first email and was informed that Steve B. and I were an 86 percent match, just as I was with George, HotRod97, BigJoe, and thirteen others who apparently also hadn't filled out the questionnaire. We had so much in common: lazy in love!

Dating was, and is, marketing. I tried to think of a new label to launch in my own rebranding campaign. "Nastalie" might deter the stalkers, but I didn't want a brand that was bait-and-witch. Was a new label really what I needed? While updating my look was easy, the scariest makeover was happening inside. I was terrified of letting my guard down again. What if I were attracted to someone and he rejected me? What if I fell in love and he betrayed me? Most terrifying, what if he actually loved me? Was there a label or hashtag for that?

#HeartbrokenButHealing

∽◎∼

While flying to New York for work in September, I leafed through the airline magazine and saw an ad for It's Just Lunch, described as "a personalized dating service for busy professionals. Quality matches. Guaranteed privacy." The ad mentioned "busy professionals" several times. The assumption was those highly successful singles had just been too focused on their careers to concentrate on the planning box labelled *Important, but Not Urgent*. Surely it couldn't be due to a driven type-A narcissism that made overachievement the only way to quiet inner demons for a few minutes?

Nonetheless, I liked that there were no online profiles. Instead, you met with a "matchmaker consultant." When I called the Toronto number, the representative, Jill, said that since I lived in Ottawa, we'd do an online video interview. I suggested that we just chat by phone. She preferred a video call, presumably to verify the goods for herself, wisely not trusting information on a form.

On the evening of my interview, I changed my blouse several times, applied extra eyeliner, then took it off, worried that I'd end up in the agency's category for Ladies of Last Resort. At eight o'clock, Jill flashed up on my screen wearing a burgundy jacket with a low-cut silk blouse. I wondered if I could also pull off the serious-but-sexy executive look.

After intros, Jill's first comment was "Nice skin, sort of British rose." A busy professional herself, she was in marketing mode. I wondered if I should tilt my webcam to give her a panning shot of the rest of the merchandise.

Jill said she would recommend men she felt matched my "life experience" and arrange lunch dates for the two of us. I was to go to the restaurant and ask for the reservation under our first names, Natalie and James (or whoever). Neither person had to divulge contact information.

Just a few months earlier, I had toyed with living single for the rest of my life. Now I realized that I'd mentally moved on from joining It's Just Lunch to wishing it were called Much More Than Dinner.

Jill casually slipped in that the service cost eighteen hundred dollars. No refunds. I swallowed hard. This was an investment in future happiness, right? A strategic demographic targeting tool. Men willing to pay this fee were successful enough to afford it and probably weren't looking for a one-night stand, which they could buy for a lot less. Then again, they could be psychopaths who stalked successful women.

Jill asked me the age range I would consider, especially since most men wanted to meet younger women. I suggested up to eight years older or younger than I was. I'd be willing to freshen his drink but not his catheter.

Jill called back a few days later with three profiles of men within my age range: Jack, a vice-president of marketing for a national coffee shop chain, who played competitive chess; Antonio, chief executive officer of an artisanal chocolate company, who loved Argentine tango; and George, an oral surgeon who enjoyed Alpine skiing.

I was cautiously tingly about meeting them. Like many people, they sounded perfect on paper. I asked Jill how long each of them had been with the dating service. She confirmed all three had registered less than two months ago.

"Oh good, those mangoes are still fresh!" I blurted out, relieved that they weren't retreads farmed out to new women members to keep them as hopeful paying clients. Most matchmaking services attract far more women than men.

Jill smiled.

I noticed they had paired me with coffee and chocolate, then a dentist. Well, not a dentist, an oral surgeon. *Oral*, I said to myself forming a delicious O with my lips.

I was more frightened than excited to date again. What would we talk about? What if I bored these men? What if they bored me? We hadn't raised a family together; we didn't meet in college; we had no history. A blank slate — like a blank page — panics me. I was putting myself back out there in the world, stripped bare of my previous labels.

Meeting a Magic Man

S everal weeks later during a business trip to Toronto, I went out for dinner with each of the three prospects. It was good to get out again. They had interesting backstories but also, understandably, the baggage that comes with age: alimony, custody, second mortgages, unresolved relationship issues.

Each was highly successful in his field and radiated confidence. I noticed how white the oral surgeon's teeth were. Every time he threw his head back to laugh, it looked like he had a few extra teeth in the back on each side. Fringe benefit, I thought, my mind drifting back to my other favourite word beginning with *O*.

While I enjoyed meeting them, I didn't feel any connections. The surgeon said that the next time I was in Toronto, we could get together. He wasn't prepared to meet me in Ottawa — he wanted a situationship. I had encountered a new breed of men that I named ZEMs: zero effort men. No more ZEMs, I thought, creating the mental hashtag #ZeroZEMs.

After more uninspiring dates, I started keeping a Man Booklet, with notes on each one. My descriptions started sounding like wine reviews, as I looked for balance, vibrancy, and full-bodied … intellect. Where was my dream man, zesty and spirited, yet also smooth and subtle? I had imagined playing the field would be exciting and glamorous. I would never need settle down again. I'd host a reality show with me telling one man each week that he had to leave the island and not call me again. In fact, it was tiring, like going on an endless round of job interviews for the same position: telling your story over and over to see if there was a "fit." Jill called back with more profiles after I'd gone on half a dozen dates, but I put them on hold.

At our next session, Miranda asked if I had considered joining an Ottawa-based dating service.

"Ottawa? I won't find anyone in Ottawa."

"Why not?"

"The gene pool." There it was: my inner snob. "What I mean is that all the men are married here. If they're not, there's a really good reason."

"Have you tested that assumption?"

"No."

"Might it be an interesting experiment to date someone local whom you could see more often?"

"Maybe." Or maybe I was afraid of a relationship with someone close by.

"All right, you might want to check out a local service called Misty River."

"Misty River? That sounds like a retirement home where love goes to die."

Miranda smiled. "I think they have clients of all ages."

The name Misty River made me imagine Cupid firing his burning arrow at my funeral pyre as it floated down the river. I would be laid on a bed of singed kindling sticks, each symbolizing the death of a past love.

A few days later, I met the owner, Linda Miller, who wore a tailored navy suit. I informed her I didn't want to meet anyone who didn't have a graduate degree or who was under six feet tall. Apparently, I still had a taste for alpha males. "I don't want to date a man I can easily throw over my shoulder," I clarified. "And no more hairy hobbits."

"No more what?" she asked.

"Short men with lots of back hair."

Hobbits are heroes in Tolkien's stories but not as a real-life dinner and dancing companion when you're almost five foot ten and his head nuzzles into your tummy or slightly higher.

"Oh, that'll be a challenge." She sighed. "At least come down to five foot eight."

"What? A guy who's shorter than I am? Can't do it, though I'll compromise on the back hair. He can shave that if he truly loves me."

She shook her head.

"I'm thinking of one man right now who might work." She seemed to be flipping through her mental Rolodex.

"Who?" I asked, leaning in.

"Someone I used to date."

"It didn't work out?" I wanted to confirm this wouldn't be some sort of weird three-way.

"No. I'll have to check with him first."

"Is he tall?"

"I'll have to check with him first." She smiled.

Later that evening, I sat down with the application. Quick tip: never fill out a personal profile, or any sort of application, after a glass of wine.

In the box for religious or spiritual faith, I wrote, "I enjoy practising the ancient bacchanalian Greek and Roman rituals for

Dionysus and Bacchus." Under hobbies and passions, I said that I enjoyed exploring the great indoors, followed by a long nap.

No way was I going to attract those outdoorsy, kayak-crazy engineers. But just who was I going to attract with this profile? I wanted the Swiss Army knife of boyfriends, an all-in-one man who came equipped with four Cs: cook, clean, cuddle, and cunning linguist. It didn't occur to me that this was likely impossible.

I emailed my profile to Linda, then poured a second glass of the Thirty Bench Pinot Noir, from Niagara. Emma Garner makes this medium-bodied wine with a liquid silk texture. Cool climates, like Canada, excel at pinot noir because the grapes don't ripen as much as they do in warmer regions. Lower grape sugar means lower alcohol and a nervy acidity that teeters on the edge of collapse but doesn't — exactly how I love my wine and my people.

It's a difficult grape to grow, dubbed the "heartbreak grape" by the self-described pathological optimists who make it. As California winemaker André Tchelistcheff once said, "God made cabernet sauvignon, but the devil made pinot noir." Pinot is my go-to wine as it packs all the flavour of a red without heavy tannin or oak. Also, I don't fall asleep on the sofa at 7:00 p.m.

∽◉∼

Too short, delete. Too undereducated, delete. Too outdoorsy, delete.

I sat at my computer clicking through the profiles of the men Linda had sent me, rejecting them as quickly as a grape picker throwing out unripe fruit. *I know, still a snob.*

The fourth profile was of the man she'd mentioned when we met. Well, if he was good enough for the founder of the matchmaking agency, he was good enough for me. Daniel's profile indicated he'd never been married, had no kids, liked to cook, didn't smoke. There wasn't a whiff of campfire or water sports.

Fortunately, my pride and prejudice couldn't kill this potential happiness. I couldn't figure out his career with the ambiguous phrase "real estate development," nor his level of education, which simply said "college."

Back at our favourite wine bar that Friday, five of my girlfriends — all married — insisted on getting every detail, making me repeat several slowly to relish them.

"We're starting a blog called 'Dating for Those Who Can't, but Who'd Like to Live Vicariously Through the Adventures of Their Newly Single Friend, Nat,'" Lindsey declared.

"Oh my God!" Lily blurted out when I showed them Daniel's picture. "Look at his eyes, look at his hands, those massive hands ... Oh, yes please!"

"Let's toast the fact that he's gorgeous." Nina raised her glass.

"Let's also toast to him not having an ex-wife or alimony payments," Cassie added, as we all raised our glasses again.

"Oh, and no kids, no baggage ... no attachments," Janice chimed in.

"He's not a vacuum cleaner," I said, as we went for a third toast.

My suspicious mind wondered if Daniel could be a Misty River Mercy Date. Did Linda keep a few stallions in the stable to trot out occasionally to keep female clients hopeful? My flaw-spotting antennae were up. I also didn't want to get hurt again so soon after my separation.

She gave me Daniel's phone number. He had a deep, worked-in leather voice and suggested we meet for coffee. Ten months after my separation, I was ready for dinner and dessert. We agreed on lunch at a downtown restaurant that Sunday. The flaming reds and oranges of fall leaves splashed across the Gatineau hills on the other side of the river.

I arrived first and took a seat at the opposite end of the restaurant facing the door, so I could watch him walk in. I'd worn my highest heels in case he'd fudged his height on the application. Then I'd stand up slowly to my full height, look down, give him the Eye of Sauron, and bellow: "Scurry back to the Shire!"

Shafts of tawny light poured in through the floor-to-ceiling windows. Suddenly, he filled the doorway. I took in a quick breath. His broad shoulders moved back and forth as he strode across the room. Was he walking in slow motion the way they do in movies when lovers first see each other?

I let out a sigh of relief — he was as advertised. A spark ran up my spine as we shook hands. He had sky-blue eyes and a quick smile. Why did he remind me of Grampy?

That aroma ... Old Spice! He used the same aftershave as Grampy. The smell took me back to when I was twelve, the summer before Grammy died. She lay on a cot in the dining room, unable to climb the stairs to their bedroom.

Ever practical, she asked Mom and me to help her sort things throughout the house. I'd run upstairs and bring back a drawer. She'd tell us who was getting that shawl or this teacup after she was gone. For a few items, she told me to ask Grampy about them. He was sitting outside on the verandah.

A ball of string, a notebook, the tiny ceramic figurine of Little Boy Blue that came inside a box of Red Rose Tea ... He held each one thoughtfully, then put it beside him, saying he was going to keep it. He didn't want to let go of anything, especially her. Theirs was the greatest love story I'd ever known.

Daniel and I ordered tea, chatting about the beautiful October weekend and family gatherings.

"What do you like most about being outdoors?" he asked.

"Coming back inside and savouring the difference."

He laughed.

"In fact, I love bed camping."

"Bed camping?"

"Yes, staying in bed all day and watching the outdoors from the comfort of your air-conditioned bedroom." I was trying to be witty and salacious at the same time.

There was that aroma again … I imagined Daniel in an Old Spice commercial. His muscular chest and biceps glistening with water as he stepped out of the shower and wrapped a white towel around his waist. I'd help him dry off … with that towel.

I ordered a small salad but barely touched it. He dug into his flank steak and fries, but his eyes held my gaze as he leaned in to listen.

"So, do you come from a big family?" I asked.

"Medium size. I have two sisters and a brother. We moved around a lot because Dad was a pilot. Mom stayed home with us."

"How did they meet?"

"Dad left Germany when they started training teenagers to fly planes for the war. He wanted to get as far away as he could, so he went to Australia, where he met Mom. They moved to Canada, where he became a check pilot — a pilot who tests and recertifies other pilots. How about you … brothers, sisters?"

"Single brat of a single mother. We moved around a lot, too. She was a teacher in Nova Scotia. We also travelled because I was a Highland dancer, so we went to Scottish games all over."

"Ah, with the kilts and bagpipes. That must have been fun."

"It was a lot of hard work, practice, lessons, but yes, I enjoyed it. Officially retired now. Traded my swords for wineglasses — I write about wine."

"That's got to be more fun."

"Yep, I drink for a living." I retreated into my jokey comfort zone. "I've had some interesting conversations with the federal tax folks: 'You want to claim all this wine under office supplies?'"

"Ha!"

"And what do you do?"

"I had my own construction company for years, but now I'm a home inspector."

He paused, his gaze falling briefly to my lips. "So why are you single now?"

"My husband ... We separated in January." I looked away. "Twenty years."

"I'm sorry to hear that. That's a long time."

As he reached for his tea, the back of his fingers brushed along my wrist, making my arm tingle.

"Yep, but I don't have any regrets." I'd learned my lesson from the whiners in Toronto not to unpack my emotional baggage on a first date. "Plus, I have an amazing son."

"How old?"

"Fourteen."

"Great age. We were in the West Indies when I was fourteen, mostly running down the beach and climbing trees. It was *Lord of the Flies* but with parents ..."

"Ha. What about you? Ever been married?"

"No, several long-term relationships. I've seen a lot of marriages from the inside, spent months in many homes renovating their kitchens and bathrooms. Years later, I'd inspect the same home for the wife and another for the husband after they split. Even my own parents were married for almost forty years but weren't really happy until they divorced. I've never been in love enough to want to spend the rest of my life with someone." His eyes softened as he looked at me.

Two hours had flown by. I felt like I was floating. Something warm bloomed inside my chest. It spread out under my arms and down through my thighs — desire.

After Daniel paid the bill, we got up from the table. Someone behind me asked, "Are you Natalie MacLean?"

I turned. "Yes."

"I loved *Unquenchable*."

"Thank you so much!"

Turning to Daniel as we walked out, I whispered, "She was a plant."

"What's *Unquenchable*?"

"My second book."

"Ah."

I loved that he wasn't from my world of wine, writing, or tech. He didn't recognize me and didn't care in a way that was incredibly freeing. He was also the first man I dated without the protection of drinking wine. I could finally get away from myself, or at least away from the me that the world had labelled.

He called that evening while he was with his siblings for dinner to say how much he'd enjoyed our time together. We chatted briefly. After we hung up, I came bouncing back into the kitchen and announced to Mom, who was visiting, "It worked, it worked!" as though I'd just snared an unsuspecting rabbit. I did a happy little Highland reel around the island. Mom laughed and clapped her hands in time to the imaginary bagpipes.

Hex and the City

————

The next day, Daniel called to arrange dinner out the following weekend. It was perfect, and yet still my neurotic mind wondered if I was about to leap too quickly into a new relationship.

"When you're house hunting, you don't buy the first one you see," I said to Miranda.

"You don't have to sign an emotional mortgage with him. Why not just have fun?"

"Sure. Maybe he'll be a weekend cottage rental for now."

I went on one more It's Just Lunch appointment that had been set up before I met Daniel. That date turned out to be with an engineer who now owned his family consulting firm. He droned on about last quarter's results and fishing trips with his buddies. It was a clincher that removed all doubts about Daniel, like the laundry detergent commercial in which the competitive brand leaves the sock dirty but our hero brand gets it sparkling clean. More than that, though, I was still thinking about Daniel's steady gaze and affable smile, which sent a delicious rush of adrenalin through me.

On our fifth date, Dean Martin's voice singing "Everybody Loves Somebody" mingled with the diners' chatter. The November chill outside made the restaurant feel cozy. Daniel had old-fashioned manners, helping me out of the car, opening doors, and insisting I go first. Even his language seemed anachronistic, with words like *dungarees* and *leotards*. Was he a time traveller?

He asked me how I got into writing.

"I can email you a link to a television video clip where I'm interviewed about my book."

"I don't want to get to know you through TV," he said gently, taking both of my hands in his. "I want to know you from you."

Damn, those time travellers were well trained on the mother ship. I melted. He seemed the opposite of Adam, who was all about performance and awards. Daniel was definitely the antithesis when it came to tech. He wasn't even on any social media platforms. I took to calling him my lovable lumbersexual Luddite.

My heart was hummingbird happy. I didn't know that someone could be interested in you for who you are, not for what you do or what you've accomplished. Sure, it's impossible to separate everything you are when you meet someone. We're always influenced by appearance, mannerisms, thoughts, speech. But what a powerful connection when someone is intrigued with your barest essentials: the most stripped-down you there is.

Dating Daniel was more exciting than having a high school boyfriend, because he brought the bonus of maturity. We also didn't have to negotiate issues like family, career, or finances. This is the joy of meeting someone later in life. You know what — and who — you want. Another bonus: Daniel had also always taken care of himself, from doctor's appointments to grocery shopping, so I wasn't the nag in the relationship having to remind him about these things.

"How 'bout I light a fire?" Daniel asked when we got home.

You already have, I thought.

"Sure."

Then he started pulling the cushions off the sofa and arranging them on the floor in front of the fireplace.

"What are you doing?"

"Well, if I can't get you out camping, I'm bringing camping to you."

"Would you like me to get some wine?"

"Yes, that's the spirit, Pioneer Nat. Rustle up some vittles, too."

"I'll get the frontier cheddar and orange wine."

Daniel had even managed to get me outside my pinot noir comfort zone. Ann Sperling makes Southbrook Vidal Skin Fermented Orange Wine, in Niagara. She has led the organic and biodynamic winemaking movement in the country, as well as the charge to create the first appellation for orange wines in the world. Let's be clear: orange wine is not made from oranges. Winemakers start out as though they're making white wine, but then they leave the grape skins briefly on during fermentation instead of removing them immediately. The wine is also allowed to oxidize during fermentation. This imparts distinctive colour and savoury flavour.

When Sperling was a child, she had a miniature version of every farm tool: a child-sized hoe, shovel, and so on, so that she could help with almost every part of tending the vines on her family's vineyard in British Columbia. Today, she says she has an intuitive feel for the vines when she walks among them and can tell within seconds their age and vitality. A vine whisperer.

Daniel and I stretched out on the pillows and talked in front of the crackling fire, sipping on the wine. I became more impressed with his deep understanding of human nature. "Where do you get these great ideas — which books?" That's where most of mine had come from.

"Life." He grinned.

Daniel was life smart rather than textbook smart. He had enrolled in a college program but dropped out to launch his construction company. He did read and, in fact, read many more books than I did. He was thawing my snobbery.

Where Adam reminded me of my father — charismatic, handsome, and unreachable — Daniel reminded me of my grandfather, who was always there for me, pushing me on the swing, sharing a peppermint, sitting on the verandah watching the sailboats glide by on Baddeck Harbour.

Grampy's father had died in rural Cape Breton in 1918, leaving his young wife with six sons and pregnant with a seventh. Grampy had to leave school at age twelve to run the family farm. He later attended agricultural college to study the science of soil management. He also became an expert carpenter, needing several jobs to support his own eight children. During the Second World War, he worked at the local ship construction company, building harbour craft for the Royal Canadian Navy.

He read voraciously and was an intellectual match for Grammy, an English teacher who didn't tolerate fools or dangling participles. She'd also sit with me on the verandah, making me memorize William Wordsworth's poems. "I wandered lonely as a cloud ..."

When I smell certain books, or even a *National Geographic* magazine, I'm right back in their home where I spent my childhood summers. I share Grampy's fascination with the magic of what soil can produce and Grammy's love of literature. Daniel has Grampy's love of building with your own hands. We both share his sense of humour.

"I'd like you to meet a friend of mine," I said to Cameron one evening after dinner. He looked up, curious.

"His name is Daniel ... perhaps we could go see *The Hobbit* movie together this Wednesday."

My dates with Daniel had so far been on weekends when Cameron was with his father. I wanted to be sure Daniel would stick around before introducing them.

"You mean on a school night?" Cameron was pleased at the unusual outing and the prospect of chocolate at the theatre.

"Yes, on a school night."

"Awesome!" Cameron pumped his fist. "Is he your new boyfriend?"

"Maybe ... I like him and I want to get to know him better, so I want you to meet him. How do you feel about that?"

"Awesome, I'm getting an extra-large Kit Kat *and* popcorn!"

That Wednesday evening, Daniel rang the doorbell. Cameron already had on his hoodie and sneakers.

"Great to meet you, Cameron." Daniel extended his hand.

Cameron looked at it for a minute, uncertain, then shook it. Daniel's grasp, I knew, would be firm and warm. He held the handshake a second longer until Cameron looked into his eyes and smiled.

"Jump in the back, Cameron," Daniel said, as we walked out to his car. "I've got that," he said when I reached for the door handle. I got in, and he shut the door. His courtly manners were new for both Cameron and me. I felt like a queen whose heir was getting an unspoken lesson in how to be Prince Charming.

Two hours later, on the way home, we talked about our favourite parts of the movie. My favourite "scene" that evening had happened as we got into the car.

∽⊚∾

"You didn't tell me about that rule." I could hear Daniel talking to Cameron two weeks later in the dining room. I was in the kitchen, where I'd lined up seventeen Chilean cabernets to taste.

"That's the way it's supposed to go," Cameron said. They were playing Axis & Allies, a military strategy board game. Cameron now often asked Daniel to play when he came over. The game could last for several hours.

"We both need to know the rules, buddy," Daniel said. I could hear the rustling of the bags of chips beside them. There were some muffled words and laughter.

I was beaming. I loved how patient Daniel was with Cameron, spending time with him, doing what interested Cameron. He was gently teaching him about fairness, graciousness in winning and losing — the rules of life.

I had learned those rules on Highland dancing stages. Mom sat in the bleachers, often burning under a blazing summer sun. She may not have been able to coach me on the finer points of my technique, but she showed me what determination looked like — and how it was a bigger achievement than any of the medals I won.

My relationship with Cameron had improved since our tough conversation about the redirected child support payments. We were spending more time together now than we ever had. We went out for dinner to his favourite casual restaurants. I even played some of his video games, though often I ended up watching him play as I sipped on a glass of wine. I was showing Cameron for the first time that a woman could be head of the household, manage and bring in the money. She could be strong, independent, fiercely loving — a warrior.

Even though we were separated, I still hoped Adam and I would discuss co-parenting Cameron like those amicably divorced television couples. Our son was in his early teens, hormones and all, and consistency on values and rules was important.

With our blow-up over the child support payments, however, Adam and I didn't speak, much less discuss parenting. We exchanged terse emails about money or pickup times on the weekends. I wish I had had the strength and maturity to rise above my anger for Cameron's sake, but it would take a few years before I could do that.

One Friday afternoon in December, Daniel joined Cameron and me on the drive over to Adam's house. Adam was usually still at work when I dropped off Cameron.

"Did you see those geese?" Daniel asked.

A V-shaped flock was crossing the grey sky ahead of us.

"Yes, they're all in a flap," I replied.

Cameron groaned from the back seat. "No, don't start again — this is worse than Mom jokes!" My Mom jokes, he had told me previously, were worse than the stereotypical, lame Dad jokes.

"So you think your mother has a fowl sense of humour?" Daniel asked. He loved puns as much as I did, much to Cameron's chagrin.

"Ughhhh." Cameron laid down on the back seat and put his hands over his ears.

"I'm not trying to ruffle your feathers, honey."

"Arghhhhhh!"

"Okay, okay, enough." Daniel laughed.

"I agree. We better stop before we get in an accident ... of course, my insurance would cover a minor dent after a small de-duck-tible."

I turned and caught Cameron grinning in the back seat. I loved that we could share such light banter together. Daniel brought out the silly side of me I'd long buried under career goals and serious talk with Adam.

As we pulled into the driveway, Adam was standing in the garage.

"Oh God, he's there," I whispered to Daniel. "You can stay in the car." Had we been rolling up on Daniel's ex-girlfriend, I would have sunk down in the seat.

"That's okay, I'll just say hello," Daniel replied, relaxed.

I smiled at him, proud to be with a grown-up.

As we all got out of the car, Adam eyed Daniel warily and didn't move.

Daniel strode up to Adam and put out his hand. "Nice to meet you, Adam."

"You too," Adam said, shaking his hand. He studied Daniel. I studied Adam.

Adam held his emotional cards close to his chest, inscrutable. I was pleased to see that Daniel was slightly taller than Adam. (Cattie Nattie.)

"Well, we're off to dinner," I announced, even though it was only 4:00 p.m.

Cameron was already bounding up the steps to the front door. Adam nodded to us.

"We're going for a walk by the river first," Daniel added, so I didn't sound ridiculous. "Enjoy your evening, Adam."

"You too." Adam turned at the top of the steps and watched us, expressionless, as we got back in the car and drove away.

~⊛~

"I want you to come with me," I said to Daniel.

"How fancy will it be?"

"Suit and tie. I'm wearing a black dress." My second book, *Unquenchable*, had been nominated in the Best Culinary Narratives category at the Taste Canada awards. The ceremony would take place in Toronto, in November 2012.

"Let's do it," Daniel said.

A week later, as we stood at the airport Starbucks counter, a long line behind us, I nudged him impatiently. "Make a decision. Move-on-dot-com."

Daniel was wavering between the croissant and the cherry tart. Now that we'd been together for a month, I was discovering some chinks in my knight's armour — no deal breakers, but still. He often waffled over decisions, going back and forth in his mind and out loud. This was the opposite of Adam, who always knew what he wanted.

"Why do you always have to debate everything?" We sat down at our departure gate.

"I like to consider my options." Daniel took a bite from the tart. "Sometimes thinking about them is as fun as getting them."

Was that why he never married? No matter. I was used to Adam's decisiveness but felt petty criticizing such a good-natured man. Over time, I would start appreciating Daniel's nuanced thinking versus my yes-or-no snappidity.

~⊚~

As we walked into the large ballroom filled with hundreds of people, I looked again at Daniel in his dark suit. The evening lights danced in his blue eyes as he smiled at me.

"You know, if I ever write another book, you're not coming on the tour with me ... women would mob you."

He smiled and squeezed my shoulder, but I could tell he wasn't entirely comfortable. I found out later that he hadn't worn a suit in years but had bought this one anticipating our lives would be one fancy gala after another. Adam had also accompanied me to events like this. He held himself with such confidence that he was once mistaken for the publisher of a major food magazine.

I spotted one of my favourite food writers and waved. She came over with her friend. Daniel said hello and stood there politely as we chatted about industry news. "May I get you ladies something to drink?" he asked during one of the few silences. After he delivered our glasses, he asked, "Do you mind if I check out what's cooking over there?"

"Go for it."

He escaped to the food stations, each featuring different delicacies by the country's top chefs. His happy place was near the shrimp table, where he chatted with the chef until the master of ceremonies asked us to take our seats.

Daniel squeezed my hand when the master of ceremonies announced I'd won the gold. For the first time, I felt I hadn't lost everything when Adam left me. I'd gained a relationship with a man who loved me for who I was. He was affectionate and retro-quirky, making this celebratory moment better than any other I had ever experienced. As we hugged, I didn't want to let him go. He gently drew back and kissed me before I went up to the stage.

Charmed

I sat staring at my computer, eating chocolate-covered almonds, procrasta-snacking.

Unquenchable had been published in November 2011. Now, a year later, as a blizzard battered against my window, I couldn't think of what to write for my third book. I had made notes, but they boiled down to a rehashed recipe of my first two:

1. Visit gorgeous wine regions, especially remote ones (aspirational travel, check).
2. Find a slightly unhinged winemaker who'll give unedited and inappropriate sound bites.
3. Share amusing fish-out-of-water experiences, such as milking goats or diving with sharks.
4. Relax with contemplative sipping of rare wine and share food porn descriptions.

5. Finish with the "realization" that wine is made in
the vineyard, not the winery.
6. Rinse and repeat.

I thought I could do my own take on F. Scott Fitzgerald's lesser-known book, *The Cruise of the Rolling Junk*. In this 1920s account, he chronicles a twelve-hundred-mile road trip from Connecticut to Alabama with his wife, Zelda. They were searching for the biscuits and peaches she loved in her childhood. She's terrible at reading maps, he's a bad driver, their car breaks down, and they encounter eccentric small-town mechanics.

I wondered if I should take a road trip across North America, visiting vineyards while driving an old car with an unruly cat in the front seat as my companion (I'm allergic to cats). I considered calling the book *Red, White, Black, and Blue* or *The Long and Wining Road*. But I couldn't write another wine book. I wasn't better than the genre, I was just done with it. I had nothing new to say. I sat marinating in my own thoughts.

In response to those who asked, I said, "I'm thinking of a travel-based approach again. This time I visit various detox and rehab centres around the world, starting with the Betty Ford Center. That's where I'm headed anyway. I'll write about the food and fitness facilities since they won't have a wine list."

I couldn't resist another quippy defence rather than answer openly that I had no clue where to go next with my writing. I felt lost. Had publishing the first two books been deceptively easy? In an industry that changed so little, where was I going to find a fresh story? I ate another chocolate-covered almond. I knew conflict drives narrative, but I had none in my happy little wine writing life at that moment, except the occasional hangover. The biggest conflict in my first two books was whether a leg of lamb went better with cabernet or syrah. In losing Adam, had

I lost the drive to write in order to please him? Had I plateaued professionally?

~~⦾~~

I loved sitting at the kitchen island chatting with Daniel as he cooked dinner for the two of us. We'd both sip slowly on our glasses of wine. Since Daniel preferred more full-bodied syrah to my pinot, I'd pour half of my wine into an empty half-bottle to save it for another night.

This made me more conscious of how much I was consuming and allowed me to fret less about wasting good wine. The half-bottle reduced oxygen exposure, so it tasted fresh when I opened it. This had worked at dinner parties, too, where I was no longer topping myself up mindlessly. I also drank a glass of water for every glass of wine, alternating between them.

One night, Daniel noticed I was watching him intently as he pounded the chicken breast with a mallet. "What I'm doing breaks down the muscle fibres in the meat, making it more tender. This is important when you have two pieces that are different sizes because they'll cook at an uneven rate. The thinner piece will dry out and the thicker one will be undercooked."

"Wait, are you foodsplaining?" I asked.

"Just in case you ever want to make this yourself."

"I appreciate your good intentions, but I'll always be cooking adjacent. You cook, I pull corks. That's why we work so well together."

Daniel, however, was willing to learn about wine. We had fun creating our own wine-tasting show, which we called *The Good Wine*, inspired by one of our favourite shows, *The Good Wife*. In each episode, Daniel tried to guess which bottle was the good wine and which one was the decoy. "Decoy wine" was a concept I had developed years ago when serving people who really didn't care about wine quality. I'd leave an open bottle within easy reach on the kitchen counter, so they'd go for the decoy wine when topping up their glass. Meanwhile, I was secretly topping up my glass with the good wine.

Our "show" started when Daniel first noticed that I wasn't drinking the same wine as he was. Now, before you shake your finger at me, understand that he came to me drinking Wolf Blass Yellow Label Shiraz. There's nothing wrong with this twenty-dollar wine. But if that's what you like, why do you need to drink my fifty-dollar E. Guigal Hermitage from the Rhône Valley?

This was the former unredeemed snobby Nat. Today, I take pride in discovering undervalued wines, just as I do when I find a designer purse marked down to 10 percent of its original price. It's not a knock-off, a decoy, or even on sale. It represents exceptional value and comes with a thrill-of-the-hunt story.

"What's that?" he asked one evening.

"This? This is, uh, just red wine."

"It doesn't look the same as mine."

"Mm-hmm."

"Can I taste it?"

"Sure."

"I like that."

"Would you like some?"

"Yep, bring it on." Daniel got himself a new wineglass. That was the start of our much more expensive and expansive life together.

We continued our TV series banter, dreaming up episodes like the one where Natalie installs a secret cellar to hide the good wine, but Daniel spots a cracked seam in the plaster. He taps along the false wall to find the secret door. In the thrilling season finale, Daniel discovers a telltale circular red bottle stain on the table. Will Natalie guzzle all the first-growth Bordeaux before he does?

Have they both crossed the thin red line in their relationship? Stay tuned!

Daniel had already learned so much about wine through our tastings that eventually, when I tried to give him a decoy wine, he would good-naturedly catch me in the cheat. He was on to me if I tried to give him anything but the best wine — usually the one I was drinking.

Decoding labels was part of our little game. Daniel learned that what's inside the bottle matters most. I discovered not to judge a person by his labels, whether they were academic degrees, career credentials, or even height. I stopped presenting my decoy self. Daniel wanted the real me. I was drunk on happiness. As we chuckled over this imaginary sitcom, I had no idea that my real life was about to turn into a horror show.

Wildfires

The Scarlet Letter *C*:
Copyright and Cabernet

———

A
s the end of 2012 approached, my life had somehow magically come back together. I'd survived the separation and found love, Cameron and I were back on the same team, I was still writing, and I had my drinking under control. For the first time in almost a year, I was happy. I didn't realize my Nightmare Before Christmas was about to begin.

It was midnight, December 15, when all through the house, not a creature was stirring, except my wireless mouse. That damn Google alert. My hands were shaking so hard that I clicked on the wrong text. The second time I clicked on the link, the scorching article on the Palate Press site came up.

It said that I "proudly proclaimed" I was the "World's Best Wine Writer" — the title given to me at the World Food Media Awards was actually World's Best Drinks Journalist — but that I had built my reputation on the work of other writers by posting their "professional wine reviews" in addition to my own, which, it noted, were often a sentence long, or less.

It added that while the quoted reviews included the writer's name, they were credited to the Liquor Control Board of Ontario's Vintages Wine Catalogue rather than to where the LCBO had sourced them.

It said that I was publishing these reviews behind my subscription wall where readers had to pay for access. They concluded that this was copyright infringement.

The six authors said they had reached out to many of the wine writers and that those writers' calls for changes from me had yielded no results. If I truly was "the World's Best Wine Writer," they wrote, subscribers would come to my site for my writing and not for that of others.

Why had they written the article? They were "committed to upholding the highest ethical standards and could not sit idly by while an ostensible colleague in oenological journalism brings discredit upon any of us by flouting those standards." It was signed by David Honig, Rémy Charest, Becky Sue Epstein, Tom Mansell, Ryan Reichert, and Gary Thomas.

Good God.

The hail of words came through the screen, stinging my eyes.

I couldn't look away. I couldn't even blink.

Wine Corp and the other Ontario wine website quoting the LCBO reviews had also posted my reviews. Neither one was mentioned in the article and, according to this gang, I was the thief.

The only thing I had as a writer was my work and my name. They were lighting a match under both. Was I about to lose everything, not just my reputation, but also my ability to earn a living to support Mom and Cameron? Would I lose Daniel and a second chance at love? Tremors ran down through my body like a tectonic fault line. My life split in two.

After my scramble to get water, I compared what they were saying with what I had published. Each page on my site started with the wine's name, vintage, vineyard, region, a bottle shot, my score, and tasting note. My tasting notes were short but not less than a sentence. What would that be — "Yum"?

There were about thirty pieces of information for each wine, from alcohol levels to maturity dates for drinking. With this much detail, especially on a mobile screen, I used acronyms for repetitive information: regional designations, such as AOC for Appellation d'Origine Contrôlée; sugar codes, like XD for extra dry; alcohol by volume was ABV; and so on. I linked to my site directory where these abbreviations were spelled out.

On the review page for each wine, under all of these details, as well as my own tasting notes, food pairings, and scores, I had a separate section labelled in large, bold font as *Other Reviews*. This is where I quoted reviews from the liquor store site. After each one was a dash with the writer's full name and my source, the LCBO's Vintages Wine Catalogue, to show this review was a quote and not my own. I made sure there was a clear division between my reviews and those quoted so as not to imply the others were my own. That would be plagiarism, which is often confused with copyright. This was not that.

The only information behind my subscription paywall was my score and tasting note for wines I'd reviewed in the past thirty days. My older reviews were posted with open access, as were the reviews from the liquor store site under the Other Reviews section, no matter the date.

Something was bothering me about the article; it was more than the differences between my site and what they wrote: This was the first time I was reading it. Before publishing, the authors had found time to contact many other writers but not the person who was the subject of the piece.

Looking at the American site, I noticed their masthead featured an old-fashioned reporter's fedora hat. Wait. Didn't journalists check their facts with the person they're writing about before they publish? Couldn't one of the six authors have reached out to me, even to give the appearance of balance?

I was grasping at anything. I could feel myself dwindling down into rationalizing what I'd done. My body was shutting down, but my mind was still casting about, looking for a way to understand.

One of the bizarre methods in the 1600s to make a "witch" admit to her crimes was called the Pressing. As she lay tied to a table, the accusers loaded heavy stones on top of her. It was supposed to make her confess, but she usually couldn't breathe, much less talk. Those doing the talking in the room were the men making accusations. Many women died this way and didn't even make it to the pyre to be burned.

That post on Palate Press, and another one coming soon, felt like my personal Pyre Press. This was where my reputation was going to die one way or another. The weight of the article's accusations was one thing, but the defamatory and sexual comments about to be posted would be truly crushing.

∽☙∾

As hail pelted my window, I wanted to escape to my prince sleeping upstairs. But that would mean telling him about this mess and blowing up my fairy tale. I sat and stewed.

Among my many mistakes was thinking of reviews as mental drudgery, the equivalent of recipes compared to great food memoirs. Yet, in hindsight, more people rely on recipes than read memoirs. The same is true of wine reviews. So what's the greater service? Talent alone doesn't define contribution, but with my writing pride and prejudice, I was blind to that.

My dismissal of reviews made me underestimate their importance to other wine critics, especially those who defined themselves professionally by them. Many were trying to provide a service to their readers. Others were in it for the status, making Supreme Court–like pronouncements on this vintage or that winery.

Were my mistakes inevitable? Perhaps. When I was ten, I overheard my dance teacher talking to Mom. "She's improving, but she doesn't have the killer instinct."

I asked Mom what that meant. "You've got to be all in, Nat. Give it everything you've got if you want to win. What do you think Karen Jackson is doing right now?" She named the girl who always came first ahead of me in competitions.

"Practising?" I felt guilty.

"Right, if you want it, you need to work harder than Karen." When we drove past Karen's hometown, she'd ask, "What's that I hear? Oh, it's the bagpipes. I think that's Karen practising."

Karen and I attended the same dance camp that summer. At the end of one class, the teacher asked Karen if she'd be willing to be interviewed on a radio show about the camp. She declined, I think, because she was shy.

"I'll do it, Miss," I said, and with her nod, went off with the reporter.

Karen became my focus for improving, rather than simply the art of dance itself. The artistic muse alone wouldn't have taken me to the world championships. I started practising four hours a day on school days, more on weekends and holidays. I honed my attention on one competitor for motivation. I found my killer instinct and finally beat Karen Jackson.

When several critics from Wine Corp joined the fray on Palate Press, I discovered that the rules for men in my industry were different from those for women — or at least getting called on them was. That killer competitive instinct might now kill my career.

Belief in witches developed because it was easier to blame a village woman you disliked for crop failure, sickness, and death than to admit it was because you planted the wrong seeds, lacked skill, or had a genetic predisposition to certain diseases. That wicked woman cursed you.

Why a woman, not a man? A woman was a ready target back then, with less political and economic status. She was also a source of particular scorn when she could do what you could not, such as healing with herbs. It was easy to isolate her and for other villagers to throw their grievances at her as well, the medieval equivalent of the online pile-on.

Had I inflamed the anger of the article's authors and their commenters because I undervalued wine reviews, both theirs and my own, assuming all reviews were as disposable as day-old newspapers? Or was this more about who I was and what I represented?

My biggest mistake was ignoring the warning signs. In October, I had received an email from Toronto wine writer Michael Pinkus. He accused me of "lifting" other reviews for which I had "failed to credit them in any way." His heavy-handed language got my back up. I believed I wasn't doing anything different from the other two review sites, both run by men. I realize now that post-separation I had fine-tuned my radar for men bullying me. My resilience was a rubber band that had snapped months ago.

I should have stopped, taken a deep breath, and waited at least a day before responding. My anger should have been a Greek chorus in my mind chanting *Danger, danger*. Instead, rage returned to me like backdraft, the explosive fire that engulfs a room when a door — or an email — opens.

"Thanks for your note." I typed furiously, throwing off decades of good-girl compliance. "I do explain all the initials for those quoted on my site to ensure full credit is given. As you may know, several other sites also quote the reviews from the Vintages catalogue and don't ask permission to do so beforehand. Fair use allows quotes of this length."

I confused the difference between the U.S. copyright law of fair use with Canada's fair dealing. (I really should have finished law school.) If you want to know how this dumpster fire escalated so quickly, you'll need to have a basic understanding of the two doctrines.

Both concepts allow for the use of copyrighted material without asking for permission if the use falls under the categories of criticism, review, commentary, or education, among others. The Canadian law states that if the work referenced is for these purposes, and the source is cited, it's legal. It does not specify how or where the source needs to be cited.

Most of the reviews I quoted were no more than a sentence or two, often representing less than 1 percent of the reviews published by that source. For example, a large wine magazine can publish over one hundred thousand reviews a year. The liquor store might quote three or four reviews from that source in a catalogue, because they quoted from many other sources. I was following what I thought was common practice back in 2012, the heyday of content aggregators like the *Huffington Post*, along with social media sharing and curating.

On December 11, Pinkus emailed me again, telling me he was "gobsmacked." This time, he copied thirty-one writers and editors of the largest food and drink magazines around the world, including Palate Press. He called for all of those copied on his email to weigh in. A few days later, he sent a second email to provoke a comment from the group, since no one had responded.

This time, I didn't reply immediately. Was I correct in my assumptions about fair use? I was worried, though not panicked — yet. I still stubbornly believed that I was complying with copyright, but I decided to get legal advice. The legal fees were beyond what I could pay, but I couldn't afford to leave the issue unresolved. I spoke by phone with a lawyer, Frank, an expert on copyright law. His partner, Ernest, specialized in defamation. Frank and Ernest agreed with me that I should do as Pinkus had requested, even though I was well within the Canadian fair dealing law.

"Tell him you're making the changes but do not apologize," Frank advised.

"Why not? Wouldn't that satisfy him and resolve this once and for all?"

"In my experience, complainants of this type are rarely satisfied even when they get what they asked for. Plus, the word 'sorry' implies guilt, even if there is none, which can have legal implications. Just say that you regret your confusion over the issue, then make the changes."

I discovered that *sorry* isn't just the hardest word to say, it's also the most expensive.

On the morning of December 12, I emailed Pinkus and those whom he had copied, confirming that I was already making the changes, including putting full names and publications after each quoted review, rather than relying on the directory. I'd start with the most recent reviews and work backward.

I confirmed this again to the same group via email on the morning of December 15 to assure them I was taking their request seriously and working my way through the reviews.

∽❧∾

12:01 a.m.

Now, fifteen hours later, as I scanned the article on Palate Press, I found no mention that I was fixing the reviews, even though I had copied Palate Press on both emails. Would that detail have made the story less juicy clickbait? Writer makes a big mistake, gets advice, and fixes mistake.

I felt flayed alive, all raw nerve endings as I continued typing a response. I wasn't a thief. My God. I assumed that if I addressed the accusations, this would all go away. Right? Small drops of blood from my palm fell on the keyboard as I typed:

 Natalie MacLean
December 16, 2012 at 12:06 a.m.

As I have already confirmed to those who suggested it, I'm in the process of adding the information that has been requested, beginning with the most recent reviews and going backward. All of the reviews that I have quoted were first quoted in liquor store catalogues, store shelf slips as well as on other wine review sites that also quote wine reviews from other wine sites and magazines.

I have agreed that I will add the information beside the quotes, including names and publications, and not rely only on the directory that has had this information on my site since I began quoting them. As I mentioned in my confirmation, I welcome and listen to feedback from both colleagues and readers and make changes as a result, including all that has been requested in this case.

Regards,
Natalie

I took screenshots of my own reviews and others on Wine Corp and the second site quoting reviews in case someone disputed my reference to them. I held a flickering hope that my comment would clarify my actions and de-escalate the situation, but I was soon engulfed in the raw force of fear. I was as naive about their opinions as I had been about Adam's feelings.

Back in my bedroom, my palm stung. Oh, dried blood … squeeze out the shard … bleeding again … tissue.

3:24 a.m.

A fiery cloud of red words swirled up in my mind, each exploding as they were replaced by others.

I dreamt of men without faces standing in a circle around me.

Bewitched and Bewildered

The next morning, I stood at my bathroom window looking down the street at homes decorated with multicoloured lights, smiling Santas, and reindeer. Then I went back to that damn computer.

David Honig, a lawyer and one of the six authors who didn't have time to contact me in the weeks before publishing the article, had responded thirty-one minutes after my post last night. He'd moved on from the attribution of reviews since I reconfirmed I was doing that. Now he was demanding I get prior approval to quote them. A few others left comments, all negative.

The anonymous comments had also started, beginning with an aggrieved wine importer who used the alias "Canadian Wine Guy." He wrote that I was "a major blemish on our industry, and it is particularly sad that she holds such sway with the average person."

Had I not reviewed his wines? Maybe not positively enough. I had no idea who he was. I'd never met most wine importers as they, too, lived in the larger cities. What could have prompted this venom?

Another man replied, "I agree that it is sad she has influence over the average person. That's a major problem today with the internet. Anyone can design a good-looking site and make people believe they are an authority."

Each man's comment felt like another stick thrown on my pyre. I sensed the eyes of those watching but not commenting. They were holding torches, waiting for their chance.

⟝⟞

Hours later, as I sat beside the TV news host, Monique, the blinding set lights flashed on. I was still staring at the bottle of pinot noir I'd brought to talk about holiday wines and spirits when Monique tapped me on the shoulder. "We're about to go live, Natalie. Are you ready?"

The producer gave us the countdown.

Mercifully, Monique didn't ask me about the accusations. I don't think she had seen them. The interview went well, but my blouse was drenched in sweat.

On the way home, I stopped to buy a syrah for dinner. As I stood in the checkout line, I remembered standing there years ago with three-year-old Cameron in my arms.

"You look like a princess, Mommy."

"Thank you, honey, but I don't have a tiara." I gave him a small squeeze.

"Princess curls," he whispered, stroking my hair. "We're gonna get married and build a house at the bus stop for Disney."

"That sounds like fun, Cam."

Was it worrisome that my most poignant memories with my son took place in liquor stores? I suppose if I'd been a carpenter, we would have been chatting in the woodshed.

When I got back home, I read a note from Mom that said she had gone Christmas shopping with Daniel. Back I went to the computer. The comments, posts, tweets, and emails were coming in fast, a denial-of-service attack on my nervous system.

Meanwhile, all the quoted LCBO reviews, including my own, on Wine Corp's website had disappeared. The company's financial backer had programmed them so they could be deleted by turning off one field. I wasn't that savvy with programming. Therefore, I would have to work backward one review at a time to update them. The second wine site quoting reviews still had them posted.

In the days that followed, I logged in every hour to Palate Press to check the comments. The angriest came from those who live closest to me in Ottawa and in my former home of Nova Scotia. Why did they have the most vitriol? Was it because we had more in common, coming from the same place, competing for the same magazines?

The wine columnist for New Brunswick's provincial newspaper, Craig Pinhey, posted, "Her current elevated status hurts almost every other writer to a certain extent, in terms of getting writing, radio, TV appearances, etc. If it was simply because she was better at it, or better at marketing herself, then we'd have no grounds to complain. It would just be sour grapes … You can't argue with her book sales though, I guess, but did anyone learn much about wine from them? I don't think so. They are more just light entertainment."

I let out a long, heavy sigh. His comments reminded me of what a morning show television producer told me as we wrapped the segment. "Finally, someone who can talk about wine without putting us to sleep."

After finishing the media tour for my second book, in 2011, I had been invited back on several shows as a regular guest expert. They were flexible in scheduling. "Just let us know when you're in town, and we'll fit you in."

Closer to home, when the *Ottawa Citizen*'s wine columnist of twenty-four years, Peter Ward, was retiring, the Food editor, Ron

Eade, asked if I'd take over the column. I thanked him but let him know that because I was writing a regular column for *Ottawa Magazine*, I believed it was a conflict of interest. I also thought that it would narrow wine opinion in the city if the two most widely read columns were written by the same person. I recommended Rod Phillips, a local wine writer and history professor whom I'd met several times at tastings. He became the paper's columnist. I didn't expect a thank you, but I noticed that as the years went by, he seemed to become increasingly antagonistic toward me.

Conversely, those who had less in common with me because of geography or high-profile media platforms didn't lash out. They didn't begrudge what I had achieved. Stacey Metulynsky, who hosted a popular wine-and-food-pairing show on the Food Network and who had co-authored the book *This Food That Wine* with Angie MacRae, emailed me: "Think about it this way. If you weren't doing great things, they wouldn't spend the time to dig into your business. You know who your fans are and they know exactly what you've been doing with reviews and obviously like it. Keep doing what you are doing and maybe someday they'll focus their energy on something half as successful as what you've built."

In medieval movies, as the witch is tied to a stake, friends wearing big-hooded cowls show up in the crowd to provide support with covert eye contact. Why didn't they just reveal their support publicly? They knew they'd be thrown on the pyre with her. The modern equivalent of that eye contact — private emails, texts, direct messages — felt like calming salve.

Outrage continued to build internationally, as more and more writers piled on. This was the delicious Christmas scandal where everyone could feast at the same table. I began and ended each day saving screenshots of the blistering tirades on Twitter and Palate Press. I felt like Hester Prynne taking sadistic selfies from atop the pyre — posting them with the hashtag #BurnBaby!

◦◦◦

"You're handling this holiday so well. I know it's your first without him. Are you okay?" Mom was sensing my stress but attributing it to my first Christmas post-separation.

"It's all good, Mom. Nothing that a little pinot can't help, right?" It bothered me I was leaning on wine again. Each night, after we'd all gone to bed, I'd lie awake until three or four in the morning with a nasty livestream running in my head, doze off for an hour or two, and wake up again on high cortisol alert. Then I'd feel the nausea twisting in my stomach, the hot tornado coming up my throat, and run to the bathroom.

I was a voyeur of my own car crash. I couldn't look away. I read the social streams each day and took screenshots. My brain had been slammed by a car door and bruised; glass shards dug into my ribs.

It came as some relief to read a supportive column on the other side of the planet. Neil Pendock, the wine columnist for the *Sunday Times* in South Africa, posted on the newspaper's website:

> The crucifixion of Canadian wine critic Natalie MacLean this Christmas by the Sanhedrin of sniffers and sippers leaves a nasty taste in the mouth. Of course, the Passion of Nats is not about wine, it's all about ego and competing commerciality, which could explain the ferocity of some reactions. If your website has 80,000 signed up purple pagers at £69 a pop ... Then competition, even from Canada, counts.

Pendock's mention of purple pagers at sixty-nine pound a pop referred to the annual eighty-five-US-dollar subscription fee to access the website of Jancis Robinson. The U.K. author had published many wine books, including *The Oxford Companion to Wine*. Although she hadn't posted on Palate Press, she replied to Pinkus's second email prodding the writers and editors, saying that she was horrified. I emailed her back immediately, confirming again that I was already taking remedial action. In 2021, Robinson sold her website to a venture capital firm for an estimated US$150–250 million, according to *Meiningers Wine Business International* magazine.

Pendock's article, though, only provoked more vicious comments. I discovered that if you don't crumble in public, you plunge down to a special category of mob loathing: The Asbestos Witch. She just won't burn.

Privately, I was having a core meltdown. Cameron, thankfully, wasn't on social media, so he wasn't aware of the mess. I still couldn't bring myself to tell Daniel. I tried imagining their reactions. Would Cameron even understand such abstract issues? What if he googled me and discovered the nasty comments? It was just wishful thinking that Daniel wouldn't find out because he wasn't on social media either. He could stumble on the news online. How long did I have before it was over?

❧

"It's the right thing to do," Daniel often said.

That phrase drove me bonkers, perhaps because it tied so closely to the suffocating small-town question I'd grown up with: "What will other people think?" Even though we'd only been together for a couple of months, Daniel mentioned it even when we discussed simple things. It felt heavy, stirring up my Catholic guilt about everything. I had started calling him Mr. Morality Clause because, unlike Santa, he brought the gift of judgment. Daniel cared a lot about what people thought and about their feelings. I loved that about him, but I also couldn't bear the idea of telling him about my online mess.

"I discovered that she had no entry in Wikipedia," Dean Tudor, a Toronto wine writer and former journalism professor at Ryerson University, posted on December 17. I felt the glass shards push in deeper.

Then, several hours later he added: "IT HAS HAPPENED!!!! Read all about it!! Hey, my idea, guys!!! My dad would be so proud of me ... LOL"

I never thought I'd be famous enough to have a Wikipedia page. But he had done it. The page had all the details from the Palate Press site. Then he condensed my thirteen-year writing career, books, magazine columns, and awards into two sentences. This was extremely destructive because a Google search on my name showed the Wikipedia entry at the top of the results. I felt I'd just been pistol-whipped with an anvil.

Tudor had used Wikipedia to rewrite my story. Why did I think this was unusual? There's a long history of men telling women's stories. We're asleep waiting for him to kiss us or we're trapped in a tower waiting for him to rescue us.

A year later, after I was sure I wasn't going to disturb the online hornet's nest, I wrote to the Wikipedia editorial board about the defamatory and misleading post. It took months of submitting evidence to undo some of the damage Tudor had done in a few hours. The editorial board finally agreed, edited his comments, and included more details about my actual career.

☙❧

Daniel and I went for a walk that night after dinner. As we stepped out into the minty fresh air, I was surprised that the real world still existed. Warm light poured out of the homes. We could see one family gathered around a table, laughing and eating dinner. Another was sprawled out on a sofa watching TV. They seemed to be from another planet.

My life had become separate livestreams: one online and the other next to it when I got up from the computer. Where did I end and online begin? I couldn't tell anymore. We had morphed into each another. When I started typing, a thousand volts shot up under my fingernails.

"All good, Nattie?" Daniel asked as he took my hand. "You barely ate anything tonight."

"Just don't have much of an appetite lately. Maybe it's all that gingerbread before dinner." I hadn't touched that either. I was tempted to tell him about what was happening but couldn't let the words out.

Later, before going to bed, I couldn't find Daniel to say good night. Then I noticed the door to the backyard was slightly ajar. I pushed it open and found him with a cigarette. He flicked it away.

"You smoke?"

He looked down.

"Why didn't you tell me?"

"I didn't want you to know." He closed his eyes.

"How long have you been smoking?"

"Since I was about fourteen."

"But you said you were a non-smoker on the Misty River application."

"I'm sorry."

"You lied to me. I wouldn't have agreed to meet you if I had known you smoked."

He looked away.

"Your father died of lung cancer when he was just sixty-eight. Aren't you worried?"

"Yes."

"Are you going to quit?"

"I'm going to try."

"I don't want Cameron to be around a smoker. I don't want smoke in the house or even outside it."

"Do you want me to leave?"

"I don't know what I want."

The irony of my concern for Daniel's health when I risked doing the same with drinking didn't occur to me then. Did Daniel have more empathy for my struggle given his own? Yes. Were we co-enablers of each other's destructive habits? I don't think so. The love and understanding we shared was a much firmer base from which to deal with our destructive habits than the emotional fracking of shame and blame.

I went upstairs and fell onto the bed, my brain feeling like it had been run through a meat grinder. Daniel had been an incredible support, yet he had withheld this truth from me as I was doing now with him. Online, the truth about who you are is delivered as search results, listed as though everything you ever did, you did just yesterday. This is who you are now, even though you may have changed. Thanks to autofill, Google will even suggest who you are before you hit the enter key. My most frequent auto-fill suggestions?

Q   natalie maclean <u>age</u>

Q   natalie maclean <u>husband</u>

I'm old enough to know that those asking this question should mind their own business. And why are women still defined by the men they're married to? Why not this suggestion:

Q   natalie maclean <u>books</u>

Google also attempts to incorporate "balance" with its algorithm. If there's anything negative about you online, it'll be on that first page of results, regardless of whether it's been fact-checked. That algorithm is the modern scarlet letter *A*. We all wear it on our virtual chests. It doesn't matter if there's more to you than those first ten results.

The short and fast world of social media doesn't leave room for nuance or complexity. Everything is black or white — a one-word answer to a novel. But you can't be defined by your extreme edges. You're not the worst thing you've done, nor the best thing. You're everything in between. It's in the grey zone that you find the shades of humanity.

Social media is an echo chamber of mindlessly forwarding falsehoods. Several bloggers, who never felt part of the inner circle of established writers, eagerly chimed in on the post. The veterans gave them virtual backslaps for their vicious comments, enjoying the fake fellowship of hating the same person. Software robots made the pile-on worse, encouraging ever nastier comments. Social media monetizes humiliation. Then it all got packaged in news digests to my contacts on LinkedIn. That's how one of my editors found out what was happening.

Pinkus was at it again on Palate Press, wondering if my writing awards could be "revoked a la Lance Armstrong," referring to the American cyclist who had won the Tour de France and been caught taking illegal drugs. I wondered how Pinkus connected the attribution of wine reviews to doping in sport. The long-form articles for which I had won the writing competitions had no short-form wine reviews.

He couldn't believe that it was possible for one person to win so many writing awards — surely it must be plagiarism. I didn't know what I was supposed to do. His venom felt personal, intimate. Bizarre for a man who'd never met me.

Pinkus also called for professional wine writing associations to remove me. This was irrelevant for the Wine Writers' Circle of Canada, from which I had finally just resigned. I had tried to resign several years earlier because most of the events were in Toronto, a five-hour drive from Ottawa. Back then, Dean Tudor (Mr. Wikipedia) was president. He demanded I provide proof of my published columns by physically mailing in clippings. The Circle executive had discussed weeding out the freeloading writers who weren't publishing but who still went on the free media trips and tastings. Instead of simply confronting those people, they created administrative work for those who had regular columns.

At the time, I was writing half a dozen columns in several of Canada's largest magazines. I was under some tight deadlines and stressed about Tudor's demand as well as the hypocrisy of hiding behind the paperwork. I emailed back suggesting that the next time he was at a corner store, he look at the magazine rack. If not, I wanted to resign. The Circle's vice-president, Shari Darling, one of the few women in the group, convinced me to stay. She told Tudor she had seen many of my columns. There was no need to mail in clippings.

This time, though, I was done with the group. It provided no value. I also stopped commenting about the issue on my site. Every time I posted, I got flaming responses from the trolls. When I didn't post, they accused me of running away from the issue.

It reminded me of one way to tell if a woman was a witch in colonial Salem: strip her down to her undergarments, bind her, and throw her into a lake. Since witches rejected the sacrament of baptism, the water would reject her and make her float. An innocent person would sink to the bottom, according to the logic.

You'd either sink and drown or float and get dragged to the stake and burned. Damned if you do, damned if you don't. Sounds like the forerunner to social media.

Hour after hour, all I could think was *Am I going to be sued? Will I lose my income? Will I lose my home?*

I was a single mother who'd left the corporate world thirteen years ago and was now a freelancer. Both Cameron and Mom depended on the money I earned from my work, and that work depended on my reputation. Daniel hadn't been in the picture long enough to share this chaos. Now I wondered if I could trust him fully given his lie about smoking. I didn't just go to a dark place; I felt fear without horizon.

Out of the Cauldron, into the Crackpot

The next morning, Daniel knocked on my bedroom door.

"Can I come in?"

"Sure."

He sat on the edge of my bed. "I'm sorry about the smoking. Do you want me to leave?"

"No. I just wish you'd been honest with me. Are you going to quit?"

"I'm really going to try, Nat. That was the first time I ever smoked here. I've always showered afterward so you wouldn't smell it. I won't do it again or let Cameron see me smoking."

"That's for sure. I've become quite attached to you, Daniel. I don't want to lose you. Smoking will kill you. It's not if, it's when."

"I know."

We hugged. The doorbell rang. I welcomed the distraction, running downstairs in my housecoat. Mike, the UPS guy, was holding a case of wine.

"Just need your scribble here, Natalie." He passed me the electronic reader.

"This oughta hold me 'til Monday." I tried to crack a smile as I handed it back to him.

"Oh, I'll see you before then, I'm sure," he said cheerfully, waving as he walked back to his van.

I remembered my friends often quipped about "helping" me with leftover wine. "That would be great," I'd say, playing along. "Bottle recycling day is a complete embarrassment."

I joked about my wine consumption with them like I did in my writing. I felt responsible for them having a good time, even when it came at the cost of my own health.

With a few glasses of wine, I'd water down my natural inhibitions. I could create the free-flowing, open version of friendship I wanted. Long before I was a supertaster, I was a super noticer. I noticed every muscle twitch in someone's expression, every change in tone. Then all that sensory input got over-interpreted by my monkey brain.

Does she disapprove of what I just said? Does she think I'm showing off?

That's probably why I was so quiet as a child and frequently got asked, "Has the cat got your tongue?"

I hated the nickname Nat the Cat because it reminded me of all the times I didn't talk when I wanted to. I was drawn to two art forms — dancing and writing — where I didn't have to speak out loud to express myself. Maybe that's why friends were always surprised at how open I was on the page. These words have always been inside me. I just didn't let them out.

Alcohol slowed down everything. It said, *Don't worry. Say what you've been wanting to say.* My shoulders melted down into safety. I felt liquid relief spread through my veins.

My friends took to calling our little circle Friends of Natalie (FONs), because I had introduced them to each other. I loved being the social connector, as I had been when selling tickets at high school dances. I just didn't stick around long enough for the scary part — deeper conversations and dancing.

There was no way this good-time gal was going to be a downer by telling them about the online mess. Why hadn't I remembered how good it felt to tell them about my separation? Perhaps I didn't want their pity when I had their admiration, at least for my career. Pity was for victims. I would never, ever be a victim. I abandoned myself, just as I had as a little girl. Told myself to buck up because no one was coming to save me.

~⚫~

As I closed the door to the UPS guy, I recalled that in my first few years of writing, I didn't accept free wine samples. I thought it would make me corrupt. I was wrong. Not accepting them would make me bankrupt. That's why it was, and still is, common practice in the industry.

Buying wines each week wasn't sustainable. Few people read reviews for wines under ten dollars, so that leaves the pricier bottles. I often needed to taste fifty wines just to find five worthy of recommending to readers.

Meanwhile, the rates for newspaper and magazine columns hadn't changed in more than thirty years: fifty cents to a dollar a word. There were fewer print columns. Wine writing was done on the web, where most people expected it to be free. Paywalls for content had failed spectacularly except for the *New York Times* and the *Wall Street Journal*.

In 2012, I charged a monthly subscription fee of two dollars to access the latest reviews on my site. This fee was about to become the centre of another tabloid-style scandal on Palate Press. My free weekly newsletter drew tens of thousands of subscribers, but less than 1 percent paid for the reviews. Everyone who signed up for my newsletter got one month of free access to all the reviews on the site. They could judge for themselves if it was worth continuing with a paid subscription. Everyone had free and open access to my reviews that had already been posted for thirty days or more.

Wineries and agencies also received this free trial. Just as they decided whether they'd subscribe to the *Wine Spectator* or *Wine Advocate* magazines, they could also determine if my subscription was a worthwhile business expense. A subscription to my site had no effect on my tasting notes or scores, as the disclaimer on my website indicated. This statement was also emailed to every winery and agency the first time they asked to send samples.

About 90 percent of the wines I reviewed, I sampled at the liquor store's monthly media tastings. I also attended some large wine shows. When I travelled for an assignment, I reviewed the wines. I uploaded this information to the site myself.

Some 10 percent of my reviews came from tasting samples sent to me by wineries and agencies, mostly low-priced bottles from large, commercial producers who can afford to provide them. For expensive wines, there was usually more demand than supply, so they rarely needed a critic's review. Sadly, the UPS guy wasn't bringing me crates of Domaine de la Romanée-Conti and Château Margaux.

For several years, I spent hours every week going back and forth multiple times with importers and wineries to chase down the basic facts about a wine, such as the product codes for the ten liquor store chains across the country, UPC codes (so that consumers could scan the bottles in my mobile apps), different prices, bottle pictures, label shots, and so on.

Eventually I realized I couldn't do this for every bottle sent to me and write the columns that actually paid the bills. I asked wineries to submit these basic facts via a simple form on the site. If I liked the wine and posted a review, I'd verify that the information they'd submitted was correct, then add my score, tasting note, and food matches. They had no influence over what I posted. They could also choose to add a note about how the wine was made or suggest food pairings. These notes were clearly separated from my own and labelled as such.

Filling out a form is also how most wine competitions work. You need to submit the details about the wine and pay an administrative fee that covers some of the cost of running the competition. Entering a competition doesn't mean you'll win or even get a medal — only that your wine will be tasted.

I didn't promise to publish a review of a wine just because a winery had submitted information on it. I also didn't indicate whether a review would be positive or negative. However, on Palate Press, my need to earn a living now came under attack.

"Canadian Wine Guy," the wine importer who had resented my influence on consumers, complained about having to pay the two-dollar monthly subscription fee to see the scores I had given his wines. He wanted to use the commercial value of my reviews on in-store shelf slips and on bottle stickers to help sell his wines without doing anything more than sending them to me. He expected me to be a free tasting consultant for his business. Another importer complained about having to send samples. Maybe it's just me, but I find it difficult to taste a press release.

All the time and money I invested in my website for a decade, the salaries of the people who worked for me, as well as my own, were beside the point. According to these importers, tasting their wines should simply be a labour of love for me.

That may be possible for bloggers who have day jobs. It's easy to confuse those of us who make wine our profession with hobbyists. Many people enjoy wine in their free time, unlike, say, having a root canal or getting their house rewired. We expect bills from the dentist and electrician.

I offer free wine-and-food-pairing classes online and forewarn those who sign up that I'll also be talking about my paid courses at the end of the presentation. It's how I earn a living. Yet there are always those who email me afterward saying they loved the free pairing tips but complain about the sales portion at the end. This is another form of misogyny. A woman selling something is labelled self-promotional and ambitious, whereas a man is regarded as a smart marketer and successful.

Below my anger was fear, pain, and loneliness. I still wasn't telling anyone, still that little girl who didn't need to bother anyone with her problems. She was just fine on her own. But was she? I thought I was shielding Mom, Daniel, and my girlfriends from this mess by keeping it to myself. Would Daniel feel the same disappointment with me that I had felt about him smoking? I mistook not letting anyone in as a defence against everything else.

～✬～

The smell of freshly baked Christmas drifted into my office. The aroma took me back to my childhood summers in my grandparents' small kitchen in Cape Breton, with the wood-burning black stove.

Mom had just taken the biscuits out of the oven. They were golden and flaky, with a heady aroma of doughy warmth. I could taste the butter melting on them.

"Love those biscuits, Mom. Grammy's recipe?"

"Is there any other?" She smiled.

After the biscuits cooled, I took one back to the office. It was the same evening the Wikipedia page went live. Now I noticed that Palate Press had published a second article about me for which they'd "unearthed new allegations of unethical behaviour."

I dug my elbows into my sides as I scrolled. The two posts had become my personal twenty-four-hour abusive news network.

Again, the writers had found time to interview various wineries and agencies to include their comments before publication, but not to speak to me.

They wrote that I required wineries to buy a subscription to my website before I'd review their wines. They concluded that this was a corrupt "pay-for-play scheme."

At the time, the cost of my website development, graphic design, the powerful server on which I hosted my site, customer support, mobile app coding, optical label scan software, and other contractors was well over three hundred thousand dollars a year. I thought about the logic of their accusation. I was going to cover these costs by selling all the wine reviews for each winery or importer for two dollars?

I wondered how that would work. Perhaps I could sell them at a country fair, like cookies. "Get your fresh batch of wine reviews here, just two dollars a bunch, and for an extra fifty cents I'll make them all nineties." (Inevitably, someone will take this sentence out of context and plaster it on social media. You're welcome for the clickbait.)

I posted a second response on their site that afternoon, reiterating the change and offering to speak with any of the six authors:

 Natalie MacLean
December 17, 2012 at 4:33 p.m.

> I am writing in response to your blog post this week-end regarding wine reviews on my website.
>
> I have now sought and obtained legal advice to ensure that I am not only doing the right thing, but also complying with any laws that might be applicable both in the U.S. (fair use) and in Canada (fair dealing). The laws differ slightly for the two countries, but I have had a thorough discussion with a legal expert on copyright and know that what I am

doing now and what I will be doing in the future is not only legal, but right. I wanted to take this advice before replying to make sure that this issue is dealt with properly.

For all reviews previously quoted, please know that I am working to revise the way I format third-party reviews to cite full names and publication details. Also know that I have never charged to review wines, and have reviewed many wines from wineries and wine agents who do not pay a subscription to my site. It's $2 a month to access the subscription part of my site, but that does not determine whether or not I review a wine.

Except for Michael Pinkus, no writer or magazine had ever contacted me to ask for a different attribution or to remove their reviews. For those who have recently, I have done so immediately. As well, my own reviews have been quoted on other wine sites and no one had ever contacted me to ask permission. I had believed that it was also fair use to quote my reviews.

I wish to thank the many wine writers and bloggers who have contacted me to show their support and understanding over the past few days. I am grateful to have this issue clarified. I hope that it helps other writers and bloggers avoid any such issues in the future.

If you'd like to continue this discussion, please feel free to contact me as I'd be happy to talk with you.

Sincerely,
Natalie

That started another frenzied round of responses. Frank and Ernest were right. Now that the crowd had circled, they wouldn't be satisfied with anything I said about changes or regret, let alone an apology. I was just giving this fire oxygen. I had to stop responding.

Jim Caudill, who had been a director and vice-president at several California wineries, posted: "For what it's worth, over the years I have shared wines with Natalie, and sometimes she's requested them, but I have never been asked to pay for that. Like others, if I wanted to look at her database, I needed to subscribe like anyone else, just like several of the top magazines whose first names start with W ... not everyone does that, but many do."

While I was updating each review, several writers continued to rant on Palate Press. I had had enough. I decided just to delete all the quoted reviews, even those from the writers who were fine with my quoting them. I was done dealing with the mob.

"Should I have stopped using the abbreviation directory right after Pinkus's first email, rather than asking him to leave it with me?" I asked Miranda at our next session. "Not that I could have done it immediately because it was going to take weeks of editing. But maybe none of this would have happened."

"That's taking too much responsibility. Let's say you did that. Do you think that would have satisfied him?"

"No, he'd be back at me for the next thing he needed me to change."

"Exactly. You're making the changes he requested. You've let him know that. Stay focused on that, then move on."

Years later, a book review column by Tamlyn Currin on Jancis Robinson's website gave me more perspective on what was happening back then. Currin wrote, "Are wine writers a particularly bitchy crowd? Or are they just insecure and scrambling for a higher spot on some proverbial human ladder that requires pissing on others to get them to move over?

"'Other wine writers' tasting notes are abysmal,'" she wrote, quoting Tony Aspler, who was considered the father of Canadian wine writing. At the end of her review of his book, she concluded, "Just found a second chapter ridiculing other people's tasting notes. Because one will not do."

Her review reminded me of Aspler's question on social media in 2011, "How do I untwitter Natalie MacLean?" He added that my posts were getting him down. Several people told him to just stop following me.

In the same article, Currin reviewed the U.K. writer Jamie Goode's book: "There is plenty ... [on] how rubbish other wine writers are. (Apparently, they write 'hideous' tasting notes ... If I collated all the passive-aggressive stabs wine writers make about other wine writers while 'inadvertently' putting their own particular style on a virtuous pedestal, they would fill a book.)"

Now I took a deep breath and looked up at Miranda.

"You need to tell Daniel what's happening."

"I can't! We've only known each other for two months. It'll destroy our relationship ... What'll he think of me?"

"You're not trusting him to be competent. If you don't tell him, he'll think something's wrong with the relationship. You can show him all the nasty bits, trust him. Use his borrowed functionality ... This issue isn't his hot button; he can take it."

"What am I going to tell him? Turns out you're dating an online pariah?"

"The words will come to you."

Daniel had started noticing something was off. He had asked several times if anything was bothering me. Were we moving too quickly into the relationship? Worry crossed his face like a cloud shadow over a sunny field. We were arguing about small things, like what to have for dinner or watch on television. I couldn't keep pretending it was a wonderful life.

The Bare Witch Project

A s Cameron and I walked through the mall, carollers sang "Silent Night." I longed for just one of those.

"Let's go in here." Cameron pulled me into the electronics store. "Santa has to know which console to buy." He winked.

My heart dropped. I had hoped he'd forget about the PlayStation. I had allowed him to play *Minecraft* online, as it focused on world building. I wanted to delay this purchase, which I imagined would take him into worlds of extreme violence and chauvinism. When Cameron asked for things while Adam and I were still together, Adam's response was "Ask your mother." I accepted my role as bad cop since I was the one who handled most of the discipline.

Once Cameron found the console, he went into sales mode, pointing out its various features to his dubious customer. His willowy frame was the antithesis of the muscular, blood-splattered game characters.

"Wow, you've really been reading up on this."

Cameron hesitated and looked at me as though he'd just eaten a forbidden cookie.

"I have one at Dad's house."

"Oh." I tried to hold back the scream inside my skull. "When did you get that?"

"A few months ago." Cameron shifted from one foot to the other.

"What do you play?"

Cameron looked down. "*Call of Duty*, mostly."

My heart dropped again. That didn't sound good. We talked about the game on the way home in the car. I didn't want Cameron thinking he had to hide this from me, so I asked him what he liked and disliked about the game, and, in a roundabout way, how he felt playing it. It didn't seem to upset him.

When we got home, I googled *Call of Duty*. It was described as a first-person shooter war game, rated for eighteen years and older based on its gore and violence. Many women who play it have since come forward to report abusive comments from male players.

I didn't want my son playing a game that inflicted violence on people without consequences. I didn't want him listening to other players, often older men, talking about women as sexual objects.

The men on Palate Press now focused on my body. They started with my hair, then worked their way down. Clive (no last name) said that he found my "hair most disturbing, it's so perfect." Another man referred to me as "Operation Peroxide." In the interest of complete transparency, I'm ready now to go public with this revelation: I'm not naturally blond.

A third man set up a Twitter account called @Nataliemacleanswig and had my "wig" post, "I'm all about 2 Italian Boys in me." This supposedly referred to my fantasy of what the two Italian men behind the wine brand Two Italian Boys would do to me. A fourth posted about my "lawsuit against those inflatable love doll manufacturers who blatantly stole my patented hair style for their own uses."

Their comments reminded me of former Secretary of State Hillary Clinton telling a Yale University graduating class in her convocation speech, "Pay attention to your hair because everyone else will." My hair seemed to play an increasingly bizarre but leading role in the posts. One friend, having read them, noted dryly, "Your hair deserves a book of its own."

My mind drifted back to a few days earlier when Mom, Daniel, Cameron, and I were playing a card game that prompts participants with personal questions.

"Recall a time you were embarrassed while playing a sport," Cameron read aloud.

"Oh, that's easy. In Highland dancing competitions, I wore a long, artificial braid coiled in a bun on my head since my hair was always tomboy short."

Mom smiled. She knew this story.

"I was in the national championships, your age, Cam. I could feel my hairpiece loosening as I swung my partner in the Reel.

"It started circling my head helicopter-style until it gained enough momentum to fly off completely and land on the floor in front of the judge. I could hear a low gasp from the crowd on the bleachers."

"What happened?" Cameron asked.

"I was mortified, but I kept dancing. I should have been disqualified, but I placed fifth."

"How'd you manage that?" Daniel asked.

"I found out later that the judge thought it was sporting of me to finish the dance rather than walk off the stage."

Cam looked at me as though I'd just levelled up my game.

Maybe my hair will write a memoir, I mused. *Loose Strands from a Tangled Life?* Or I could offer my Hairstyling Tips for the Persecuted. These would be inspired by the great witches of literature, movies, and television, starting with Morticia Addams from the 1960s television show *The Addams Family*. Her family tree traced back to Salem, Massachusetts, and the witch-burning trials. Her hairstyle? Nice & Sleazy, but He's Not Worth It. You'll look sleek in a midnight black dress because you ARE worth it.

Then there's Wicked Wanda's Wash & Go. Whether you're moving into a new house or lying trapped underneath one with just your red shoes sticking out, you'll want a cut that's low fuss. This style works with all internal and external weather, including tornadoes, cyclones, and tsunamis.

Finally, my favourite, the Singed Fringe. Even if you're not yet strapped atop a burning bonfire of mixed hardwoods, you can still achieve the singed look for your bangs with a small blowtorch, like those used to caramelize crème brûlée.

~ஒ~

As the men worked their way down my body, humour escaped me. Tudor, the former journalism professor, envisioned me as "Warden Gnat in black boots and leather with a whip encouraging reviewer guys to 'come' more often."

Another man wrote that I needed a "spankin." A third suggested, "Bring on the Vincotto and Feathers!" Vincotto is a sticky, thick paste made from cooked wine in Italy. I guess that's the vinous equivalent of being tarred and feathered.

Sonoma writer Ron Washam's posts about my "hooters" eviscerated me more than the others. When *Red, White, and Drunk All Over* was published, the *New York Times* wine columnist Eric Asimov had written in his review that "Ms. MacLean is the disarming Everywoman. She loves wine, loves drinking ... ultimately, it's a winning formula." Washam rewrote that review: "Nat is the most loved and respected wine writer alive, and what knockers! — Eric Asimov, author of *How to Love Wine, and Nat's Knockers.*"

As I read the comments, a ghostly version of myself stepped out of my body the way they do on medical dramas when people are dying and watch themselves on the operating table. I had lost nine pounds in one week. My skin was barely holding me together; I was afraid my vital organs would drop out.

Hugh Johnson, editor of *The World Atlas of Wine*, had described my second book, *Unquenchable*, as "There's everything here: old stories and new, an enquiring mind and lots of enthusiasm." Washam changed this to "Nat is not only one of the great palates in the wine business, she has fabulous tits. — Hugh Johnson."

Among those cheering on Washam in the comments was the *Seattle Times* wine columnist, Paul Gregutt: "You have certainly captured her bra-zen pose (I mean prose)." Several years later, Washam won the best online communicator of the year category at the prestigious Louis Roederer International Wine Writers' Awards.

As my eyes ran along their words, I felt their hands sliding over my breasts and down my body. They dismantled me part by part in public. The more they described what they wanted to do to me, the more I wanted to have nothing to do with my body. Instead, my head rolled on alone through their groping gauntlet.

My photoshopped head on a bikini had followed me around the internet for years. Now this. There's no better way to strip a woman of her intellect than to go after her naked body.

At night, I thought about Cameron growing up in this world. Could I even counter the sexist narrative online that had also been part of my separation in real life? The message: Women are valued for our faces and bodies, not our minds. Men are entitled to comment on us freely. When our shelf life expires, they find a new one.

I lay there in wordless grief.

～◎～

I never wanted to be considered sexy. I wanted men and women to fall in love with my mind. But my body betrayed my desire for intellectual respect.

There had been a string of red-faced moments throughout my life, from snide comments in graduate school about why I was on the Dean's List, to my husband's Bay Street colleagues leering at the Christmas office party photos: "Wow, I never realized how *buxom* your wife is."

I "bloomed" at eleven years old and was taller than anyone in my class, including the boys, so I started slumping early to hide my blossoms. I remember the day when Mom and I went to shop for my first bra. I couldn't look at the saleswoman in the department store.

As a teenager, I taped posters of ballet dancers en pointe, arms extended, to my bedroom wall. My ideal of beauty was a dancer's linearity, from the tip of her fingers to the end of her toes. One long line without interruption or speed bumps. When I competed in Scottish games, I bound and taped my chest with just enough room to breathe.

As an adult, I did a full fitting at a specialty bra store when I couldn't find regular bras with enough support. They told me that my measurements fit their Goddess category: 34G! Keep going past triple D, triple E, and triple F. I felt like a freak.

These specialty bras had better infrastructure, with heavy wiring, but they dug into my shoulders and set off metal detectors at airport security. As I looked past the burly guard in embarrassment, I'd murmur, "It's not my boots, it's the bra."

My tops were always larger than my bottoms, draping and loose, camping-tent style. These were like the dresses Grammy wore. In her early fifties she had developed a "dowager's hump," a postural kyphosis. This curvature of the upper spine near the back of the neck resembles that of the Quasimodo character in Victor Hugo's *The Hunchback of Notre Dame*. Many factors play a part in developing this hump. Slouching is one of the major ones.

It wasn't until 2017, when a talk show host was brave enough to speak about her own breast reduction surgery, that I thought, *Yes, that's it — I'm going to do it*. Perhaps I shouldn't have been surprised to learn that provincial health insurance covered the full cost. It's considered a health issue, not cosmetic like breast augmentation, given the associated symptoms of bad posture, red welts, and constant sweating. As well, there was the searing back and neck pain every night after a day at the computer, even after using various ergonomic chairs and a standing desk.

It surprised me that the surgery was three hours long, required general anaesthetic, and a six-week recovery period. It went well. Post-surgery, I was free — weightless. People finally saw "me" first.

In 2012, the weight of those comments landed heavily on my chest as various men continued to discuss my body and comment on what they'd do to me in raw, intimate detail. The violence directed at women online and off is more sexual than it is for men. Cyber-misogyny goes beyond cyber-bullying. It can include stalking, sexting, and revenge porn.

The crudest commentators often use the classic justification: freedom of speech. Shouldn't they be allowed to express their opinions about you, no matter how vulgar? Isn't it their right to say what they think? But one person's right to say anything online can terrorize another person into silence.

I had no words in response to a direct message on Twitter: "If you do not shut up, you will be raped."

It broke me.

That evening, I sat on the edge of my bed, still shaking from the threat. I thought about my failed marriage, my ruined reputation, the toxic pool of stress my son was swimming in, and how I was about to tank this new relationship either by keeping this soul-sickening secret or by sharing it.

How could I live in a world with people who hate me so much?

I took a Zoloft. The open bottle was still in my hand as I slid off the bed onto the floor. My legs folded tightly against my chest. My forehead pressed down on my knees.

What if I took them all?

The Howling

———

"... I need to tell you something." My voice trembled as Daniel and I sat in the living room in front of the fireplace. The fire snapped and sparked up into the black chimney. On the stereo, Frank Sinatra was singing "My Foolish Heart."

I'd opened my eyes that morning to see the Zoloft bottle on my night table. I was now a week into the attack.

Daniel had asked three times in the past few days if something was wrong. I was still trying to keep my Little Miss Perfect tiara intact. But I was scalped raw. I could no longer face this alone.

Daniel looked at me worriedly as we sat there on the sofa.

"Something's happening to me online ... have you seen it?"

"No." He put his arm around me. "Tell me."

"The whole world hates me!" I burst out sobbing, choking in breaths. The tears I'd held back now flooded my vision.

I wept for release. I wept for reprieve. I wept for redemption.

It was another twenty minutes before I calmed down enough to speak in sentences. My head felt split open like a watermelon.

"They're saying it's plagiarism?" Daniel asked.

"No, it's copyright, but everyone gets it mixed up with plagiarism. Plagiarism is pretending you wrote something that's not yours. This isn't that. This is about quoting someone else's opinion."

Daniel pulled me closer to him.

"What are you thinking?"

"I think I'm glad you shared this with me, Nattie." He gave me a long hug. I couldn't believe he wasn't shocked and appalled. His judgment-free empathy made me break down again.

"Please, please don't leave me," I whispered.

"I'm not going anywhere. Why would I do that?"

"Look how awful I am! My father left me, my husband left me, my son will leave me."

Daniel hugged me tighter.

"I guess you could say I have abandonment issues." I sniffed, trying to lighten up a bit.

"You'll always have me, Nattie." Daniel rubbed my back. "I've never met a woman who loves as fiercely as you do. You and me, we're in this together."

I never felt so loved and so miserable. Sharing this crisis with Daniel deepened our bond as much as sharing my divorce had with my girlfriends. I could no longer hide behind the public relations–version of myself, shedding it like an old skin — more exposed and more closely connected.

Daniel's loving acceptance gave me the courage to tell Mom the next day what was happening, without the weeping that might make her heart condition flare. She, too, gave me a big hug. I felt less alone. I didn't go into detail with Cameron, but just let him know I was dealing with some online issues that were stressing me a bit but had nothing to do with him. Everything would be okay.

But would it? Even as I said the words, I didn't believe them.

༺ა᠅ᡅ

"Did you report that rape threat on Twitter?" Miranda asked.

"Yeah, but they couldn't trace it beyond an anonymous email address that didn't respond." I sighed heavily.

"How are you feeling about it now?"

"Sticks and stones will break my bones, but words will never hurt me, right?"

"Sexually violent comments can have a real physical impact, especially on the mind."

"What, you think I have PTSD or something?"

"Perhaps. There was a man in a depression study who decided to commit suicide by taking all his pills at once and then was admitted to the hospital. The doctors were convinced he wouldn't survive because his vitals were crashing. When they did blood work, they discovered he was taking a placebo, sugar pills. Once he was told that, he recovered."

"All my life, I've been taught to be strong, never be the victim. Single child of a divorced mother and alcoholic father? No problem, you can overcome anything; all things are possible, just work harder than everyone else. PTSD sounds like blaming someone else."

"The mind is powerful; it creates our reality," Miranda said. "MRI scans have shown that when someone who survived a near-fatal car accident reads a script to trigger those memories, their brain activity is similar to actually experiencing an accident. They're not remembering the trauma, they're *reliving* it."

"I just want to know who sent me that message on Twitter." I wrapped my arms across my stomach. "At least I'd know where he is ... I keep wondering if he's behind me in the parking lot."

Even now, ten years later, I still slip into the present tense when talking about the attacks. The body remembers what the mind wants to forget. When I scroll down through the old social media screenshots, I'm back there. My heart races, my breath catches, dread seeps through me like blood into white linen.

Online attackers never see how the abuse adds up across different websites and social media channels. They're aware of only the stone they throw. That's why they often assume that they didn't do any real damage. They justify their demonizing language because they don't want to feel like they're bad people. They rationalize their actions by believing the internet isn't the real world. The person attacked can just turn it off.

But my work was entirely online. Day after day, I drank the venom. My personal drinking habits also couldn't be dealt with separately from the samples that surrounded me unless I walked away from everything I had built professionally. The internet had helped me create a career, and now it could destroy it.

I've since consciously uncoupled with those who are toxic — and liberally block them online — for sound mental health. I've also stopped minimizing what happened as a "social media attack." They were attacks, with real-life damage. Back then, I had no perspective or understanding of why I was so shaken.

In 2013, a high-profile columnist for the *Times*, Caitlin Moran, organized a twenty-four-hour boycott of Twitter to protest its failure to deal with violent threats against women. Although thousands participated using the hashtag #TwitterSilence, not much changed.

"Why don't you take a break from that." Daniel came into my office.

As usual, I was doomscrolling through the comments.

"Here, let me give you a shoulder massage." He tried to pull me from the computer.

"Stop! My world is falling apart. You can't make this go away with a shoulder massage."

Daniel was trying to fix the situation because that's what Prince Charmings do. Now he stood there, uncertain what to do, which made me even more cross. I wanted him to be bold, strong, and decisive — a hero. What did I really want? I didn't even know anymore.

"I'm just trying to help." He raised his hands and backed away.

I felt guilty for snapping at him. I was starting to see patterns in my own behaviour. I had withheld the truth from Daniel, just as I withheld remedial action on the reviews initially. Was this misplaced ferocity about doing things on my own really an inability to cope with other people's disappointment in me?

It reminded me of my helplessness as a child when I couldn't fix Mom's grief and anger. Had I misplaced compassion for myself as a little girl? I shut down that sadness. Now I was feeling sorry for myself as an adult when I should take responsibility? My thoughts were a bubbling broth, but I hoped that what might arise from them would be a magic potion to create a stronger, truer, better me.

∽◉◦

Night after night, my heart raced. At first, I thought this was a normal response to what was happening, but it wouldn't stop. It seemed to skip beats sometimes. Mom suffered from atrial fibrillation, an irregular heartbeat, with surges over two hundred beats per minute. It can be fatal if not managed. I thought I should get it checked out.

The next morning, the cold metal of my doctor's stethoscope pressed on my chest. In the silence, I could hear it thumping as though it were pleading for an end to the chaos: "Make it stop, make it stop, make it stop."

"It's definitely irregular," my doctor said. "I don't want you to worry, but I'm sending you for an ECG so we know what exactly is going on."

"ECG, that's a heart monitor, right?"

"Yes, an electrocardiogram shows the electrical activity of your heart. You have a family history of heart disease. Your mother has atrial fibrillation so this is important to diagnose early."

I tried to slow my breathing, so I didn't flood my heart with stress.

Breathe in 1, 2, 3, 4.

Hold 1, 2, 3, 4.

Breathe out 1, 2, 3, 4.

Hold 1, 2, 3, 4.

Breathe.

When my doctor received my results, she confirmed I had developed a heart murmur. She said the stress was making it worse. Anxiety was constant in my life now, a background hum that never went away. My right hand had developed a tremor.

I was living too much in my head. As a child, I expressed myself through dance, letting my body say what I was feeling. As an adult, I expressed how I felt through my writing, but my body still had something to say. I just needed to listen to it.

∾⊚∾

"You need to get away from this." Daniel wrapped his arms around me from behind. It was December 27. I was still spending hours on social media.

"Let's go to Montreal for a couple of nights," he suggested.

"I can still log on there." I stared at the feed.

"Well, I'm going to keep you so busy you won't have time for that," he whispered into my ear, turning my chair around. Daniel had been trying in gentle ways to take my mind off my mind. We went for daily walks and watched the retro movies he loved, like *My Fair Lady* and *Miracle on 34th Street*. Anything to get me away from the computer.

I agreed reluctantly. When I told Mom and Cameron, they immediately started talking about which movies they'd watch together while we were gone. I packed my bag but forgot my phone charger. My mind was still scrolling through the feeds.

The next morning, as the train gained speed on the track, all we could see was the blizzard outside. On arrival, we jumped in a taxi. A record snowfall of sixty centimetres had encased Montreal in a thick white blanket. Our greystone hotel in the heart of old city had a giant red sculpture of the word *LOVE* outside.

In the lobby, a large fireplace crackled with inviting warmth.

"How fantastic!" Daniel exclaimed. "Let's go for a walk!"

"Are you crazy, it's a blizzard out there."

"Exactly! We have the whole city to ourselves. Put on your mittens, kitten. Let's go!"

We walked down the middle of the street, our tracks the only ones visible. The Christmas lights in the small storefront windows blinked in the crisp evening air. Flakes were falling more gently now. The cars parked along the sides were entombed in snow, like sleeping furry white animals with their side mirrors resembling ears still perked up, listening to our chatter.

We ducked into one of the small bistros still open and sat at a wooden table by the window. Soft strains of Édith Piaf singing "La Vie En Rose" seemed to come from an old record player in the kitchen. We warmed ourselves with large bowls of steaming French onion soup. The wine list was small, but the owner mentioned he had one bottle of champagne in the fridge. I nodded without asking what it was.

He brought out Veuve Clicquot Non-Vintage Champagne. As I wrote in *Red, White, and Drunk All Over*, Barbe-Nicole Clicquot Ponsardin was just twenty-eight when her husband died of a malignant fever in 1805, leaving her with a six-year-old daughter. Madame Clicquot took control of the château to produce some of the most prestigious wines in the world in an era when few women were in business at all.

Only weeks after the funeral, the widow (*veuve* in French) arranged a shipment of twenty-five thousand bottles to Russia — an extraordinary feat given the uncertainty of trade during the Napoleonic wars. Her wine got through. Years later, her champagne was so popular in Russia that Pushkin, Gogol, and Chekhov all wrote about it.

Madame Clicquot wasn't just a saleswoman. She was also an inventor, developing the technique called remuage, or riddling, to remove sediment from the wine — a method that was quickly adopted throughout the Champagne region. The second fermentation in the bottle that gives champagne its bubbles also creates sediment. This imparts an unsightly cloudy appearance. To clarify it, Madame Clicquot drilled holes in her kitchen table and inserted the bottles upside down. The sediment gradually collected in the necks, where it was disgorged while the bottles were still upside down. The bottles were then turned upright and re-corked.

Eventually she switched to racks shaped like pyramids, which took up less space in the cellar. (And presumably, Madame grew tired of balancing her dinner plate on her lap.) I loved the story of this feisty single mother running a wine business for more than sixty years, until she died in 1866, at eighty-nine.

Daniel and I clinked glasses. The bubbles tickled my nose. Its aromas of lime zest, green apple, and freshly baked bread paired beautifully with the crusty bits of baked cheese I chipped from the sides of the bowl.

As we walked back out into the night, Daniel lay down in the middle of the quiet street and made a snow angel. I laughed. The fresh, clean air felt good. We wandered around our ghost city for an hour. We felt like the last two people on the planet — exactly what I needed.

Into the Legal Woods

Back in Ottawa after our trip, Daniel and I went for an evening walk. It was a mild evening. I was shivering even though I wasn't cold.

When we returned home, I still had my coat on as I logged into Palate Press. Several commenters were egging each other on, asking who had contacts at Ottawa- and Toronto-based newspapers. They wanted to get the story published in my hometown newspapers as well as those in Toronto, where my editors lived. I was to be dragged to the village square whipping post for a little more public humiliation before I burned.

Someone called Wino-fred confirmed that the editor at the *Ottawa Sun* had been sent a link to the Palate Press site. Their editors would decide if they'd run it. Others had contacted Canada's most widely read wine columnist, Beppi Crosariol at the *Globe and Mail*.

Crosariol's email popped into the top of my inbox.

"Can we talk?" he asked.

Oh God.

A molten lump of fear moved slowly from my stomach up through my chest and lodged in my throat. We scheduled a call for the next morning. I called the lawyer, Frank. I was willing to cash in my retirement savings in this fight for my name. It's all a writer — or anyone — really has.

At nine that night, the sixteenth-floor legal offices of Frank and Ernest were in shadows except for a few desk lamps. One illuminated the poinsettia at reception. City lights dotted the landscape below.

Frank brought me into a conference room. We sat down opposite each other at a long table. After reviewing the issues, he said, "Let's role-play. I'll be the reporter."

As we went back and forth on potential questions, he advised, "Slow the interview down. Stop the momentum, throw a question back at him … Could you clarify what you mean by that?

"You'll be nervous, so every once in a while, ask yourself, Am I talking too much? Then shut up. Just answer the question and no more."

Then he started a rapid-fire mock cross-examination. When he was done, I was sweating. He had more advice. "Don't let him go on an open fishing expedition with vague questions that you're left to interpret and answer. Absolutely no guessing or speculating on questions that aren't your expertise or about the future or others' motives. You simply say, 'I am not knowledgeable enough to answer that question,' or 'I need time to think about that and to get legal advice on that before deciding what to do.' Be friends with silence."

"What if he asks me if I did the right thing?" I asked.

"Just say, 'Well, I feel I'm doing the right thing now.'"

"Does that mean you were doing the wrong thing before?" I shot back, now playing the reporter.

"Very good." His eyes warmed up to this mental chess.

For a moment, I felt very Alicia Florrick from *The Good Wife*. But this wasn't a game. This was my life.

I drove home late that night, sick with nerves. Daniel was standing in the hallway as I came in the door. We hugged silently for a long time.

Lying in bed, the question came back to me: Did I do the right thing?

No, I hadn't. I had let my competitive instinct get out of control. It was no longer a healthy prompt to work harder but now a compulsive need to win. I should never have started posting other writers' reviews on my site, let alone not spelling out the writers' full names, even if these were noted in the directory. It didn't matter who else was doing it or that I became the lightning rod for the issue. I was wrong.

I made the situation worse by being defensive and resisting the initial calls to make changes. I didn't understand copyright but should have taken the time to learn about it sooner than I did.

I also had to acknowledge both my attraction to and repulsion from alpha males. They triggered something inside me. Was it a yearning for a father who didn't care enough to be in my life? Was it the anger I held for Mom toward my father?

I had been drawn to Adam for his unfettered confidence, then was sad when he left me. I should have been angry. Instead, I stockpiled that anger and let it blind me when I was bullied by aggressive men.

I also tried to handle everything on my own instead of trusting that Daniel would not leave me when I told him about the attacks. I was reliving the old stories about the men in my life, not considering this man might be different.

I was exhausted, heartbroken, shattered. I didn't want to live this way anymore. Even when love sees all of me, love might stay.

❦

The next morning, I woke up remembering the call scheduled with Beppi Crosariol. My stomach heaved. He was also editor of the Business section of the newspaper and a twenty-year, full-time employee, not a freelancer. Though his reviews were published on the paper's website, he didn't have his own competitive website dedicated to wine. He was at the top of his game, with the most respected wine column in the country.

The cinnamon notes from Mom's mulled wine warming on the stove filled my office as I picked up the phone. I took a deep breath trying to unclench my body.

After a brief greeting, Crosariol asked me what had happened and what I had done since. He kept to the facts and asked succinct questions.

"What started this?"

"What did you do in response?"

"What's happening now?"

A long silence followed, then he said, "I was discussing this with my editor. It's so inside baseball with these writers. I don't think readers really care."

I bit my lip and shut up but mentally agreed with him. What might have been of greater interest to his readers was the deep-rooted misogyny in the wine world, but no one was talking about it back then. I sure as hell wasn't going to bring it up and jump into the next boiling cauldron.

After a long pause, Crosariol said, "I think that's it. I'll let you know if I have more questions."

"Thanks." We hung up.

"How do you feel?" Daniel asked as I dropped down beside him on the sofa. He paused *An Affair to Remember*. Ripped wrapping paper from opened presents was still scattered on the table.

"Like I got up from the stretch rack just before my arms and legs were pulled off."

Daniel put his arm around me. We sat there for a while in silence as my breathing slowed. Then he put the movie back on. We watched someone else's happy ending.

Days later, Crosariol emailed me to say he'd decided not to write the story. The *Ottawa Sun* also didn't publish. I felt deep down, cellular relief.

~~~

It occurred to me that this whole mess had clarified my friends and foes. The first to condemn were those who had grumbled about many things on social media. They seemed to enjoy bingeing on the carcasses of other people's reputations, pecking from the sides, trying to pull out a strand of carrion to fortify themselves.

Those who were more senior and successful in the field, like Crosariol, believed there were always two sides to a story and actually asked me for mine. They didn't get to where they were by assuming the worst about everyone. They gave people the benefit of the doubt and recognized their own humanity in other's vulnerability.

Patrick Fegan, wine columnist for the *Chicago Tribune*, posted on Palate Press: "Curious to see that Natalie MacLean is in the Palate Press's list of contributors. I'm just wondering why this could not have been handled at first on an 'in house' basis (or was it and with what results?) or why PP did not acknowledge her as a contributor in the above piece."

David Honig, the first to respond to my initial comment, replied that he hadn't noticed that my name was still on the site and so he removed it. He did not answer Fegan's question.

As Steve Heimoff, then a columnist for the *Wine Enthusiast*, one of the largest U.S. wine magazines, wrote on his own website,

"I thought there was some piling onto Natalie by elements of the blogosphere and wine media, and I didn't want to be part of that ... [She] has repented and asked for forgiveness. That she hasn't groveled is beside the point. She is now listing the full names and publications of the critics she quotes — which, by the way, is called 'buzz' in some circles. She should have done that from the beginning, but who among us hasn't erred in some way? Let everyone now stop casting stones."

Rocks and witches have a long history beyond stoning and pressing. The witch-stone, or hagstone, was a pebble with a natural hole in the middle worn as an amulet to repel witchcraft. I prefer the crystals witches themselves used to heal and transform. I still have a piece of amethyst I found on a beach in Nova Scotia as a child. It sits on my desk, glittering violet rays on the wall in the morning sun, protecting me from evil spirits.

୭

I opened the giant fridge door at the grocery store, staring at the eggnog, Grampy's favourite holiday drink mixed with rum. When I was a child, I loved his tales about rogue elves that got into mischief but were forgiven by Christmas Eve.

"They were buthans and bumlers," he said in his deep voice, using Gaelic-ish words he made up for scoundrels. "Like you." He would tweak my nose, pretending to steal it.

The clink of ice cubes in his glass; his sweet, toffeed breath.

"Are you buying eggnog or making it?" Mom came up behind me.

"I'm smelling Christmas past." I snapped back to the present, taking a carton.

"Grampy's favourite," Mom said. "You don't drink eggnog. Does Daniel?"

"No, I just want one in the fridge." I yearned to go back in time before this mess. I also wanted a reminder of the first good man in my life.

～☙～

Now that Heimoff had published his piece, I had a new comments section to scroll. This time, there were supportive posts. One reader, Ian Tarrant, wrote, "Thanks Steve … Only one word has come to my mind in relation to the Nat 'scandal' … Jealousy."

A glimmer of positivity — and time — were starting to help. I was eating breakfast again, though I still often forgot small tasks I had started, like putting the garbage in the garage. I'd stand for a few minutes in front of the big bin, then look down at the bag in my hand, wondering how it got there.

Shari Darling, a syndicated wine newspaper columnist and the woman who had convinced me not to leave the wine writers' association several years earlier, wrote on her website,

> Just this week a wine writing colleague of mine has been thrown into the deep end of boiling hot water. She is weathering a storm of legal and ethical allegations. I am so sad that she must endure this scrutiny. It is an example of how any writer can find him/herself in legal trouble by overlooking or simply not paying attention to details.
>
> The grey area, in the case of this Canadian wine writer, is that these wine tasting notes had already reached the internet by way of the Liquor Control Board of Ontario and are within public domain. Hence are they not up for grabs? There is

no clear-cut answer to this question when it comes
to blogging.

I wished I had gone to journalism school or had an editor tell me
about the nuances of copyright attribution. The editors for whom I
wrote articles as a freelancer didn't have time for coaching. However,
my misunderstanding of copyright and lack of journalistic training
were not excuses. I had to take responsibility for what I'd done.

Ian D'Agata, author of several award-winning wine books and
also a medical doctor, emailed me:

> I am Ian D'Agata; as you know, I write about the
> wines of Italy, Alsace, Bordeaux, and Canada for
> Steve Tanzer's *International Wine Cellar*, and also
> contribute to *Decanter* and France's *Le Figaro* daily.
> I am also one of the wine writers whose tasting
> notes you quoted over the years in your website.
>
> I am sure that your quoting other's tasting
> notes with only abbreviated initials of the wine
> writers you were quoting was only done in good
> faith and I for one cannot see how anybody could
> ever have mistook those reviews for your own.
>
> Besides, you have now taken steps to amend
> anything that might have ruffled a few feathers,
> for which you are to be commended. Ours is a
> tough business because we're all critics. I wish you
> and all your loved ones a very happy holiday sea-
> son. Keep up the good work.

His words meant everything to me. I thought I was alone, but
the supporters had been there all along. Now they were stepping
forward from the shadows.

∽☙∾

"I have declared this matter closed in the Circle committee," Stuart Walton, the chair of the Circle of Wine Writers, emailed me. The Circle, based in England, is the largest worldwide wine writing association, with 276 writers from more than a dozen countries. Members include Jancis Robinson, Hugh Johnson, Oz Clarke, and others, including me. "Whatever other comment you receive, or are made party to, does not carry the CWW imprimatur. I hope you will be able to put the whole issue behind you in the new year. On which note, my compliments of the season to you, and all best wishes for a successful 2013."

While this wasn't absolution — nothing goes away on the internet, ever — it felt like papal forgiveness. The Circle sets strict ethical guidelines and standards for the wine writing profession. I'd been a member since 2004 (and still am). In 2020, they featured me in their magazine as their Member of the Month. I know, I'm still a sucker for recognition, but it's on a shorter leash now.

I posted a comment on my own site that the chair of the Circle of Wine Writers declared the matter closed. I didn't name him, as I didn't want the mob going after him. In response, W. Blake Gray, former wine editor for the *San Francisco Chronicle*, posted a long screed about how I was telling yet another lie.

All I could think was *It. Never. Ends.*

Years later, at a wine media conference, Gray would deliver a speech entitled "Reporting Techniques for Better Wine Writing." Leaning into the camera, he warned the audience about the importance of reliable sources and accurate reporting: "You've got to get your facts right. If you have one fact wrong in there, everyone's going to dismiss your opinion … Moreover, they may dismiss you entirely because you got a fact wrong."

A Discovery of Bitches

A few days before the new year, Daniel and I lay on the living room sofa, my head on his chest as he stroked my hair. The lights on the tree blinked as "Auld Lang Syne" played softly. I couldn't imagine ever returning to the "olden days" before this mess. They wouldn't be long since forgotten; they belonged to another life.

"I've got another call." I dragged myself up.

"Who?"

"*Toronto Star.*"

Nancy White, a writer from the Lifestyle section, had asked to speak to me after some of the commenters on Palate Press contacted her. As the call began, my hands trembled. I tried to slow my heartbeat, now a hammer hitting my solar plexus.

She asked similar questions to those of Crosariol. I told her I was fixing the reviews and focused on the facts. To wrap up the interview, White asked, "Is there a third book in the works?"

"I'm gathering material for it now." I was joking. I had no intention then to write about this mess. She laughed.

White's piece came out on New Year's Eve. It was mostly a recounting of the facts. She quoted Michael Pinkus, who had sent me the accusatory email and copied the writers: "She did not seem apologetic ... Her attitude was tee hee I made a mistake."

The only thing more bizarre than Pinkus's mind-reading skills, surprising given we'd never met, was that White didn't challenge him on the mind-reading quote.

In colonial Salem, men said they could just "tell" that the women they accused of being witches were secretly mocking them. Even before this, in 1484, Pope Innocent VIII's papal bull ordered clergymen to rid their parishes of witchcraft. He added that women were unfinished animals made from Adam's rib and therefore naturally deceptive.

This fervour for hunting witches spread across Europe. Despite its small population, Scotland put more suspected witches to death than any other country. This fascinated me, given my Scottish heritage. Some thirty-eight hundred, mostly women, in the country, were tried as witches. Two-thirds were strangled, hanged, drowned, or burned at the stake between 1563 and 1736. By contrast, in Salem, Massachusetts, nineteen people were executed.

One of the most famous cases in Scotland was Lilias Adie, who was charged with causing her neighbour's hangover. I wouldn't have survived a fortnight back then. The last Scottish woman to go on trial for witchcraft was in 1944. Elizabeth Johnson, the last woman condemned as a witch in Salem in 1693, was exonerated in 2022.

I've always been interested in the Druid priestesses, the prophetic seers of the ancient Celts, who were part of my ancestry. They, too, were accused of being witches. That's why I love the TV series *Outlander* and the book series of the same name by Diana Gabaldon — well, okay, also because of the broad-chested, kilt-wearing Jamie.

Were Scots more prone to accusations — or being accused — of witchcraft? Seems like we had, and still have, a special talent for it. The tradition continues, but now the pitchfork pack has gone online.

∾◉∿

I was beginning to understand that the men who made the sexually explicit comments saw nothing wrong with their "banter." Pinkus had characterized the vicious slurs as simply "unfortunate."

Perhaps it shouldn't have been a surprise when he described on his podcast, in sexual detail, what his co-host would do to a chardonnay. The wine was made by a young woman, a rising star in the winemaking industry, whose name I refuse to put in the same paragraph with this sexist sewage.

I heard about his remarks because someone had shared a review of his podcast on social media: "Disgusting. It's 2020, guys. Some potty humour is expected but when one host says to the other, 'You're going to pull out your penis and jerk off all over this wine,' it's too much. Absolutely disgusting behaviour from two supposed wine professionals. FYI, this system forces you to give a star minimum in order to complete a review, but this is worth -5 stars."

In another episode, Pinkus and his co-host interviewed Grant Westcott, the owner of a different Ontario winery, Westcott Vineyards. Grant spoke with respect about how his wife, Carolyn, had named their wines after women in history she admired.

This included Lilias Massey, the daughter-in-law of Vincent Massey, Canada's governor general in the 1950s. Lilias had served as the chatelaine or hostess of Rideau Hall for diplomatic entertaining since Massey's wife had died just eighteen months earlier. Lilias also accompanied Massey on his rugged trips across the frozen North in dogsleds and tri-motor airplanes. She was as game as he and his men were for the adventure. Well into her eighties, she piloted a twenty-six-foot triple-cockpit motorboat with a high-speed aircraft engine.

Carolyn named another wine Violette, inspired by Violette de Sibour (née Selfridge), daughter of the Selfridges department store founder in England. She flew a propeller airplane across Europe and Africa ten years before Amelia Earhart flew across the Atlantic Ocean. She also marched on the streets of London with the suffragettes in the 1920s to protest that women should be allowed to vote.

As Carolyn later told me, "These were strong-willed women fighting for women's rights, trying to make the world a better place."

Pinkus described these wines to Grant Westcott on the podcast as he tasted them: "These ladies give it up one sip at a time ... They take off a sock, they take off a glove, they take off the kerchief from their head ... Slowly she's getting undressed ... I really can't wait until I get the bra and panties on this one."

Grant Westcott was silent for several seconds until Pinkus asked if he had hung up on him. His response: "Not quite."

As of this writing, Pinkus and his co-host continue to write about wine for *Toronto Life*, one of our country's largest magazines.

～⊛～

After I posted my response to the second article on the Palate Press site, the men stopped disputing the facts. Instead, they demanded that I send them the private emails of supportive writers. They had moved off the original issue since I had removed other writers' reviews from my site. This time I didn't respond. As the weeks went by, without the fuel of my engagement, the comments slowed like dying embers.

In January 2013, someone who created an account called "Is that it?" posted, "We rant and rave and everything calms down … Seems a shame that it all ends like this."

The comments stopped, though I kept scrolling as though looking for the skid marks showing where the eighteen-wheeler went off the cliff. I didn't feel relief, just an absence of constant terror.

Could I ever get back to "normal"? At any moment, there might be a new post about God knows what. I finally had the mental space to consider what had happened. Frank and Ernest told me I had clear grounds to sue for defamation. I just wanted it to be over. If something similar happened today, I'd consider the legal route, especially if it could raise awareness of these issues in my industry and help other women. In 2020, a media company purchased Palate Press, letting go all staff except for one woman.

While the biggest toll had been on my mental and physical health, I also lost two magazine columns and three speaking engagements. It took five years to replace them. It took longer for the Palate Press and related articles to drop off page one of Google's results. I'll never know what else I lost because potential editors and event organizers searched my name.

What I didn't lose was my love of wine and the people in the industry. Most of my experience in the wine industry has been positive, filled with moments of sensual delight, creative challenge, and human kindness. It allowed me to explore the world, travelling to places I never could as a child. It also made me more worldly, experiencing cultures so different from my small-town upbringing. Just as I lost faith in the Catholic Church but still wanted spirituality, I turned away from the closed attitudes of some in the wine industry but still yearned for connection with so many more who have broadened my mind.

It strikes me that Wicca, the practice of witchcraft based on pre-Christian traditions of nature worship, shares much with Catholicism, from the robes and relics to candles and incantations with ritual celebrations of life, death, and rebirth. The biggest difference seems to be that Catholicism is based on the history of men with special powers, whereas Wicca is based on women. Witches are healers connected to the earth with their herbal remedies. They can also heal themselves.

I recalled that Jesus said he was the "true vine." Those who remained faithful to him would bear fruit, while those who did not would be thrown into the fire and burned. That connection to nature appealed to me. Perhaps I needed to create my own blend of spirituality with what resonated for me from the Bible, Wicca, and the Romantic poets.

In turn, I believe I've broadened the minds of those who read my work. Many of them, including me, would never read a thick tome on agriculture, commerce, history, politics, law, religion, relationships, or sexism. But they learn about those topics in my "wine" books. You could create a liberal arts degree with wine as the hub connecting the spokes of all human endeavour.

That broader perspective helped me realize something else. The male critics had depersonalized me so they could project on me whatever motivations they wanted. But hadn't I done the same thing to them? I had labelled them all as sexist aggressors.

"Grant that I may not so much seek to be understood as to understand," Saint Francis of Assisi said in the thirteenth century. Wisdom worthy of an Instagram quote card.

I hadn't taken the time to understand how important the wine reviews were to these critics. Perhaps the way they approached me was the only way they knew how. I'm not excusing bad behaviour, theirs or my own, but as the ashes blew away, I saw more clearly, almost face to face, that we all struggle and fail. It's what we do with failure that counts.

One of the most powerful parts of Catholicism is the desire for forgiveness. Without it, there's no desire to change. You'd just give up trying to be good. During Lent, the forty days leading up to Easter, we had to forgo something, like candy, to show our repentance. That's when I became a professional at picking out my sins and feeling terrible about them.

The priest would rub the ash cross on my forehead.

You are dust, and to dust you shall return.

Black cross, scarlet *A*.

Dust, ash, rise again, second chance.

Without forgiveness, there is no redemption. Without redemption, there is no rising again, no life after death, no change, no hope.

The price of forgiving myself was forgiving my father, Adam, and the men online. I couldn't hold all that hate. As I let it go, I breathed in deeply, released from the heavy stone I had placed on my own heart.

They're Creepy and They're Crawly

―――――――

The attacks in 2012 opened my eyes to hatred and its lingering impact. This experience changed how I experienced everything else.

It wasn't until 2018 that Karen MacNeil, author of *The Wine Bible*, became one of the first women to speak publicly about the rampant misogyny in the industry.

"Is there a Harvey Weinstein of wine?" she tweeted.

She later elaborated: "When everyone's job involves drinking — when the professional and social contexts are blurred — how do you determine where the lines should be drawn? And even if you were sure when those lines were clearly crossed, wine often enters the equation again to serve as the perfect 'cover.'"

Why is it, I wondered, that predators can point to alcohol as an excuse when they sexually harass someone? "Sorry, I wasn't myself.

I had one too many to drink." Do we exonerate someone who drives drunk and kills someone?

She also spoke about how much women have achieved in the industry but that there's still work to be done: "Some day, women in wine will be able to put down their guard, but as every woman in the industry knows, that time hasn't come yet."

The restaurant industry had exposed the sexual harassment by celebrity chefs and restaurateurs such as Mario Batali, Ken Friedman, and others, including Ottawa's Matthew Carmichael, the chef-owner of Riviera, El Camino, and Datsun restaurants. The wine industry, however, is much smaller and less formalized than the restaurant industry. That makes it more prone to these abuses — and less likely to admit them. In such a clubby industry with a powerful social grapevine, you can quickly be ostracized.

More than 80 percent of U.S. and Canadian wineries are tiny, producing less than five thousand cases a year and with fewer than twenty employees, according to industry statistics. Most don't have a human resources department, let alone a harassment policy. Even when there is one, it's often not communicated to employees. In the drinks business, like others, the cultural norms are established at the top.

Entry-level winemaking, sommelier, and other positions are apprenticeships with a mentor rather than conducted via group training. Even candidates with a college or university education must still apprentice. They're often young and relying on their boss to refer them to their next position. These close, one-on-one work relationships with great power differentials can easily be manipulated.

In the magazine *SevenFifty Daily*, Amy Bess Cook wrote about a 2018 survey by Unite, a U.K. hospitality industry union. It revealed that 89 percent of hospitality workers and 80 percent of female agricultural workers reported on-the-job sexual harassment, statistics that don't even include other forms of power abuse.

As MacNeil has clarified, sexual misconduct is not about sex and not a mere misbehaviour: "It's about using your gender to undermine, intimidate, and put someone in their place. It's about abusing your power to render someone else powerless."

Cook believed that MacNeil didn't get responses to her question about the wine industry's Harvey Weinstein because the industry lingers in silence. Cook founded Woman-Owned Wineries, an advocacy group that includes a U.S. winery directory, storytelling project, and wine club through which members can buy wine made by women. She's dealt with hundreds of wine industry professionals: "I encountered persistent power abuse that touched every aspect of my life. My repeated attempts to seek help were met with derision, stonewalling, and — ultimately — retaliation."

She quoted Hope Ewing, author of *Movers and Shakers: Women Making Waves in Spirits, Beer, and Wine*, who says that employees who must confront or report their superiors contend not only with backlash but with guilt as well. "People self-silence because their abusers might also have helped their careers along at some point — or those of their close friends. This is not only deeply confusing on its own — He's not all bad! What if no one believes me? — but throw in the fact that we're surrounded by alcohol and all the stigma that still comes with it, and you've got a hothouse of shame and denial."

These men had picked me. I felt ashamed for being attacked. How could Daniel, Mom, and Cameron understand the dynamics of this industry? This was another reason I waited so long to tell them what was happening.

~◎~

Karen MacNeil's provocative question on Twitter came back to me in 2019. Norman Hardie made wines I admired. I often gave them scores in the 90s. His pinot noir was a personal favourite. I purchased it by the case for my off-duty drinking.

My jaw dropped when I read the front-page headline in the *Globe and Mail*: "Canadian winemaker Norman Hardie accused of sexual misconduct: A *Globe and Mail* investigation reveals a wide-ranging pattern of alleged sexual advances and sexual harassment by Hardie, a major player in Canada's food and wine industry."

After a six-month investigation, Ann Hui and Ivy Knight reported twenty-one allegations of sexual misconduct against Hardie. As the journalists observed, his winery was a hub for celebrity chefs and industry power-players in the posh, pastoral enclave of Prince Edward County, just two hours east of Toronto.

As I originally mentioned on my podcast, Prince Charles and Camilla (now King Charles and Queen Consort Camilla), as well as Prime Minister Justin Trudeau and his wife, Sophie, had visited Hardie's winery. Over dinner at Montreal's Liverpool House, chef-owner David McMillan (also proprietor of the renowned Joe Beef restaurant) served Trudeau and U.S. president Barack Obama the Hardie Chardonnay. The *New York Times*, *Wine Spectator*, and *Vogue* had all written about his wines.

Dubbed the "King of the County," Hardie, then fifty-two, hosted late-night parties on his estate and, according to the *Globe* report, at a "secret beach" nearby with the understanding that "what happens in The County stays in The County." Newly recruited employees stayed in rooms in his home filled with bunk beds nicknamed the "Normatorium."

Daniel and I were visiting Mom in Halifax when the article came out. I was sitting at her kitchen table when I read, then reread, the multi-page exposé.

"What's caught your eye?" Daniel came into the kitchen and leaned over me.

"A winemaker's been accused of sexual harassment." I scanned the paper.

"Do you know him?" Mom asked as she turned around from the coffee maker.

"Not really, but I love his wines." I shook my head.

"Hmm ... are you going to say anything?" Daniel asked.

"I don't know ... I'm sure as hell not drinking his wines anymore."

Several days later, Jen Agg, owner of Toronto's Black Hoof restaurant and author of the memoir *I Hear She's a Real Bitch*, wrote an editorial for the *Globe*: "I know my industry well enough to know if I'd tried to go up against the brick wall that is Norm Hardie Inc., I'd lose. The restaurant industry is slow as molasses to change, and just as sticky with secrets and lies. Powerful men such as Mario Batali and Ken Friedman think they can just waltz back in, business as usual."

Hui and Knight interviewed over fifty people in a six-month investigation to report on the twenty-one women willing to come forward with sexual allegations against Hardie. Many of the women interviewed told the *Globe* they wouldn't have gone on the record about Mr. Hardie before the #MeToo movement. Sarah Reid said she was just twenty years old when Hardie put his hand up her shirt and then down her pants while sitting beside her at an event. When asked by the *Globe* about the wine industry, she said, "It's like no other business that I know. And it's accepted like no other business I know."

The *Globe* had contacted Hardie about the investigation several months before publishing the piece to give him a fair opportunity to comment. At first, Hardie denied the allegations in a letter, but after the story was published, he posted an apology on his website, saying that he was "approached several years ago by trusted colleagues who expressed concern about our work environment becoming too familiar and, specifically, with my behaviour and language. I was also told that the socializing and overly-familiar bantering with colleagues needed to stop … some of the allegations made against me are not true, but many are."

Overly familiar bantering?

Would that refer to unwanted requests for sex or to groping women's breasts?

Both the LCBO and Société des alcools du Québec (SAQ) stopped stocking his wines on their shelves. This was a major economic blow given that both retailers sell most of the wine in their respective provinces. Marquee restaurants, including Joe Beef, the Black Hoof, Treadwell Cuisine, Raymonds Restaurant, and Soif Bar à vin, the latter owned by Véronique Rivest, who placed second in the Best Sommelier of the World competition, also removed the wines from their lists.

Days later, the Ontario Wine Awards organization stripped Hardie of the Winemaker of the Year title. The award, whose mission statement is to recognize and celebrate the excellence of the province's Vintners Quality Alliance (VQA) wines, also includes the need to provide a safe and respectful working environment.

Less than six months later — just in time for the holiday-buying season — the LCBO put his wines back on the shelves, stating that it would "leave the choices to purchase Norman Hardie products in the hands of customers."

In a *Globe* article, Elizabeth Renzetti wrote about the scandal that we "fixate on the tremendous suffering of men who have behaved like predators (at best) or criminals (at worst) … Is it because we cannot fathom a world in which men's material wealth and status might be stripped away as a consequence of their terrible actions? I have no idea. But I do know that we seldom give as much thought to what women have lost, through no fault of their own — physical and mental health, job security, professional advancement. There's a hole in the world where their accomplishments should be, but we'll never see it."

While I wasn't physically assaulted, I saw the impact that ignoring chauvinistic behaviour can have on both women who are silenced by it and men who continue to perpetrate it. That's why I'm writing about these subjects more broadly here than simply what happened to me. I believe in post-traumatic growth (PTG) by casting light on secrets and shame — even if it takes a bonfire to do it.

⮵⧟⮴

When the Hardie story broke, I was floored. I'd often mentioned his wines on social media and in my newsletter.

Now what?

I certainly wasn't going to review his wines in the future, but should I remove my previous reviews from my site? Didn't I still believe that his wines were well made? I did. Blood diamonds are beautiful, but we don't buy them because of the unethical practices used to mine them. That's why fair-trade, cruelty-free, and sustainably produced food and drink are on the rise. There's more to a product than the product itself, especially if we believe that every bottle of wine tells a story.

Next, I had to consider that Ontario wineries producing expensive wines, like Hardie's, depend on critics' scores to sell them. I concluded that any economic impact on him as the winery owner was fair given that Hardie had used his position and power to harass women. Did this unjustly punish those working at his winery, including the women?

This was a tough one. On a much larger scale, Western countries impose economic sanctions on regimes that violate the human rights of their own citizens, even though those innocent citizens will suffer. It's impossible to separate the two and achieve change. I contacted the Prince Edward County Wine Council to offer assistance. They were helping the women at Hardie's winery to find counselling and positions at other wineries.

I decided to prioritize tasting wines made by women and wineries owned by women in that region and elsewhere, such as Lynn Sullivan, at Rosehall Run, and Deborah Paskus, at Closson Chase, among others. Their wines would no longer sit in my two-hundred-bottle backlog. This didn't mean they'd get high scores, just the opportunity to be tasted. Of course, I still reviewed wines made by men, as the majority were good men and trusted mentors.

I planned to remove Hardie's wines from my website and mobile apps until the winery was under new ownership. I'd been reviewing his wines since he launched the winery in 2004, as had many of the bloggers who posted on my site. In total, I deleted more than five hundred reviews. Before doing so, I shared my decision with my 230,000 subscribers, as many of them had saved these wines in their virtual cellar accounts on the site:

> In light of the recent allegations of sexual harassment levelled at Norman Hardie, winemaker and owner of Norman Hardie Wines, reported in the *Globe and Mail* this week, I will be removing all listings and reviews of these wines from my website and mobile apps.
>
> I believe in the right to be presumed innocent until proven guilty, however Norman Hardie has subsequently published a statement confirming that many of the allegations are true.
>
> Immediately thereafter, I started determining how to do this quickly and effectively within our database, which contains hundreds of reviews of these wines from our team of writers.

As well, there are thousands of listings from those of our members who keep cellar journals on our site.

Therefore, I wanted to let you know that these listings will be deleted to give you a heads-up in case you'd like to save your cellar notes or wine reviews elsewhere.

Actions speak louder than words, so I'll keep my own words focused on this action, and leave the excellent editorial and reporting to Ann Hui and Ivy Knight of the *Globe and Mail*.

Sincerely,
Natalie

Over three thousand replies flooded my inbox, most supporting my decision. There were about a dozen angry comments and people choosing to unsubscribe. #GoodRiddance

One reader wrote, "I fully support what you're doing, but surely Hardie isn't the only winemaker guilty of sexual harassment. Are you going to remove wines from other predators too? What about wineries historically built on slavery and other abuses?"

I wrote back that I would remove the wines as I became aware of existing issues and if they had either admitted to their abuses or were convicted in court. I added that I couldn't retroactively fix all historical wrongs, but I could act here and now with the information I had.

Drink local; act local.

Several months earlier, I had purchased four cases of Hardie wines for my personal consumption. When we got back home to Ottawa, I asked Cameron to help me load them into the car. As we drove to the liquor store, I explained the situation to him.

"That's awful. What are you going to do?"

"I'm going to return the wine. I may not be able to change everything that's wrong in my industry, but I can change who I support economically. Also, the LCBO isn't a mom-and-pop store; it's government-owned."

Cameron was silent, thinking.

When we hefted four cases up on the customer service desk, the rep asked, "Are they faulty?"

"No, but I believe the winemaker is."

Cameron was watching me closely.

The rep looked at me quizzically, so I handed him the receipt. He looked at it closely, then said, "It's been two months since you bought these. That's outside our thirty-day policy, so you can't return them."

"I'm returning them on principle." My voice was rising. "The winemaker has admitted that many allegations made against him are true."

That's not exactly something you announce in the middle of an LCBO.

Cameron took a sharp breath.

The rep froze for a few seconds, then stammered something about getting the store manager.

"What seems to be the problem here?" the manager asked.

I repeated that Hardie had admitted to the allegations, and I didn't want to support a business with those values.

"Oh, that issue has been resolved," he said.

"How has it been resolved?"

"It wasn't true," he told me.

"Many of the allegations were true, and he admitted to it."

The manager stared at me for what seemed like five minutes. I held my gaze.

"Aren't you that wine writer?"

"Yes, Natalie MacLean." I extended my hand.

"Right, we have your scores posted on the shelves all the time."

"Thank you."

He turned to the customer service rep and said, "Please take care of Ms. MacLean's return."

What would this exchange have been like had he not realized I was part of the media? I'm not sure. Why did I do this when I didn't work for the winery? We're all involved when one of us is involved. Otherwise, we stand alone and watch each other burn until it's our turn.

Why not just dump the wine or give it away? That wouldn't have had the same economic impact, however small. Returning it sent a message to the store staff, the LCBO, and Hardie that products made in an unethical workplace don't sell. When consumers do this as a group, we can make real change.

Best of all, Cameron was looking at me with new respect. It almost made up for that time six years ago when he had looked at me in quite the opposite way after Adam had forwarded my email about taking him to court if he didn't reinstate child support payments.

As of this writing, Hardie's wines are not on my site but are still sold in the LCBO. Wine Corp has since awarded his wines several medals in their competition and his wines remain on their site.

In 2019, John Szabo, a Toronto master sommelier and lead critic at Wine Corp, praised Hardie's pinot noir grapes on social media while visiting the winery. Jen Agg commented, "Very unsurprised by John Szabo ... supporting Norm Hardie ... It would be great if everyone who sees this were to let him know how misguided and misogynist that post is."

Agg's comments and the Hardie scandal reminded me of my first industry-tasting event. I spotted a woman writer I knew and gave her a big hug. Right behind her was a male critic I had never met who said, "Oooh, gimme some of that, gorgeous." His greedy fingers groped down my spine and around my waist. "Mmm, mmm, yes, ma'am."

I wanted to go home and burn off my epithelial layer. I just stood there flushing, angry with myself for saying nothing.

Men like him, mostly in their fifties and sixties, were used to the smiling attention of several young, attractive publicists. While I respect all women in the public relations business, many couldn't easily speak their mind to these gatekeepers for fear of reprisal. The wines they represented could be trashed or ignored. I started thinking of these men as COGs (creepy old guys).

Today, I'd tell that male critic, "Stop referring to my sexuality in the workplace. Comments like 'Sorry you're married,' 'Hey, beautiful,' and 'I wish I were thirty years younger' as you leer at my breasts are a power play that you'd never use on another man. I don't care if you're a 'nice guy' or from a different generation. You're a journalist who should know better. I am here because of my professional achievements. I have a job to do, so get out of my way and keep your hairy hands off me."

❧

In 2020, the *New York Times* published Julia Moskin's scathing, multi-page exposé of the wine industry's rampant sexism, with twenty-one women reporting that they had been sexually harassed, manipulated, or assaulted by male master sommeliers. The article noted that the abuse was a continuing problem of which the Court of Master Sommeliers leadership had long been aware. Women who had had relationships with the men were called "sommsuckers."

The fallout was swift. Seven master sommeliers were suspended or stepped down for sexual misconduct, including the chairman of the organization. There were calls for the entire board of directors to resign and to disband "the court." Many of those interviewed in a series of follow-up *Times* pieces believed this was only the beginning for the last pale, stale, male preserve now imploding with its own #MeToo revelations.

In North America, there are 165 master sommeliers, of whom just 28 are women. Karen MacNeil believes they're turned off by what they see as a "pin-kissing bro culture" among male sommeliers. Those who pass the exams are awarded a coveted lapel pin.

The master of wine ratio has a closer split, with 151 women of a total 450 masters, perhaps because it has a more academic focus. The two organizations are separate. The Institute of Masters of Wine is based in London, England. The Court of Master Sommeliers is headquartered in Santa Barbara, California.

Master of wine candidates must write an in-depth dissertation on an original wine research topic that synthesizes ideas and research. Their papers are graded anonymously. The judges don't know the name, race, or gender of the authors. In contrast, master sommelier candidates are tested on their recall of facts and a service exam that not only reveals who they are, but also who they know among the judges.

The pass rates for both exams are notoriously low, less than 10 percent on the first try. Candidates spend years, and tens of thousands of dollars, preparing for them. It strikes me that the master sommelier isn't so much a professional degree, like an MBA, but appears to be more of a private club to keep certain people out, especially women and people of colour.

My view has been influenced by the documentary *Somm*, which came out during my disastrous vintage, 2012. The film helped elevate sommeliers to rock star status beside bad-boy chefs. It also chronicled the gruelling journey of four candidates, all men, studying for the final exam. Their wives and girlfriends were largely ignored or tasked with emptying spit buckets.

The wine world seems to create elites in many aspects from these special designations that are almost impossible to achieve to the 1855 ranking of Bordeaux wines based largely on their prices. Only five wines today are called first growths among those produced by more than two thousand wineries.

The *New York Times* articles seemed to prompt a change in tone from Master Sommelier Szabo, who wrote on Facebook, "I understand the apparent hypocrisy in my recent post in support of the women featured in the NYT article, while at the same time reviewing Norman Hardie wines, who was accused of similar charges."

He promised to stop reviewing new releases, welcomed a "spirit of open dialogue for positive change, and not just more hate." He asked readers "to create space for more conversation."

I wondered where the space for open dialogue and conversation had been when he wrote about my "substandard ethics" in the *National Post* without contacting me. As Szabo concluded in his piece on me, "That's the beauty and the curse of the Internet. It has always behooved us to check into our sources ... Transparency is also critical."

Was he truly changing or just cornered? If I wanted the benefit of the doubt, I had to give it to him.

Hardie has kept his position as winemaker and owner of the company. In 2022, among 185 wineries in Ontario, his was one of 17 representing the province and country at the Canadian embassy in London, England. Hardie poured his wines for media, sommeliers, wine store buyers, and government dignitaries.

Despite twenty-one victims coming forward to report a wide-ranging pattern of unwanted sexual contact, groping, lewd comments, and requests for sex, and despite Hardie's own admission that many of the allegations were true, no charges were ever filed. According to the *Globe*, his victims received no amends.

Personally, I had hoped that Hardie would set up a fund for women in the industry or donate a portion of the proceeds from his wines to a similar cause. Yes, that would have drawn more attention to what he had done, but it could also have been one of the greatest turnaround stories in our industry. Hardie had enjoyed a cult-like following. Using his leadership platform on this issue could have prompted so much positive discussion and change in the industry.

The Hardie and master sommelier situations illuminated for me just how much of a status-driven, rule-bound business wine is — from medals and scores to stratified classifications, the lowest of which translates to peasant wines. This country-club culture of power and control fosters silence and abuse. That hierarchy is the antithesis of a product that's so cyclical and seasonal in nature. The movement of wine isn't from top to bottom, it's around and around, whether it's in your glass as you swirl it or when you revisit a wine you had years before and taste it as if for the very first time.

Farm-to-table stories bring the humanity back to wine. These stories, often told around the table, strengthen our connection with each other and with those who made what we're now making part of us. Creating and consuming wine as communion.

When I went from tech to wine, I left a *Brave New World* and stumbled onto the set of *Downton Abbey*. Tech urged me to break the rules; wine clamped down on me to keep them. Prohibition was about power and not letting us make adult choices with alcohol, especially women, for whom it was thought unseemly to drink when there were children to care for. That corseted culture still pervades the attitude toward women who work in this industry.

◈

I sat with Cassie in my living room on a frosty evening in January 2013, mesmerized by the flames in the fireplace licking at the darkness. We sipped on a glass of Sul Vulcano, from the Sicilian winery Donnafugata, whose name means "woman in flight" or "fugitive woman" (*donna in fuga*). Sul Vulcano means "on the volcano," so this woman was both on the run and on the hot seat. Perfect pairing for the moment.

The name *Donnafugata* refers to that story of Maria Carolina of Austria, Queen of Sicily and Naples. During the French invasion of Naples in 1798, she fled to the Sicilian countryside where the vineyards are planted today. Conniving men plotting her overthrow tried to hunt her down. She survived and returned triumphantly to her reign. In her honour, the winery has an illustrated woman's head with windblown hair on every label.

The vines for this robust wine grow in the volcanic soils of Mount Etna, where they struggle but become stronger for it. Given the sporadic eruptions of fire and brimstone, those vines, like people, don't take survival for granted.

José Rallo is co-owner with her brother, Antonio. She has received the Premio Bellisario award for her contribution to supporting female entrepreneurship. Theirs is the fifth generation of the family to make wine, a legacy that's lasted for 170 years.

"Maybe I should just get out of the industry." I sighed.

"Really? After all the years and work you've put in to build your business?" Cassie asked.

"I just want to run away." I rubbed the stem of my glass. "I feel like the word *crushed*."

"Where would you go?"

"Back to tech marketing."

"But didn't you tell me there was plenty of sexist crap there, too?"

"Yeah, guess there's no escape."

"Remember how excited you were when you first started writing about wine?"

"Yeah." I smiled at the memory of sloshing through muddy vineyard rows with Anne-Claude Leflaive, of Domaine Leflaive, in Burgundy. The rain bucketed down on us. She had offered to stay inside, but I wanted to go out into the fields. We bent down at several places, picking up handfuls of rich, thick soil, smelling the fresh promise of life. I wanted to eat it.

I literally felt grounded for the first time in my life. Maybe it was because Mom and I moved so often when I was a child. Perhaps it was a generational desire from Grampy's love of soil. Could it go back further to when my ancestors were evicted from Scotland in the nineteenth century during the Highland clearances and immigrated to Nova Scotia? I felt connected to the land wherever I travelled in the wine world. Home became a place rooted inside me.

I still felt as deeply about my *why* when it came to wine and writing. I just needed a new *how.*

"You'll figure it out, Nat," Cassie said, touching my forearm. I felt her strength like a lining under my skin.

A New Season's Growth

Round About the Cauldron We Go

—————

It was just after 6:00 p.m. in mid-February, 2013, about two months after the attacks started. The guardians of gotcha hadn't run out of steam, but they had found another witch to burn. I didn't feel strong enough yet to enter the fray to defend her, but I sure as hell wasn't going to be part of the encircling mob.

As I was mindlessly scrolling online, the doorbell rang.

A man in a black suit asked, "Are you Natalie?"

Then I noticed six more suited men behind him.

My God, what is this? I took three steps back, ready to run.

"Please, come in." Daniel came up behind me, his arms encircling my waist.

The man who had spoken now brought a rose out from behind his back and gave it to me as the men came in and arranged themselves into a semicircle.

"Hmmmm," the first man intoned.

Then their rich baritone voices filled the front entrance as they sang, a cappella, "Heart of My Heart."

I had forgotten about Valentine's Day, but Daniel hadn't. Love had been waiting for me to catch up.

They sang another four songs, taking my request for "Stand by Me" and Daniel's for "This Magic Moment." Then they wished us a good evening and left.

Daniel guided me to the kitchen, where he had prepared a candlelit dinner of honey-glazed salmon and roasted parmesan fingerling potatoes. I opened a bottle of Pommery Rosé Champagne. In 1858, Louise Pommery was left a widow with two young children only a year after her husband had bought the champagne house. She built Pommery from a small winery into one of the world's most respected brands and created the first dry style of champagne.

Daniel and I toasted to the fact our love had come along — at last. It wasn't guaranteed happily ever after, but it was happy in this moment.

Even though I was stronger and more confident after the attacks, I still felt the need to entertain everyone, including Daniel, at my own expense. In my personal life, I undermined myself with a nervous chuckle after almost every sentence when talking to someone new. That little laugh came out even when I was talking about something serious, as if to erase what I'd just said. I hated that it was almost reflexive, out before I could stop it. Prior to each podcast interview, I put a sticky note on my computer that read *Don't be a chucklehead*.

When did I learn I was a joke? Was this me gaslighting myself? How could others take me seriously when I couldn't do that for myself? Mom shared this anxious tic, but I took it to a new level professionally. Could I entertain without stepping on a verbal banana peel every time? Could I be personal and vulnerable without hiding behind humour?

On my podcast, I asked Karen MacNeil, author of *The Wine Bible*, what she'd advise young women entering the wine industry. I was really asking for myself as I needed a new approach.

"Be more serious about business. Be ambitious," she said. "I can't tell you how many business cards I have from professional women who call themselves Wine Chicks, Wine Goddesses, Wine Divas, Wine Dolls. Language can marginalize."

Ouch. My email signature was Chief of Wine Happiness. As women, we're taught to be caregivers, which is easily manipulated. Is the desire to be liked or, at least, to not appear threatening, part of why women in the wine industry belittle their own skills and experience with cutesy names?

I asked her if we make wine more accessible with self-deprecating humour?

"No, not unless you're already in a position of power."

True, we don't see those monikers with men: Harvest Hunks, Wine Warlocks, or Stainless-Steel Studs.

Then there's the title of this book. Language can marginalize, but it can also reclaim lost meaning. As I wrote my story, I also wanted to counter the old narrative about wicked witches, just as I wanted to be professional without depersonalizing myself.

MacNeil told me women also overexplain and second-guess themselves. I call it talking past the sale. This is made worse with what MacNeil describes as an insidious and often subconscious form of harassment: "Being belittled, ignored, talked over, looked past, demeaned, interrupted, reprimanded, corrected, or addressed as a junior, among countless other slights and abuses — takes a toll on anyone's confidence."

There it was again: gaslighting. Both MacNeil and I make our living by giving our opinion on wine. The challenge is owning your expertise when you're constantly undermined.

"Give a lot and ask for a lot," MacNeil said. "Take risks. Adopt a professional, business-oriented tone of voice and dress the part. Take control when you can and when it's appropriate."

MacNeil's words resonated with me, not just professionally but also personally. It was time to take myself seriously, not to be so jokey and deflective about my accomplishments. If I started appreciating them more, perhaps I wouldn't always be hunting for new ones. After twenty years of being in a marriage where I doubted my thoughts and feelings, it was time to rely on my intuition. There are more than five hundred million neurons in our stomach lining, which is why it's often called the second brain. It's also where 90 percent of serotonin is produced. I had to stop second-guessing myself and start trusting my gut — it was the smart thing to do.

༺ঌ༒ঌ༻

As I poured my second glass of Carmen Stevens Wines Petite Sirah in the kitchen, I lost myself in the mellow voice of Nat King Cole singing "Unforgettable." Cameron was upstairs doing homework. Daniel was making roast beef for dinner.

Carmen Stevens is considered South Africa's first female winemaker of colour, a term that includes not just Black people but also many other races in the country that former president Nelson Mandela described as a "rainbow nation." I visited her when she was the winemaker at Amani Vineyards, on the southern slope of Kanonkop, near Stellenbosch. *Amani* is the Swahili word for peace.

In 2011, Stevens founded her own winery, the first 100-percent Black-owned winery in Stellenbosch. The label bears a tiger that's a composite of four figures: a person on the right side of the animal's face, a bird with a red beak on the left side, and a face of a dog between the two, all atop the body of the tiger. Stevens says it represents how different people experience wine: "Some people pick up a glass and identify all characteristics, while others take time to see all the wine is expressing in the glass. The tiger is very special to me. My eldest daughter, Caitlin, painted it at school when she was only six years old. I love it!"

Stevens's petite sirah has a luxurious palate weight, with layers of peppered raspberries, black cherry, and mocha spice. A smoky, velvet plum heart slowly emerges. There's nothing petite about this wine. It's full-bodied, deeply concentrated, and it growls with pleasure beside roast beef.

I wasn't drinking as much as I had been in December during the attack, but it was still too much for a woman who wanted to stay within the bounds of moderation — and who didn't want to say stupid things to her partner. Apparently, one night I informed Daniel that he was the *luckiest man on earth* to be with me ... three times.

As the years passed, my tolerance for alcohol decreased. I didn't have the "Teflon liver" of my Scottish relatives. After two glasses, I became buzzed. I was a tightrope walker afraid of heights.

I got saucy when I drank too much, surprising myself at what came out of my mouth ... and what went into it. I'd play along with Daniel the next day, pretending I recalled the entire evening, hoping he'd tip me off to what I had said or done, watching his reactions like a hawk to see if I was in trouble.

At first Daniel said nothing. But after a few months, he started making some gentle comments about my drinking. He understood my impulses better than anyone I'd known because of his own struggle with smoking.

I knew I still had work to do on my relationship with wine. I needed to get away from the high of alcohol and return to the sensuality of wine; to move from the anaesthetic to the aesthetic. I wanted my experience to centre on who I was with rather than what was in my glass. More importantly, I had a young son who was watching my every move. Did I want him to develop the family disease?

Fortunately, my relationship with Daniel was closer than ever. He was now sleeping over most nights though still in the guest room. He snored like a small group of woodland creatures. I was an insomniac. The heating vents in the room didn't work, so it was often colder than the rest of the house. He joked each evening that he was checking into the Econo Lodge.

⚬⚬⚬

"Have you booked the flight?" I asked Daniel. We were making plans to go to New York City together for a long weekend in March.

"Can you do it? You're always on the computer."

"No. I've booked the hotel and restaurants. You said you'd book the flight two weeks ago."

"But you're so much better at this than I am."

"I am not better at it. I don't like doing it anymore than you do."

"You're so much faster at it."

"I'm not going to be your social secretary. Book it or we're not going."

Daniel glared at me, but I wouldn't budge. I wouldn't slip back into old roles. Sharing tasks made me less resentful and more connected with Daniel, and he with me.

With our flight booked, I thought about how I'd handle wine before and during our trip. Thank God, Daniel drank moderately; otherwise I might be writing this memoir from the Betty Ford Center. I still wanted wine, but I wanted other things more, like the restorative power of a good night's sleep and waking up fresh in the morning to write, rather than searching my brain fog about last night's gaps in the timeline.

Wine is a diuretic. We urinate more fluid volume than the alcohol we drink. It rouses you in the middle of the night not only to pee, but also because you're dehydrated, so it raises your heart rate.

It also fractures the sleep you do get and often prevents deep sleep. Losing weight is easier without alcohol because the body burns alcohol before fat. It's also easier to go into ketosis, the metabolic state when the body burns fat for energy because it doesn't have enough glucose. This prompts the liver to produce ketones, which help the brain function much better for certain periods of time — a better mind for writing.

I realized I wanted my evenings back. I had to tell myself that the night wouldn't get any better or more fun with more wine. I'd just end up saying things I'd regret, fall asleep early in front of the TV, wake up in the morning gutted.

I also wanted to command my own boundaries rather than worry about developing a soggy reputation with friends. *She sure likes to have a good time, wink, wink.*

Most of all, I wanted good health, the scaffolding of happiness. I wanted to get out from under the wine-soaked cloud of depression and not die of breast cancer.

Now that I had my why, I just needed the how. The challenge was making it through the arsenic hour around 5:00 p.m. when there's a natural dip in serotonin, the hormone that stabilizes our mood and sense of well-being. I had no commute to separate work and home. My office was just another room in my home. The key was giving myself a permission slip to quit work for the day at 6:00 p.m.

I also had to convince myself that chemical relaxation wasn't Natalie relaxation. I had to change my thoughts from *I need a drink to relax* to *I'm taking care of myself in a different way this evening* and *I'm treating "future Nat," who'll thank me tomorrow.* I had to rewind to the thought that was just before the thought that said *I need a glass of wine.* Usually that instigating thought was prompted by worry, anger, or despair that I wanted to water down with wine.

When the urge for a glass of wine seized me, I asked myself, How am I feeling now in this moment? I put my hand on my heart to reconnect with myself physically, to stop running back and forth across the icy attic of my mind and come back down into my body and feel my own warm flesh.

I decided not to have wine the next evening. That night I made a green tea and sat down to watch *Suits*. Yes, I still tasted wine daily, but that was spitting, not drinking. It felt luxurious to enjoy three to four hours of full energy after dinner. I read books again without falling asleep. I had complained for years I didn't have time to read. What I didn't have was an unmarinated brain.

Practising this reset at restaurants was harder because of their strong association with wine. I don't open up as much as I'd like until I've had a glass or two. I also feel trapped in restaurants since they're not my home environment, where I can roam freely. That's why I'm too feral to work in a corporate office.

First, I had to stop "pre-drinking": having a glass of wine at home to sand down the edges before going out. Daniel had caught on to what I was doing and asked me to wait until we got to the restaurant.

"Stop judging me. I just want to relax."

"I want to share the same reality with you." He put his hands on my waist. "Let me keep pace with you so we share the experience ... When you have a glass before we go, we're not on the same plane."

God, I love that man when I think about this now, though at the time I called him Buzz Killington.

With his support, I stopped the pre-drinking habit. At restaurants, I had to be vigilant with those small sips, and alternate them with sips of water. I made sure servers weren't topping up my glass too quickly, allowing them to refill only when I had finished a glass completely and stopping at a couple of glasses. If we didn't finish a bottle, I asked for it to be recorked to take it home — a treat for another night.

In New York, we skipped Broadway and splurged on dining at chef Daniel Boulud's restaurant, Daniel. Dinner was our theatre anyway. My Daniel seemed to be reading a novel as he "perused his options" with the menu. I took out my phone and started checking emails.

"Okay, hon." He closed his menu.

I ignored him.

"Natalie." He put his hand gently on my wrist.

"What?" I snapped. "The man is ready now to engage so the woman has to drop everything and entertain him?"

"Nat, I know you've been wronged by some men in your life, but I'm not one of them." He put both his hands on mine. "Some of us are good guys. I want to be in your life, but I'm not going to force my way in."

Tears welled. He was right. I had been unfairly generalizing about men. I relaxed. I also realized that once I got out of my head and into my heart, my drinking pace slowed. I took my time, ordering wines by the glass, which also made it easier to track how much I was drinking. I paired a briny Austrian grüner veltliner that tasted like ocean spray with chef Daniel's "Sea Scallops in Black Tie" — thinly sliced scallops interspersed with slivers of black truffles drizzled in a beurre blanc sauce.

When we returned from New York, the next challenge was socializing at friends' homes. Could I be real without too much wine, fully present and relaxed? It helped not being around the high-powered tech crowd. At a birthday party for one of Daniel's relatives, I basked in their warmth. They were more interested in me than in what I did. They asked about my family, how I spent my spare time. (Spare time?) They worked to live. I recalled the plastic lawn chairs of my childhood and my own extended family of uncles and aunts — carpenters, mechanics, people who worked with their hands — much like farmers and winemakers.

At more gussied-up dinner parties, Daniel was my wine wingman, tapping me twice under the table if I started getting too loose with my comments. Though once I turned to him slowly and said in a voice everyone could hear, "Please stop tapping my thigh to warn me I've lost my socially acceptable inhibitions."

Daniel always had my back, and my heart.

~☙~

Dinner parties at home with Daniel were decidedly different from those with Adam. We never hired a caterer because Daniel loved cooking. We'd sit around the kitchen island with his friends rather than at the more formal dining-room table. The conversation was often about family and travel rather than business and tech.

I socialized more often with Daniel than I had with Adam. Although I liked Daniel's friends, I struggled with adapting to a new group and managing my wine intake in these situations. I kept everyone's glasses topped up and retreated into Tasting Alley to top up my own glass more frequently. I drank faster than everyone else, even the men. I needed a few glasses to relax down into myself.

The pop of the cork. The bottle, an extension of my arm, tilting, promising. The long stream of jewelled red liquid as it touched the side of the glass, circled down and around, up the other side. The fresh berry aroma of the wine bloomed around my head as I raised the glass to my lips. That first taste, my mouth watering. The wine slid down my throat, the warmth seeping down my arms and legs, then finally up to my brain, flooding it. It whispered, I'm here, let go.

Ahhhhh.

The chatter and clinking glasses reminded me of the Celtic kitchen parties, ceilidhs, in my grandparents' home. Our Scottish and Irish ancestors mastered toasting life and death with alcohol, whether it was a wedding or a wake. But were they celebrating or blunting feelings?

My relatives laughed and kept time to the fiddle music with a hand or a foot. I'd be bouncing on the knee of an uncle whose beery breath warmed the back of my neck and circled down and around my ears, under my nose. I loved the smell of alcohol long before I drank it — it was the aroma of happiness as much as the salt air and Grammy's homemade quilts.

When I got a little older, Mom would give me that look that said, "Dance for your grandfather." While I had no problem dancing in front of anonymous crowds, I hated being drawn out in front of my family. It was too intimate. Still, I was a good girl and did as I was told. The joy in Grampy's face helped, but I wanted to stay on the sidelines with the other cousins. I didn't have a drink to help overcome my shyness.

Now I did. And I was still the performer, cracking jokes to keep everyone amused, diving into conversational gaps so no one felt awkward. The wine also allowed me to retreat mentally to the sidelines so I could watch me in the centre entertaining.

Earlier in the year I had cut back on my solo drinking to cope with the heartbreak of separation. Now I was drinking more with company to blunt the anxiety. At first, when we'd chat the next morning, Daniel would suggest gently I slow down. As I drank, I lost my inhibitions completely.

"Spaghetti, Daniel?" I asked one evening as eight of us sat around the kitchen island. "That's lazy. Even I could cook this."

I noticed the flood of embarrassment on his face, but I thought it was funny. Our friends smiled uncomfortably. After they left, Daniel was the most ticked off with me he'd ever been — our first fight. We argued in circles, then he walked out of the bedroom. After ten minutes of continuing the argument in my head and winning, I ran downstairs to the front window.

"What are you doing?" He came up behind me.

"Checking to see if you left."

"I'm not happy about tonight, but I'm not leaving." He put his arms around me. "I love you."

"I'm sorry."

A few dinner parties later, I woke up on the living-room sofa the next morning.

How did I get here? When did everyone go home? Oh my God, what did I say? What did they think?

I walked into the kitchen where Daniel was scrambling eggs. His look leeched all the colour out of me.

"We can't have friends over if you keep doing this."

"I know, I know, I'm sorry." I sniffled. "What did they say?"

"Nothing."

That was more devastating than any criticism. I sobbed with embarrassment.

Daniel hugged me for a long time. I felt his tears on my neck.

Dinner parties weren't the only thing I could lose.

"It won't happen again," I whispered.

With Miranda's help, I slowed my drinking during dinner parties. I got better, then worse, before I got better again. It wasn't a tidy linear progression. At first, it felt like physiotherapy after a car crash: holding the handrails, taking mincing steps. As I stopped repeating the old behaviour, I weakened those old associations in my brain. My resistance grew stronger. It was like lifting weights to break down and build muscle: rip and repair.

Two things slowed me down enough to stay connected with my body. The first was the guided sessions on a meditation app. As my mind quieted, I found the spiritual silence I missed from Mass. I realized my anxiety about drinking too much was sometimes more the issue than was the actual drinking.

The second was walking in nature. Forests, mountains, and moving water all create charged particles that are good for our bodies. The Japanese coined the term "forest bathing" in the 1980s to combat tech burnout. Those particles help increase our natural level of serotonin, which, in turn, alleviates stress and depression. I felt energized after walking along the river. That's why I loved strolling in the vineyards, too. My body felt grounded in the earth's body.

～∞～

I didn't just need to reset with wine; I also had to reset with writing. I've always loved food memoirs in which the author finds healing in the kitchen, kneading dough or eating a chin-dripping plum. These writers dove deeper into their subject to find peace. I couldn't drink more wine, so I had to savour the words. Writing was healing for me, and the more I did it, the less I needed wine.

Words have life-force power; they define our reality. Grabbing the chaos out of my body and putting it into words is healing. Research shows that when we label feelings, we move from our fear brain (amygdala) to the rational, calm frontal cortex. We can make sense of what happened and diminish its emotional scalding. We can't control what happens to us, but we can change how we think about it.

In fairy tales, the witch's curse is often broken with a spell — powerful words that release the victim. Shameful secrets are modern curses. When we name what's happening to us and how we feel about it, we often feel a release. That's why memoirs are so powerful. People feel seen and heard in someone else's experience, someone who has put it into words for them.

I had to find meaning in the act of writing itself, not in the awards. It took me back to how I felt about Highland dancing before I fixated on my competitor, Karen Jackson. Hours of practice didn't lead to a professional career or a Johnnie Walker sponsorship. It was simply the pure joy of doing something well, like landing a leap without faltering.

I've always thought of writing like my bolder friend who spoke up for me when I couldn't. I write to see how my mind works. For the tough issues I faced in 2012, I didn't know exactly how I felt or what I thought until I wrote about them. When I double down and write so that there's nothing left, it's an exposing business. Everything's on the page.

I lost touch with the joy of writing and got swallowed by the business of production. This, too, was part of never enough. I had to stop trying to collect as many subscribers as I could and start connecting more deeply with fewer of them — my people.

To get right with writing, I had to make an appointment with myself every morning. I blocked it off like a meeting. That twenty minutes before the official day started — before I was lost in the froth of email, social media, phone calls, voices, colours, sounds, smells — became sacred. Gradually, I returned to my highest calling, the best thing I do.

The modern writer Roger Martin builds on the poet John Keats's concept of "negative capability." In *The Opposable Mind*, he writes about the brain's ability "to hold two conflicting ideas in constructive tension." We make better decisions and generate more ideas. He challenges us to ask these questions: What if the opposite of what I think is true? What if I set aside my ego to envision something (or someone) that's contrary to what I believe? You can create something you never thought possible. That's what I had to do: write this book rather than just bury the past.

Getting to know people before forming an opinion is the opposite of the rush to summary execution on social media. That pause usually comes from those who acknowledge their own mistakes. They have compassion for themselves and others.

These ideas, though, weren't going to help me with the wine reviews. I wanted to convey the joyful, wordless abandon of drinking wine. I've always found wine deeply personal. You blend in your own experience with what you're drinking so each wine means different things to different people and at different times. When you describe a wine, you reveal something about yourself.

Some critics, however, embrace their authority to "call it" by some objective international standard. There was, and is, a strong tendency toward binaries in the wine world: typical or atypical, great or not, 95 or 85. Many consumers want these reviews. How could I reinvigorate my version of them? I tried telling stories about each bottle, adding history or bits of trivia. I hid odd phrases in the middle of reviews, little Easter eggs, the way software programmers do in their code.

The grapes for this Niagara pinot noir are hand-harvested by particularly picky people who create a wine of silk drapery to slide along your tongue.

Tight and tannic, this cabernet needs to relax like a newly minted Manhattan socialite … nothing that a flash sale at Saks can't solve, or two hours' decanting.

I started thinking of each wine review as a mini sonnet or vinous haiku: the creative challenge of how to pack density of thought and whimsy into a small space.

Lemon zest for the spotless mind in this riesling. Laser acidity pierces through creamy dishes and bad moods. Finishes with the snap and bite of a green apple after a spring rain.

Gorgeous depth and plushness in this Argentine malbec! Like diving tongue-first into an ocean of plum pillows. Feel your way through this red that gently brushes your senses. Woodsmoke and whispered campfire stories circle your head as you listen with drowsy eyes. Just the right amount of oak, like a loosely thrown shawl over your shoulders.

This full-bodied California zinfandel is purple-built for pleasure. Perfumed with violets and black roses. A cherry river of hedonism runs through it. Eyes wide shut.

Was I a hypocrite for writing these after criticizing Jim Murray's whisky reviews? I think there's a difference between sexist, sexy, and sensual writing. The first subjugates someone as purely a sexual object. The latter two talk about personal desire without doing that. The same standards should apply to both women and men, but I think we're less comfortable traditionally with women expressing sexual desire. Thus, the cougar. We're stalking sexual prey rather than just expressing a healthy sexual appetite as a mature woman. More often, older women are stereotyped as having neither sexual desire nor sexual attraction. Thus, the old hag or witch.

I do, however, realize now that even joking about UPS delivery guys, kilt-wearing heroes, hobbits, or short hairy men was a double standard when I didn't want my own body sexualized. It belied my insecurities as I looked for love again. I focused on height because at almost five foot ten I felt too tall to be feminine. But I didn't need a man to make me feel small and delicate. I needed to embrace my own powerful body.

Was it a contradiction that I fell in love with Daniel and his old-fashioned manners, language, movies, and music after complaining about being caught in a 1950s time warp in my marriage? I don't think so. These aspects of Daniel's personality made me feel loved and supported without diminishment.

One more hypocrisy while we're at it. I urged others to explore many wine styles, yet I drank mostly pinot noir. I loved — and still love — the liquid velvet mouthfeel of this wine. Its acidity can make it hard for new wine drinkers to love. That's why it's also considered an intellectual wine, blending perfectly with the rest of my snobberies. It was time to get out of my pinot rut, at least occasionally.

Is there any real value to wine reviews? I'd say yes now because it's such a confusing category. There are exponentially more choices in wine than in television shows and movies. There are more than a million wineries worldwide who make anywhere from five to twenty-five different wines every year from various grapes and blends. Contrast that with a television producer who creates one show a year if she's very productive. (I'm looking at you, my beloved Shonda Rhimes.) When someone watches that show many years later, it'll be the same as when it first aired. One winery's cabernet made in three different years will change each year. Even that same cabernet from one vintage will taste different as it ages. I woke up to that fact when I discovered a wine importer was using my review of a previous vintage on the current vintage, which was a disaster by contrast. I asked him to use the correct review.

Reviews of restaurants share more with television shows than they do with wine. There are far fewer restaurant openings in a city than wines released in its stores. It's good to know which restaurants to avoid when there's a high likelihood you might have dined there if you weren't warned. Plus, there's the *schadenfreude* of reading a deliciously nasty review. One of my favourite restaurant critics is the *Guardian*'s Jay Rayner, who once wrote that his pigeon entrée was "so pink it just might fly again given a few volts."

Highlighting good wines is a service to consumers. It supports winemakers doing a good job. But tearing down a bad wine is like stepping on a beetle. What's the point? It just seems mean, especially when there are so many of them. That's why I don't review poor wines.

When my dance teacher asked me to stop looking down, I'd overcorrect and look at the ceiling.

I realized that my own pride, arrogance, and naïveté had blinded me to the value of both others' reviews and my own. Those plodding workhorse reviews were of greater service to consumers than my long-form thoroughbred narrative. Just as I had to stop living in my head and get back down into my body, I had to embrace all parts of my identity.

Trolls Just Wanna Have Fun

—————

While the focus of sexism in the wine world is often on men, it's just as vital that women support each other. As Madeleine Albright, the former U.S. secretary of state, said, "There's a special place in hell for women who don't help other women."

This made me rethink how I supported women in the industry. While I hadn't knowingly undermined other women, I hadn't made a concerted effort to help them. That had to change.

I started giving several of my regular columns in the *Windsor Star* newspaper and the *Huffington Post* to women trying to get published for the first time. This meant convincing my editors to take a chance on these new writers. I edited their work at first to ensure it met the publication standards.

I also transitioned several of my regular segments on television shows to other women. Getting a column or a segment gave these women media credentials. That opened more doors for them in the industry. When wine councils invited me on all-expenses-paid media trips to regions around the world, I asked that one of these women go in my place. She would write about it on my site.

Next, I encouraged bloggers of all genders to post wine reviews on my website, to help raise their profiles. Their full names, headshots, and links to their websites were posted beside their reviews. I also commissioned several women to write articles on the site, so that they could develop a portfolio.

When I hired employees and contractors, I gave priority to women and people of colour who had the same potential as other applicants. There was no shortage of candidates, no pipeline issues. I trained them to meet my standards and paid for them to take courses. The satisfaction I felt brought back feelings I'd had training young dancers. Was this discrimination against men? I don't think so. I was hiring based on the merit of anticipated contribution to the business and of supporting my values as the owner. These new hires had more potential and a drive to work harder to prove themselves. As of this writing, all my employees and contractors are women or people of colour.

Beyond my team, I started looking to support those publishing their first books. One such was Victoria James, author of *Wine Girl: The Obstacles, Humiliations, and Triumphs of a Young Sommelier.*

James believes people started listening to women's stories in the hospitality industry with the revelation of celebrity chef sexual assaults. When I interviewed her in 2020 on my podcast, *Unreserved Wine Talk*, she observed, "Since those scandals, I don't believe that any real structural change has occurred. Women are still afraid to speak out." She believes that the wine world was — and still is — an old boys' club.

So how will change happen? James thinks that restaurant owners need to take a firm stand against workplace harassment with staff training and zero-tolerance policies. She also founded Wine Empowered, a non-profit organization to offer free wine classes to women and people of colour who could not otherwise afford the training.

I started supporting industry organizations for women, both financially and personally, with my time. The Catholic in me is yelling, "Stop writing about this!" since these efforts are more worthy if they're done unseen (more heaven points). But I think there's a greater good in talking about them now.

Today, there are a dozen groups that advocate for women's issues in the industry, which I've noted at nataliemaclean.com/resources. I wish they had existed in 2012. Perhaps things wouldn't have turned out any differently, but I wouldn't have felt so alone. A decade after the attacks, I still feel the sexism fermented into the wine industry.

During the pandemic, I wrote on Instagram about how we need to support local wineries. Their tasting rooms were closed and their other major source of income disappeared when restaurants shut down. Many of these family businesses relied on online sales alone to survive. The post had lots of comments and questions from my followers. I included ten related hashtags to help spread the word.

Wine Corp's vice-president, David Lawrason, had been the *Globe and Mail*'s wine columnist for fifteen years before Beppi Crosariol replaced him. Lawrason wrote on my account: "How many hashtags does a girl really need?" Then he liked his own comment.

At first, I was angry. I'm a grown-ass woman who has been writing about wine for twenty years. I wanted to tell this seventy-year-old boy to eff off and block him. After a few minutes of deep breathing, I thought, no. I'll let it sit there in contrast to the rest of the discussion for others to see for themselves.

In another post, just for fun, I paired my Canadian-designed Fluevog shoes with a Canadian wine. My followers loved the playfulness, especially during the bleak days of the lockdown.

Lawrason wrote on my account again: "Is this a paid advertising post? And is it about boots or wine? Or both? Hard to tell in the fake era. And does anyone care about the difference?"

This time, because he was attacking my integrity, I responded. Anger became my friend. It's a hotter emotion than sadness and the necessary fuel for justice.

"This post is not paid for by @township7 or @fluevog or any other organization. I love the design of these shoes and so do those who follow me. I'm just trying to share a little levity and light in my community. Sounds like you could use a little too."

Lawrason didn't respond.

Sexism is one thing, but does it even matter if wine writers are unbiased? Unlike stockbrokers who are influenced by company freebies and then recommend stocks that wipe out your life savings, the greatest danger from a biased wine writer is that a high-alcohol chardonnay ruins your sea bass.

After all, it's just wine. Or is it?

Critics comment on many of life's pleasures — wine, food, movies, theatre, music, books, and travel. These are the things we work hard to enjoy. Yet most of us don't have the time, money, or interest to sort through the thousands of options in each category to find the best. That's why many of us trust critics to do this for us. When we drink a poorly made wine or dine at a restaurant with sloppy service that was recommended by biased writers, we stop trusting them. All criticism is debased. It's the same effect as every movie getting two thumbs-up. We may then trust only certain critics, but searching them out becomes time-consuming. We may not bother.

Conversely, when we trust a broad spectrum of critics, we're better able to recognize and demand ever-higher levels of quality and taste. This prods these industries to higher standards. A good reputation means more sales, higher margins, stronger exports, more jobs, and a more pleasurable experience for the reader and drinker.

Wine is a product. Recommending it is a commercial activity. Lifestyle journalism is transactional. As writers, we want information or samples from the source, and the source wants coverage for their products. U.K. wine columnist Malcolm Gluck wrote that the wine trade and wine writing are "twin cheeks of the same backside." Commercialism is a slippery slope down that backside. Criticism requires judgment not just in assessing wines, but also in how we come to assess them. Objectivity may be impossible but striving for fairness and balance is what we owe to readers, or we deserve a kick in the pants.

Several years after the attacks, I was asked to do a television interview featuring the wines of a large winery sponsoring this advertorial segment. It wouldn't have the variety of wines that I always presented based on an editorial theme, such as pairings for Thanksgiving or Valentine's Day. Sponsored segments are common on television shows. Hosts often participate to promote a variety of products, from makeup to food delivery. I think this is fine. However, as a writer critiquing wines, including those from the corporation, I decided this was a conflict of interest for me, and indeed, a pay-to-play. The winery was paying for the show. If I accepted the segment, I'd be paid more than the usual appearance fee of three hundred dollars, which didn't even cover my overnight stay in Toronto. I declined the opportunity and others that followed.

In my own segments, I could choose the topics and wines as long as one wine out of the twelve was from the large winery. I could live with that, because I chose a wine that I had reviewed positively and independently from their portfolio.

The drinks columnist for the *National Post* newspaper at the time agreed to act as the wine expert for the sponsored segments. I was surprised not only that he did so, but also that no one in the writing community posted anything about it.

Several other wine writers were, and still are, brand ambassadors for particular wines or regions, while still reviewing the wines of both their clients and their competitors. A brand ambassador is hired by a winery or wine region to promote that brand to media, trade, and consumers. That seems at odds with a balanced assessment that consumers expect from reviews.

In 2020, Wine Corp's Lawrason became part of a public relations agency representing wines while maintaining his role as vice-president and lead critic at Wine Corp, as well as being a judge in wine competitions. The agency noted in their press release: "David Lawrason, the most respected wine writer and judge in Canada, heads up our Canadian team from his base in Toronto. In every major Canadian city, we have local market managers who have their finger on the pulse. They also happen to be the leading wine expert in town."

This seemed akin to a lawyer marketing himself to clients by adding that he was also the presiding judge in their cases.

In Salem, the men who accused the women of being witches were often also their judges, prosecutors, and jury. The women were forced to submit to them. At least on social media, I didn't have to listen to every Tom, Dick, and Harry. I could just block them.

Behind the Curtain

"**D**on't go," Daniel said softly. He put his arm around my shoulders. We stood on the back deck in the April sunshine, breathing in the fresh, green spring air. It smelled like everything could start over.

I had mentioned I was thinking about attending a large tasting in Toronto in a few weeks' time. The men who had attacked me on social media four months before would likely be there. I'd never met most of them in person.

Daniel didn't want me to face more harassment. The mob's maelstrom had subsided only a couple of months earlier. I still had the heart murmur and constant dread every time I went online. Should I even return to that hostile world? Sometimes I still thought I should go back to the safety of marketing at a packaged goods company. Then I remembered what I'd lose: the freedom I found working for myself, the natural high of writing, and my love of wine's sensory delights beyond the buzz.

Running away from the wine world was also an unnecessary defeat. After all, I had survived. The voices of Mom and her teacher friends singing Helen Reddy's "I Am Woman" came back to me. These men had bent me, but they did not break me.

Since the attacks, many women in the industry had privately shared with me their own experiences of sexism. What I did now mattered as much for them as it did for me.

"If I don't go, then they're still bullying me."

He sighed. "Go get 'em, tigress."

I smiled tightly. My throat was dry at the thought of walking into the tasting room at the head office of the LCBO. I could barely swallow.

I emailed columnist Shari Darling, hoping she was going to attend so I'd have at least one friendly face there. She couldn't make it, but sent back this story:

> When former disciples targeted Buddha in a temple one day, calling him names, Buddha did nothing and said nothing.
>
> A loyal disciple said, "Buddha, they were yelling at you and showing such disrespect. Why did you let them do it? You did nothing. You let them get away with it."
>
> Buddha said, "If they had come with a basket of oranges, a gift that I did not accept, then what?"
>
> The disciple said, "Well, they would have had to leave with their oranges."
>
> Buddha said, "Exactly. They came with their abuse. They stayed with their abuse. They left with it. I do not accept it."

This helped, but I still imagined walking into that room, their heads turning, their eyes narrowing. What would they say?

∿◉∿

It's Friday morning, the day of the tasting. I get out of the taxi and walk across a busy parking lot. Delivery trucks back up and beep. The concrete LCBO head office is penitentiary grey. Inside, security buzzers go off. Doors slam.

I check in with the gruff guard at the front desk who asks for ID, then pushes the sign-in sheet toward me. I see the names of seven of the men who had been vicious online.

My heart lurches. I'm about to walk into a hellish furnace ... The real-life version of the comments section.

The guard gestures upward, mumbling fourth floor. I want to drag him with me as my bodyguard.

I get in a small, creaky elevator; a metal coffin. On the fourth floor, I walk down a long hallway. When I grab the doorknob to the tasting room, it just spins. My hand is slippery with sweat. I wipe my palms on my pants, then use both hands to get it open. I slide inside the room.

There they are.

There are thirteen men, no women. I recognize these men from their social media profiles. As I look around at them, I remember their malicious comments, each one a knife wound.

Mr. Wikipedia, Dean Tudor, seemingly made of gristle with a grey moustache and beard, is a few feet in front of me. Across the room, Master Sommelier John Szabo wears a buttoned-up waistcoat similar to his Twitter picture in which he's emerging from a red sports car. In the corner is Michael Pinkus, with an intense black-eyed stare.

I breathe in slowly. They're smaller than I imagined them. Or am I just taller than I thought I was?

Mom's calm voice reading *The Wizard of Oz* comes back to me. My heart raced when the great and terrible wizard was revealed as nothing more than a man without special powers. I'd rest my small hand on her forearm, the other on the open page, trying to absorb more of the story and her strength.

Now I feel the strength of my own story. I pull myself up to my full height as the famous line from the movie echoes in my mind: "Pay no attention to that man behind the curtain."

The online curtain has been pulled back. I stand face to face with those whose voices had boomed on social media like angry giants. Now that they can't hide behind their online avatars, they're silent. I imagine @ signs on their foreheads, like tiny bullseyes. Where is their keyboard courage?

Pinkus looks up, then away.

Tudor coughs. Or did he catch his breath?

Szabo seems to choke on his tasting sample.

Am I blushing? When I'm stressed, I turn deep red because I have rosacea. When I drink wine, or even taste it, it makes it worse. I end up looking like a radioactive lobster.

Whatever. Let my face show my fire.

I stay just inside the door for a few agonizingly long seconds, not dropping my gaze. I will not scurry in. I have the urge to click my heels three times.

One by one, they drop their gaze. They can't look at me, it seems, much less say anything. As they lose their voices, I get mine back.

The white walls of the room are lined with a tasting counter holding some seventy bottles, a backup infantry standing shoulder to shoulder. I walk over to an empty place and start tasting, quivering with relief.

"It's quite the lineup we have in here," I say to one man who hadn't been involved in the online fracas.

"Yes ... a new vintage of sour grapes." He smiles back at me.

As the day goes on, there are a few whispers. I overhear one grump muttering to another: "Well, I guess life does go on."

Indeed, it does, gentlemen.

Tudor is making his way down the line of bottles toward me quickly, because he isn't spitting or taking notes. Szabo had tweeted at him after a previous tasting: "Hey, saw u guzzled 2 glasses of Krug [an expensive Champagne] on your way out of the lab, some writers missed the chance to taste, please forward ur notes."

At last, he gets to the bottle between my laptop and the wall. He pauses. Coughs. It's impossible to get it without asking me to move. I stay put, even though I've tasted all the wines in that area.

He coughs again, walks over to another section of the counter, then returns to where I am. Cough. His throat must be getting sore.

I hold my ground.

He moves away to another section to taste.

This is the former journalism professor who had been so bold in writing the defamatory Wikipedia page and then bragging about it to his buddies. He's the one who had fearlessly characterized me as a leather-bound dominatrix, urging male critics to ejaculate. Now he can't even ask me to move down one spot on the counter.

Social media had given these men their "courage," but when faced with the reality of the woman they had attacked, they are silent.

As I continue tasting the wines, they keep shrinking in my mind. Why had I been so afraid of them? I'd stayed awake nights thinking about what they'd say next. Why hadn't I been able to see them for who they were — or who I was?

Then I remember my favourite scene in *The Wizard of Oz*, but I imagine the good witch, Glinda, is talking to me, "You've always had the power, my dear. You just had to learn it for yourself."

The Social Spell

That man is whipping the crowd into a frenzy.

Blood pounds in my ears, making their shouts spike up and down like sirens. Blinding white lights flash on, still visible when I squeeze my eyes shut. I don't want to go out there. Don't want to face the mob again. The difference this time is that I'll confront them while on national television. Damn. Why am I here after everything that's happened?

It's September 2013. I'm shaking in the wings on the set of CTV's *The Social*, Canada's most popular television talk show. Like the American show *The View*, four hosts interview guests and discuss issues, some of which are controversial.

Filmed in Toronto before a live studio audience, it's broadcast to 3.2 million viewers across the country in real time — no editing. Audience members, here and at home, post their views about each topic on social media, tagging CTV. Those comments — both positive and negative — are displayed onscreen.

Negative comments. National television. Oh God.

This is my first time on the show, but that's not the reason I'm nervous. Several weeks ago, I had cold-called the show's producer via email. I suggested today's segment on pairing wine and fast food: Drinking Outside the Box. Pitched it as shabby-chic combos — fried chicken and champagne, like ripped jeans with rhinestones.

She loved it.

They hated it.

Some of those male wine writers told me so on social media when I posted about it.

Then it hits me.

I'm throwing myself on national television as troll bait.

What the hell am I doing here?

My pulse galloping, I recall Dr. Brené Brown in her book *Daring Greatly* quoting U.S. president Theodore Roosevelt:

> It's not the critic who counts; not the man who points out how the strong man stumbles or where the doer of deeds could have done them better. The credit belongs to the person who is in the arena. Whose face is marred with dust and sweat and blood; who strives valiantly ... who at the best knows in the end the triumph of high achievement, and who at the worst, if he fails, at least fails while daring greatly.

The show's audience warm-up guy has done his job.

The crowd is chanting.

The music is blasting.

My legs are moving.

My red shoes are itching to walk even further outside my comfort zone before going back to the safety of home.

I find myself in front of a packed house on their feet, a sea of flashing phones in front of their heads. Celebrity hosts stand to my right and left, blazing lights, a dozen large cameras zooming in and out, and now the prospect of getting shamed on national television.

I think I've taken the whole arena thing too far.

I have two choices: melt into a puddle of neuroses with a shaky little-girl voice or forget myself and focus on making this a great experience for the audience. No half-measures. I must be all in, even risking the odd little quip that could fall flat. Entertain before you educate.

"Why is sauvignon blanc a good match with poutine?" Melissa Grelo, one of the hosts, asks, taking a sip of the wine.

"We have a lot going on in poutine: fries, gravy, cheese. The acidity in the wine cuts like a knife through all the richness and fat. It gets you ready for the next bite. You don't satiate out. You can have more poutine because you've refreshed your palate. You taste the wine, then go back to the poutine, then back to the wine."

"So we can have more poutine and wine?" Traci Melchor, another host, asks, as she snags a fry.

"That's the magic of food and wine pairing. They elevate each other, creating new flavours and tastes."

"Yes! More wine, more poutine," the women cheer.

As we move from one pairing to the next, the cameras move in and out. I bathe in the adrenalin rush. Even the viewer comments running across the screen are positive.

I shiver with relief.

Out of the corner of my eye, I see the floor director making circular arm movements to wrap up the segment. One host thanks me, the audience cheers. It is done. The camera lights go from red to black. We walk off the set for the commercial break.

I recall another quote from Dr. Brené Brown regarding what she calls "Twitter thugs":

If you are not in the arena also getting your butt kicked, I'm not interested in your feedback. There are a lot of cheap seats in this world where you can just sit back, never risk anything, and throw cheap criticism at people who are trying. I think being vulnerable feels dangerous, and I think it is terrifying. But I don't think it's as dangerous, scary, or terrifying as getting to the end of our lives and wondering, what if I had shown up?

Backstage, my heart is still a fist pounding against my rib cage. I taste the sweat on my lips — and savour it. The producer is smiling.

I'll soon become the show's regular wine expert. My next segment will be pairing wine with Halloween treats. The hosts will wear costumes. Naturally, I'll dress as a wine witch.

~◎~

I'd love to tie everything up emotionally with a red bow. All better now! But maybe I haven't actually "fixed" all my flaws. Maybe I'll backslide into perfectionism or competitiveness. I worry about having revealed them to you because this time you'll notice and wonder if I learned anything from my mistakes.

I'm more confident about managing my wine consumption as I've honed techniques from meditation to mindful drinking. Low and no-alcohol wines are now part of my repertoire. You'll find these in the free companion guide for book clubs and wine groups at nataliemaclean.com/witchwines. My tips and health-related information in both this book and the companion guide are not medical advice or a substitute for it. I hope they're helpful in some way and encourage those who need professional help to get it.

Moderation became much easier after I dealt with the depression about my divorce and the anxiety from the online attacks. I first had to go on my own journey to Oz to reunite my head, heart, and courage.

I used to make my drinking habits fodder for humour. Now I hope they'll fuel discussion on overdrinking. It's a topic we don't talk about in my industry. Drinking is viewed as an occupational duty or there's shame in admitting a problem. U.S. Department of Health and Human Services statistics indicate that the hospitality industry, which includes wineries and restaurants, has the highest rate of substance abuse among all professions. Some of that stiff jargony wine writing is rooted in the fear of liking wine just a little too much.

I'm happy to add that Daniel has quit smoking. His struggle was much harder than mine. We keep each other on track.

After twenty years of second-guessing myself, I still do it. I still catch my breath when I drop something. However, I've discovered that the goal isn't the absence of self-doubt but how I deal with it. I've learned to exhale.

On the business front, I'm now a regular guest expert on half-a-dozen television shows. More than 320,000 wine lovers subscribe to my free newsletter. My online wine and food pairing courses at nataliemaclean.com draw people from around the world. The *New York Times* selected my podcast, *Unreserved Wine Talk*, as one of the seven best in the drinks category. Oh yeah, still loving that glitter glue, but in smaller dabs.

I was on a panel discussion recently when the moderator asked, "How does it feel to be in a position of power?"

I almost looked behind me to see if she was talking to someone else.

Power? Me?

Overcoming self-doubt also means accepting your power, seeing yourself as someone who can lead, and trusting your intuition.

When I sense a feeling about something or someone, I now go with it. It's often the right decision for me.

While meeting Daniel helped, I realized that *I* was the one I'd been waiting for. I had been there all along, just too bound up in worry knots to see my own strength.

It wasn't just naïveté that made me miss the signs that my marriage to Adam was in trouble; it was also pride. I wanted it to be perfect. When it wasn't, I ignored the problems. Gaslighting works particularly well on those who want to believe what they're being told.

I used to think I'd failed the Marriage Test. Now I know the divorce is part of who I've become. A successful marriage doesn't necessarily mean for life. It can also be successful because I have a son I love who also loves me.

As time passes, I look back on my earlier self as a younger sister, trying to do the best she could at the time. Maybe a memoir is a hug for your past self when you needed one but were alone.

I regret the later years I spent in my marriage, but I'd do it again to bring Cameron into this world and to rebirth myself. It's only because I had to fight for my emotional and financial freedom that I know who I am.

I also remember all the good times Adam and I had together, the spicy sweetness of talking for hours into the night, the high of circling his charismatic orbit. He made my weather. We fetishized intelligence starting when we were in business school talking about which professors were blue-flame thinkers. I never thought the stabilizing base for our relationship might be emotional. With Daniel, feelings are as important as thoughts — mind, body, and soul are a rock-solid foundation.

I may always feel twinges of sadness about Adam. A decade later, he still jokes about his "wandering eye" in the occasional email we exchange. I want him to be happy and to have a strong relationship with Cameron, as much as I want those things myself.

While I had never been close to my father, I was struck by something I learned when he died a few years ago. It was several days before they found his body in his apartment. Family members told me he had taped my magazine articles to the fridge. I think he did the best he could, too.

Now Cameron is grown up and a man himself. We talk about relationship issues often. I don't think we'd have such a close bond without what happened in 2012. I'm proud of the values he wants in a life partner and of who he wants to be as a husband and father.

I've learned to soften my reactions, not lashing out at men bullying me and accepting love without suspicion from those who support me.

It's like the optometrist's vision test. With one click, a fractional change of lens, you see the fine lines between confidence and arrogance, vulnerability and naïveté, humility and self-doubt.

When the Hurly-Burly's Done; When the Battle's Lost and Won

I t's just before midnight on December 31, 2013. Daniel stirs the beef bourguignon on the stove as the savoury aroma fills the kitchen. I'm warmed by his smile. He talks about our plans for winter vacation.

It's only been a year since the meltdown, but it feels like a decade ago. I've finally realized that vulnerability is the only defence. Little Miss Perfect can't control what others think of her, only what she tells them. So why not tell them lots, without editing out the nasty bits? That's how I connect with others — not through perfection but through sharing my flawsome tendencies, which they see in themselves.

My relationship with men has healed, too. I used to focus on the men in my life who have told me I couldn't do something: the

Rhodes Scholarship judge, the marketing professor, the McKinsey partner, the supercomputer company boss, the wine critics, Adam, and my father, whose alcoholic life made me fear my own DNA.

Now there is the stronger presence in my mind of the men who lifted me up: my grandfather, many male teachers and coaches, friends, Cameron — the young man of whom I am so proud, and, most of all, Daniel. To paraphrase myself, I'm the luckiest woman on earth to have met him. He sees all of me, dark and light, and embraces it all.

Even though the separation and the attacks felt so different at the time, I realize they shared many similarities: hitting me out of the blue, threatening the life I'd spent decades building, and undermining my self-worth. My disastrous blend of pride, self-doubt, competitiveness, and perfectionism made me an easy mark for both crises. They humbled me not just because they took place when I thought I had "made it" career- and family-wise, but also because I was pushed to realize I couldn't deal with these issues on my own. The lifelong outsider — the kid who never answered the door — had to let others into her life to survive.

Mom, Daniel, Cameron, and I sit around the island counter. I top up the adult glasses with Featherstone Joy Premium Cuvée Sparkling, made by husband-and-wife team David Johnson and Louise Engel, in Niagara. Every April, they allow lambs to wander through the vines to eat grass and clover. They stay until early fall, also munching on low-hanging vine leaves. The grapes are green and bitter then, so they're of no interest to these lamb-mowers. They reduce the farm's environmental hoofprint as part of the circle of life and rebirth each spring.

The Joy sparkling wine is named after David's mother, Joyce, a woman he says exuded charm, finesse, and the cheerful character in this wine. Joy is made from chardonnay grapes, using the traditional champagne method of the second fermentation in the bottle.

It's a toasty, crisp bubbly with aromas of freshly baked bread, green apple, and sun-dappled happiness.

My computer has been off for hours. The evening glitters around me. I'm wearing the fiery red number with clashing orange Fluevog shoes. #WhoCares!

We play a card game that prompts participants with personal and holiday-related questions.

Mom asks me, "Who was the Christmas Witch?"

"Oooh, I know this one," I say.

"Unfair advantage," Cameron declares. "You know every witch that ever existed."

"Yes, it's one of my special powers." I smile.

"Befana was an old Italian woman covered in soot who visited children. She gave them candy or coal. Sound familiar? She actually predates Santa and used a broom rather than a sleigh. Children left her wine and local food rather than milk and cookies. My kinda woman."

Cameron rolls his eyes, but smiles.

In 2012, I felt like a witch in the worst ways: outcast, despised, scorned, hunted. But I'm not equating my experience with the horrors women faced in the seventeenth and eighteenth centuries. Rather, their stories rekindled my desire to call out the sexism and misogyny that still drive unfair, and often cruel, treatment of women today. The methods now are far more subtle, but the results can still feel devastating.

I've also come to realize that fire can be good when it illuminates darkness and shame, when it burns away the parts you no longer need, allowing you to rise from your ashes. I'm on fire now, no longer afraid of my own fury. I'll never stop burning.

Cameron reads aloud: "What do you know about yourself based on what you know about one of your parents?" His brilliant blue eyes shine at me as he says, "That I could become a Navy SEAL if I wanted to. You know, sit in the cold ocean for hours and the other crazy stuff they do because they don't give up ... they've got grit."

Grit.

His word for me has changed from *vicious* to *grit*. I'm flooded with pride.

I read my card: "What's one thing you don't regret that would surprise other people?

"Suffering," I say. "Good Catholic answer, eh, Mom?"

She laughs.

"You mean what doesn't kill you makes you stronger?" Cameron asks.

"Yes, it's why vines starved for water make the best wine. They have to dig deeper to stay alive ... that's how they get more flavour into the grapes."

Cher's singing "If I Could Turn Back Time" from our New Year's–themed playlist. As painful as 2012 was, I realize I wouldn't want to turn back time. I am who I am because of it. Banishment can be a gift. It gives you time to peel off the old labels and create your own.

Extreme failure made me face something I never want to return to, but it also gave me a taste of a full life I never want to lose. When the angry online mob shoved me up against a wall, I had to ask myself, Am I really this person? Am I who they say I am?

Yes, no, and something more.

Hester Prynne was forced to wear the scarlet letter *A*. She embroidered it ornately with golden thread, making something creative out of her shame. She transformed a badge of humiliation into an emblem of individuality, the only way she had to take back her story.

We change with our experiences. Each brings out different things in us, just as syrah and shiraz grapes express themselves as different wines in the soils and climates of the Rhône, Barossa, and

Okanagan Valleys. Each season, the vines must adapt to different weather, one year a killing frost; the next, a drought. They thrust their roots farther down through the cracks in another layer of rock to find the nutrients they need to survive.

The winemaking term *dry extract* refers to the essence of the wine's flavour components when all the moisture has evaporated. Dry extract is in us, too, whether it's salt from tears or ashes from fire. It's what's left after life has burned us down to our essence. If we hold on to that, we can rise again.

I've reclaimed what I almost lost: my family, love, health, and career. My roots are deeper, my wisdom fiercer.

Daniel serves the beef, its savoury thyme aroma wafting up from our plates. I top up the glasses. We all sit down at the dining-room table and dig in. A few minutes later, I look around at Daniel, Mom, and Cameron, laughing, talking, eating.

Daniel notices my eyes watering.

"Everything okay?" He takes my hand in his.

"Yes," I whisper. "It's perfect."

Mom and Cameron are watching me closely now as well.

"Hey, Mom," I say. "Remember Helen Reddy's song you used to sing with the teachers?"

She smiles.

"I do," Daniel pipes up. "Even I feel like a strong, invincible woman after hearing it seventeen hundred times" — he grins — "and I'm still a man who has a long, long way to go."

Cameron rolls his eyes again, but he knows this golden oldie because it became my anthem after the separation. I played it at full volume over and over on the stereo.

We all belt it out together.

My voice is on fire.

Post-Morticia

I didn't want to share this story. I couldn't even look at notes I'd locked away for years. It was too exposing, too shameful. I'd be vandalizing my own privacy.

Memoirist Glennon Doyle advised, "Write from a scar, not an open wound." But why even write about it after the healing is done? Poet Sean Thomas Dougherty had the answer. "Why bother? Because right now, there is someone out there with a wound in the exact shape of your words."

My memoir gathered different parts of my life that I thought were separate, but were just two sides of an open wound. Words were my sutures to sew my life back together. The scars they created are now patterns of meaning that are stronger than the flesh before the injury.

After talking with many women who had similar stories but not an outlet to share them, I decided to write this memoir. A book can travel so much farther than I can with this message.

I still found creative ways to delay finishing it. I wanted to keep editing it to be perfect; triple-checking every detail. Perfectionism is procrastination in disguise. Perfectionism and competitiveness coil together like a cobra and a boa constrictor. The first bites you with envy, the second squeezes the joy of life out of you. Together, they're the undisciplined pursuit of more.

Damn all that effing glitter glue — it's so sticky. But I think it's the struggle that counts. Now there's a person behind the person who was all about perfection and winning. This quieter self sees me striving and says, "Relax, sister, I've got you."

Some may read this as a revenge book. Others may read this as a book of healing, and I hope it is that for them. How you see it depends on who you are. But it's neither for me. This is a coming-of-middle-age story about creating my own labels rather than accepting those that others slapped on me.

This book is for Mom and for all those who have watched the world tell their story, wishing they could let their words out. It's also an invitation to you to join me for a glass. I'll bring a bewitching wine; you bring your magical self.

I'd love to hear what you thought of the book, if you found a typo, or if you'd like me to meet your wine or book club gathering virtually. Heck, I might just jump on my broomstick and join you in person. Email me at natdecants@nataliemaclean.com or visit my website at nataliemaclean.com.

Natalie

P.S. What's happened since? Cameron has grown up to be an empathetic, engaging young man who has graduated with a degree in computer engineering from the University of Waterloo. He now works in that field. Mom is in good health and continues to say that what the mind can conceive, the body can achieve. I wrote that on a sticky note for my bathroom mirror. Meanwhile, I'm still living happily ever after with Daniel, a.k.a. Prince Charming.

Acknowledgements

Thank you to the many women in the wine industry who told me their stories long before I dared to share mine. You gave me the confidence to write this memoir. To my sister in wine, Felicity Carter, thank you for having my back in the trenches.

I appreciate the winemakers who welcomed me into their homes, lives, and thoughts over the years, allowing me to tell their stories.

I'm grateful to the lawyers who combed through every line of the manuscript to ensure there was no clause for concern.

The incredible work ethic of my assistants Andrea Shapiro, Helena Cody, Karen Mitchell, Ellen MacDonald, and Deb Podurgiel allowed me to focus on this book.

I'm deeply grateful to the beta readers who suffered through the early drafts of the manuscript yet remained encouraging.

Many great bottles are owed to Allyson Latta and Kathryn Willms, who together, performed triple-bypass surgery on the manuscript, ensuring it had a strong heartbeat when we sent it out on proposal.

The generous financial backing of Randall Howard, Jason Martin, and Lorne Wallace enables Dundurn Press to publish Canadian voices, like mine. A special thank you to Randall Howard for his mentorship.

Russell Smith at Dundurn Press may look like an everyday, successful acquisitions editor, but he actually has secret superpowers that he used to make this memoir better than I could have dreamed. Thank you for your patience, Russell.

Robyn So is a copy editor par excellence. Any remaining errors are entirely my own — she could only do so much given what she had to work with (especially with a writer who likes to end sentences with prepositions).

Project editor Erin Pinksen's irrepressible zest for words and wine carried me through the entire publishing process.

The supporting team at Dundurn used their magical skills for the greater good of this memoir: Elena Radic, Megan Beadle, Laura Boyle, Karen Alexiou, Eva Svec, Kathryn Lane, Chris Houston, and their fearless leader, Kwame Scott Fraser.

Once the book was finished, marketing and publicity wizards Kendra Martin, Alyssa Boyden, Rajdeep Singh, and Maria Zuppardi ensured that this memoir, and its message, reached more readers than I thought possible.

I owe a great debt to my literary agent, Sam Hiyate, who believed in this book when it was still a tangled mess of emotions. He shared his vision with me that this could be more than just my story, and that it could help others. His warmth, humour, and genius make him the best agent in the business.

Miranda, consider this book a three-hundred-page thank you note. You know what I mean. You always have.

Thank you for your enduring friendship, Cassie, Nina, Janice, Lindsey, and Lily. See you Friday at our favourite wine bar. The first round is on me.

Grampy, I remember those long summer afternoons when you gave into "just one more" push on the swing, and then another. Grammy, thank you for planting a love of language so deep inside me that our roots in words are forever entwined.

Cameron, I'm incredibly proud of the man you are today. Thank you for all the hugs (and hug coupons at Christmas), and for my favourite phrase, "You've got this, Mom."

Thank you, Daniel, for loving me warts and all. I love you more than words can say, which is a humbling admission for a writer. You still sweep me off my feet.

Most profoundly, I'd like to thank the woman to whom this book is dedicated, my mother, Ann. Thank you for not buying that dress so that I could have a kilt, for spending your weekends taking me to competitions instead of finishing your favourite books, and for loving me into the woman I've become. I did it, Mom. I let the words out.

About the Author

Natalie MacLean's previous books, *Red, White, and Drunk All Over: A Wine-Soaked Journey from Grape to Glass* and *Unquenchable: A Tipsy Quest for the World's Best Bargain Wines*, were each selected as one of Amazon's Best Books of the Year. She was named the World's Best Drinks Journalist at the World Food Media Awards and has won four James Beard Foundation Journalism Awards. She is the only person to have won both the M.F.K. Fisher Distinguished Writing Award from the James Beard Foundation and the M.F.K. Fisher Award for Excellence in Culinary Writing from Les Dames d'Escoffier International.

Her work has appeared in *Bon Appétit, Food & Wine, Wine Enthusiast,* the *Globe and Mail, San Francisco Chronicle, Chicago Tribune, Star Tribune, St. Louis Post-Dispatch,* the *Sydney Morning*

Herald, the *Age* (Australia), and *National Post*. She's the regular wine expert on several television shows.

Natalie is the host of *Unreserved Wine Talk*, selected as one of the best drinks podcasts by the *New York Times*. She interviews the most colourful people in the wine world and chronicles her journey in publishing this book and the next one. She offers online food and wine pairing classes where she connects personally with those around the planet who share her passion for wine at nataliemaclean.com.

CPSIA information can be obtained
at www.ICGtesting.com
Printed in the USA
JSHW080151300523
42398JS00001B/1